MW01623574

PAUL
HEE

THRE

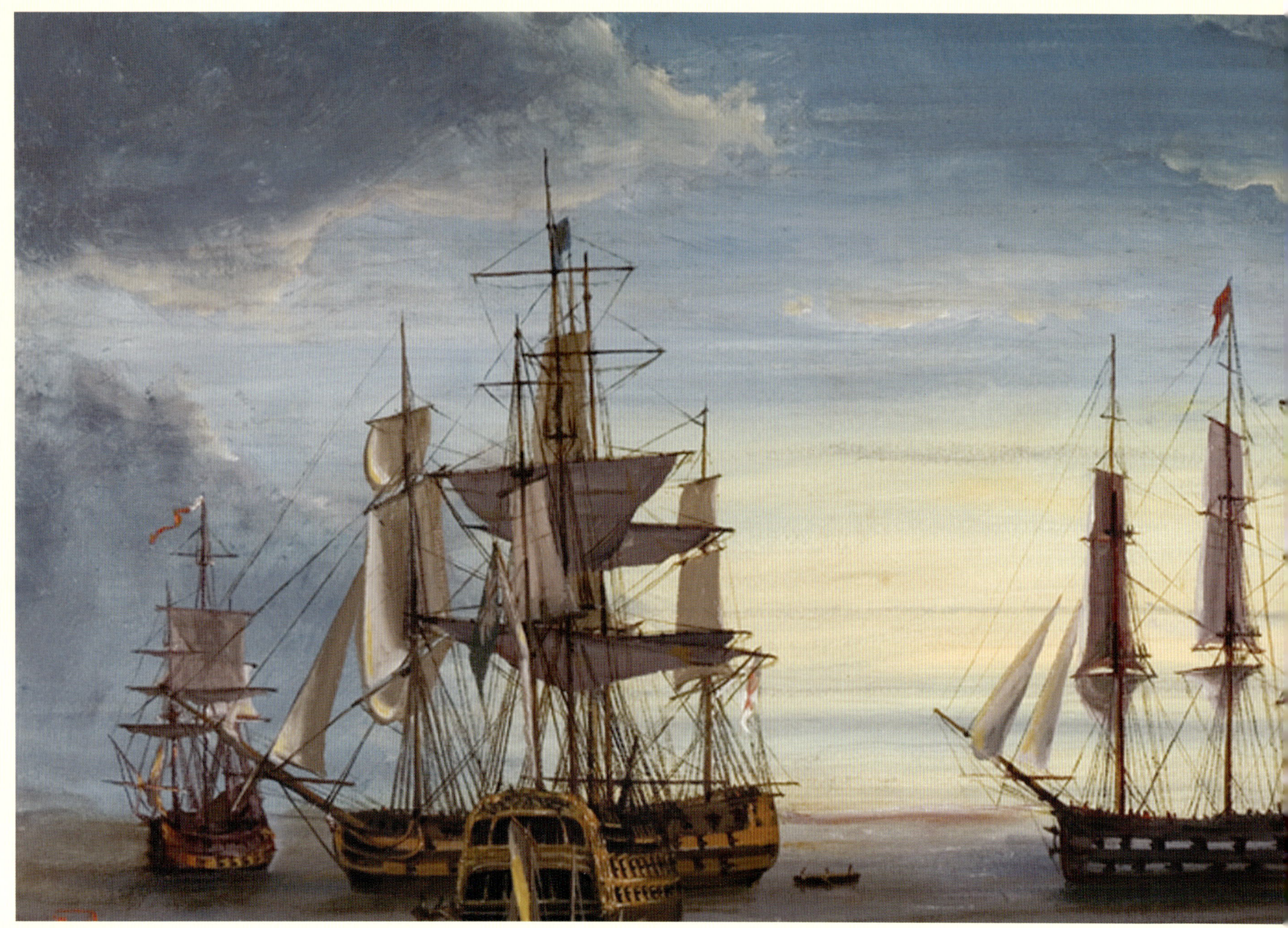

CENTURIES OF SEAFARING

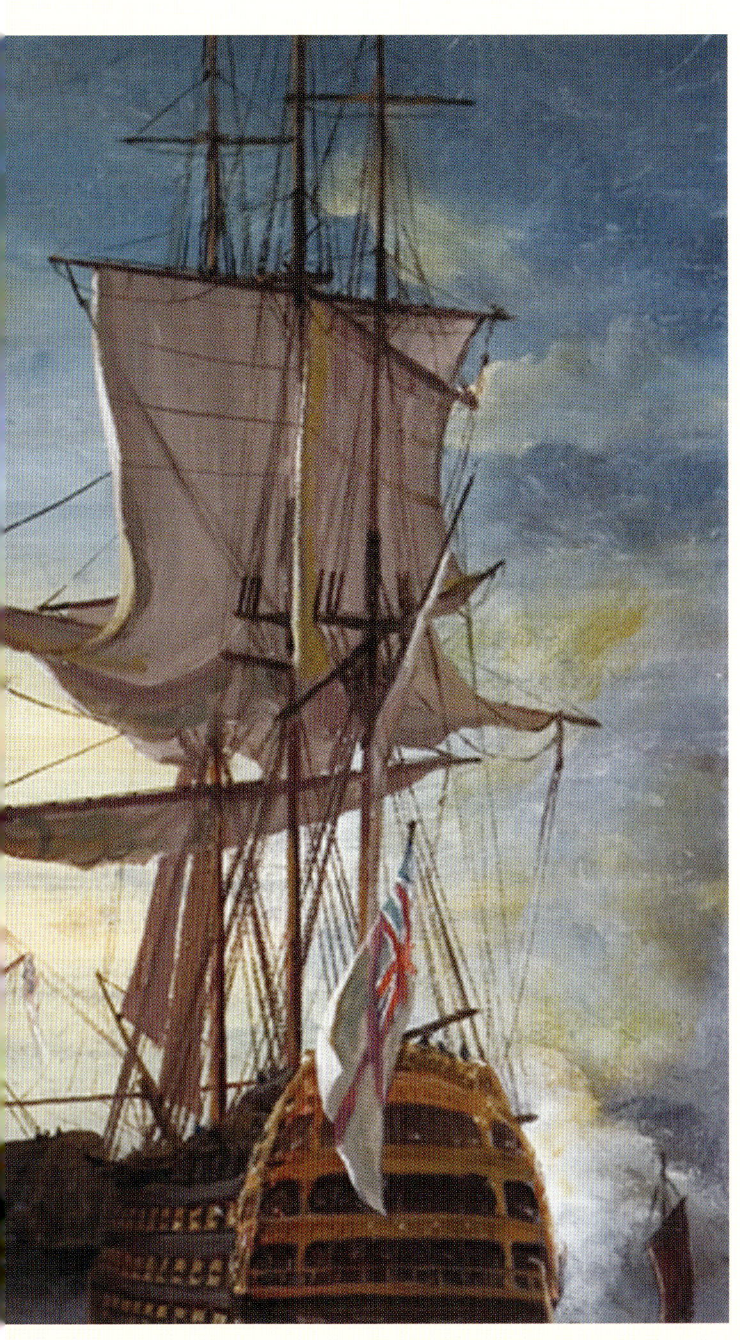

THE MARITIME ART
OF
PAUL HEE

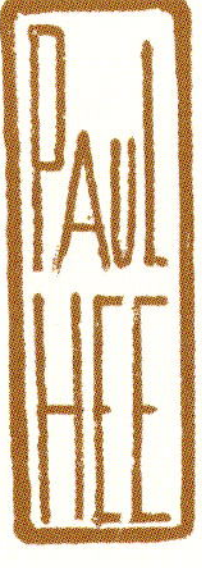

Three Centuries of Seafaring: The Maritime Art of Paul Hee

Published in conjunction with Paul Hee retrospective exhibition at the North Carolina Maritime Museum, Beaufort-by-the-Sea. (October 2009-March 2010).

Published in the United States of America by Fish Towne Press with Friends of the North Carolina Maritime Museum, Beaufort-by-the-Sea, North Carolina.

Design: Rebecca McMillan, Eastern Offset Printing Company, Atlantic Beach, North Carolina
Digital Photography: Scott Taylor, Beaufort-by-the-Sea, North Carolina
Text: Rick Carroll and Marcie Carroll, Fish Towne Press
Preface: North Carolina Maritime Museum Director Joseph Schwarzer
Foreword: North Carolina Maritime Museum Curator Paul Fontenoy
Printer: Jake Park, MiraeN Culture Group Co., Seoul, Korea

Hee, Paul.
Three Centuries of Seafaring: The Maritime Art of Paul Hee. —1st ed.
p. cm.
Exhibition Catalog
Includes bibliographic references and index.
1. Art, Maritime - Exhibitions. 2. Art, Ships - Exhibitions. 3. Art, Maritime History. I. Title.

Library of Congress Control Number: 2009935139

ISBN: 978-0-9796186-2-8

First Edition

ON THE COVER
Evening At Anchor
Five warships commanded by British Naval hero Horatio Nelson, who died in the Battle of Trafalgar aboard the 100-gun ship *Victory,* seen here with the 64-gun ship *Agamemnon*, and the 74-gun ships, *Captain, Vanguard* and *Elephant.*

"Of wrecks in the great September gales,

Of pirates coasting the Spanish Main,

And ships that never came back again..."

—The Building of The Ship

Henry Wadsworth Longfellow
(1807-1882)

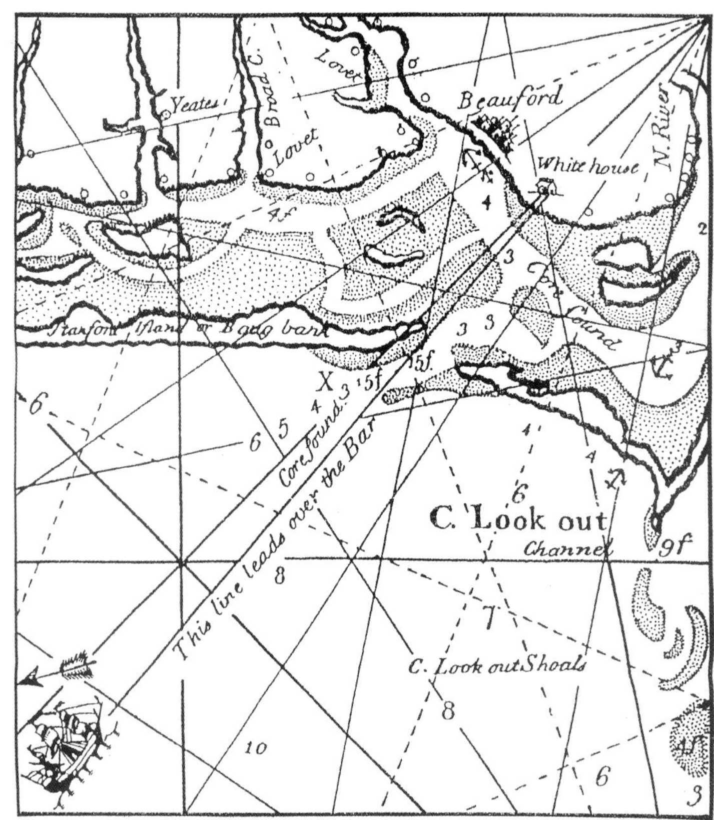

James Wimble Chart, 1738

dedicated to
all the seafarers who
have come and gone
from these shores

Three Centuries of Seafaring

The Maritime Art of Paul Hee

Fish Towne Press
Beaufort-by-the-Sea

Table of Contents

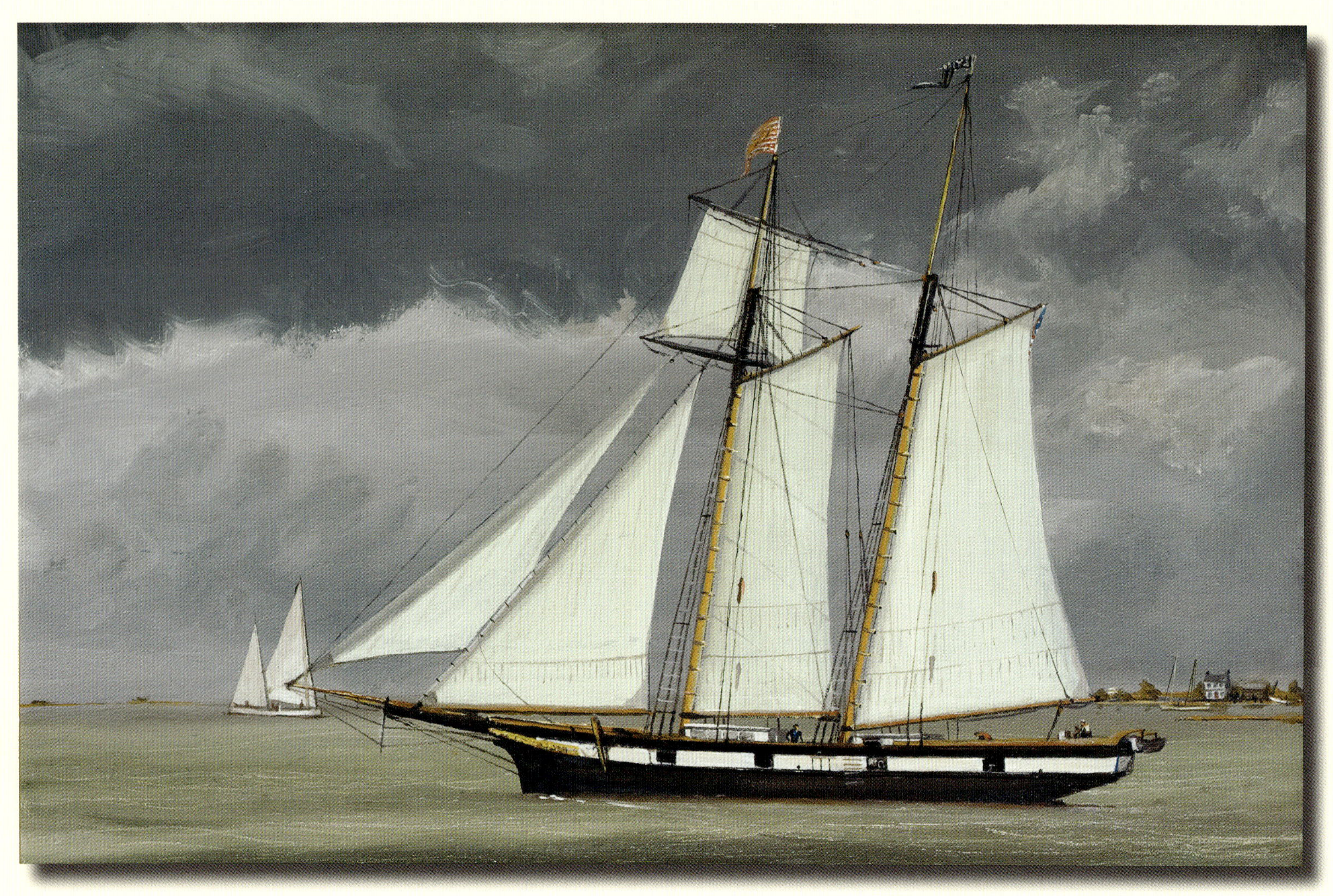

Lynx, Topsail Schooner in Beaufort Harbor

Published on the occasion of the exhibition

Three Centuries of Seafaring: The Maritime Art of Paul Hee

by

THE FRIENDS OF THE NORTH CAROLINA MARITIME MUSEUM

&

FISH TOWNE PRESS

To celebrate the
Tricentennial Founding Anniversary
of Beaufort-by-the-Sea,
North Carolina

Exhibit Organized

by the

North Carolina Maritime Museum

October 2009 - March 2010

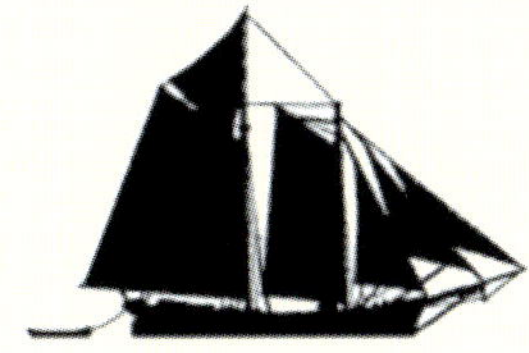

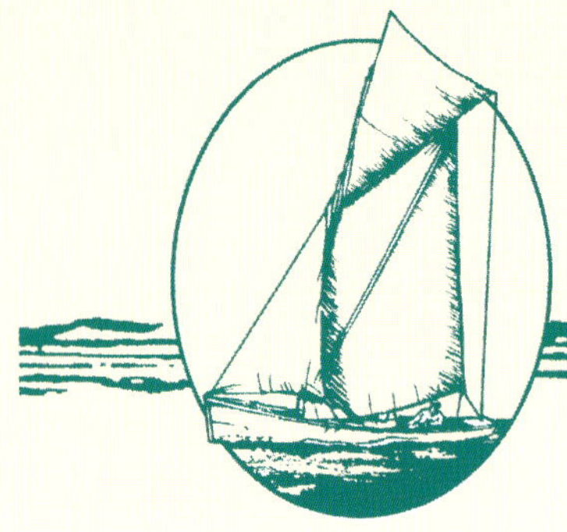

North Carolina Maritime Museum

In celebration of the three-hundredth anniversary of the founding of Beaufort, North Carolina, the Friends of the North Carolina Maritime Museum at Beaufort and Fish Towne Press have collaborated to showcase the art of Paul Hee.

Many generous supporters have contributed time, effort, and money to make *Three Centuries of Seafaring: The Maritime Art of Paul Hee* a reality. Few projects could more accurately communicate the fundamental nature of the Beaufort community.

Established in 1709, the small settlement that would become Beaufort rapidly grew into an important seaport and bore witness to critical stages of state and national development. The Tuscarora Wars, piracy and privateering, the Revolution, the War of 1812, and the Civil War all affected the growth of the town. In 1722, Beaufort was appointed a port for the unloading and discharging of vessels.

The historic Ward-Hancock house served as a customs house for the emergent *entrepot*, and commercial fishing continued to thrive and expand as a principal industry. This rich heritage is evident throughout present-day Beaufort. A walk down Ann Street takes the visitor past 18th and 19th Century houses, historic churches, and the Old Burying Ground.

Locals are justly proud of their past and are dedicated to preserving the timelessness of the community. Numerous volunteer organizations and attractions, such as the Beaufort Historical Association, Friends of the North Carolina Maritime Museum, Beaufort Woman's Club, and the North Carolina Maritime Museum, are committed to this goal.

The Museum is particularly pleased to have worked with the Friends on this project. Since the early 1900's, the Museum has researched, preserved, and interpreted the remarkable maritime history, culture, and environment of coastal North Carolina.

The maritime art of Paul Hee is an integral part of that history and culture. Past president of the Carolina Maritime Model Society, frequent Museum visitor, volunteer and member of the Friends, Paul is part of that indispensable group of community supporters who have helped to make the Museum one of the finest maritime museums in the country.

Every year the Museum conducts more than 300 public programs and numerous exhibitions and has more than 200,000 visitors. This year, one of those exhibitions will focus on the maritime art of Paul Hee. The exhibition will run from October 3, 2009 through March 7, 2010. This volume will serve as an overall introduction.

In one way or another, Paul Hee has spent much of his life on or near the water. A native of Long Island, he served in the Navy during World War II, and was finance director for a Miami cruise line. After selling and racing imported sports cars (MGs, Maseratis, Lamborghinis and Ferraris), he retired in 1988, studied art and moved to Beaufort to pursue his lifelong dream of capturing America's maritime heritage on canvas.

His subjects range over three centuries from the Golden Age of Sail to the heyday of steam. Each ship is exhaustively studied. Exact specifications are drawn from sources in museums and libraries, and his compositions are rendered in a style that is historically correct, visually stunning, and luminescent. Even more extraordinary, each of his compositions, from 17th Century battle pieces to 19th Century broadsides, evokes the *zeitgeist* appropriate to the subject.

As testament to his success, his paintings are highly prized and can be found in private collections, galleries, and museums across the nation. This is the first attempt to provide a catalogue of Paul Hee's maritime paintings. Quality digital reproductions by Scott Taylor, historic vignettes by Rick and Marcie Carroll of Fish Towne Press, and an Introduction by Paul Fontenoy, internationally recognized maritime historian, combine to present a unique overview of the artist's work. The resulting detailed analysis and historical insights constitute an appropriate tribute to the Beaufort community and the town's tricentennial.

August 2009

Joseph K. Schwarzer, II
Director
North Carolina Maritime Museums

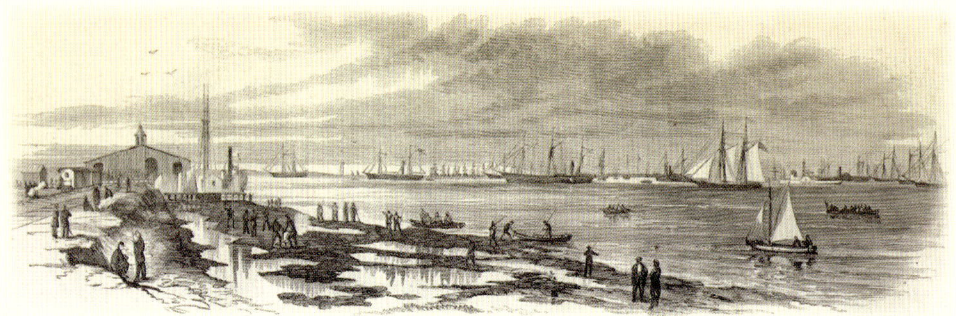

Great Southern Fleet Calls on Beaufort, North Carolina -Harper's Weekly, February 21, 1863

315 Front Street Beaufort, NC 28516-2124 *phone:* 252.728.7317 *email:* maritime@ncmail.net www.ncmaritime.org

Acknowledgements

Back in winter 2008, Rick Carroll reminded me that several years ago we'd talked of publishing a collection of Paul Hee's paintings. For various reasons, the project was shelved at the time. Wouldn't 2009, the year of Beaufort's 300th anniversary, be a good time to revive the idea? This local book – painted, written, photographed and designed right in the neighborhood – would be a fine memento of the town of Beaufort's 300th anniversary.

As a member of Friends of the Maritime Museum board, I thought the book would be a natural for the Museum. Rick and Marcie Carroll's Fish Towne Press would produce the book and the Friends would sell it. After paying the artist, printers, and publishers, profits would go to the Museum. We wrote out a business plan and it looked like a winner, with residual income for the Museum potentially for years. Paul Hee was enthusiastic, too.

Our first decision, before presenting the project to the Friends board, was to raise enough money in advance to cover costs of production. We designated the first 500 copies of the 3,000 press run as a limited edition, to be numbered and signed by the artist and delivered in a slipcase. We took advance orders. We signed up sponsors. We encouraged Museum supporters to become patrons. And many friends of the Museum and Paul Hee's fans joined this labor of love.

Our patrons and sponsors are listed below. I'd also like to thank those who gave generously of their time and enthusiasm to get this project underway: Joe Schwarzer and Paul Fontenoy of the Museum staff contributed the preface and introduction, respectively. Fellow Friends board members Rich Olsen, Bruce Chadwick and Larry Gross, Friends Director of Operations Brent Creelman, photographer Scott Taylor, designer Rebecca McMillan, and, of course, Rick and Marcie Carroll of Fish Towne Press. We also had enthusiastic assistance from Ray Voelpel, at Tidewater Gallery in Swansboro, N.C.

In addition to the contributions listed below, the book project was buoyed by anonymous grants of $5,000 and $1,000, for which we are truly grateful.

David DuBuisson
Secretary, Friends of the Museum
August 2009

Sponsors

$1,000 Level

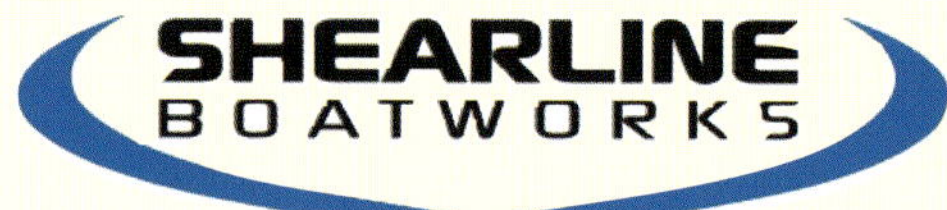

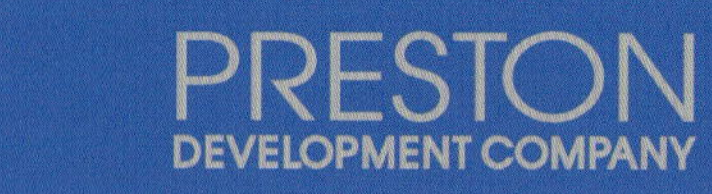

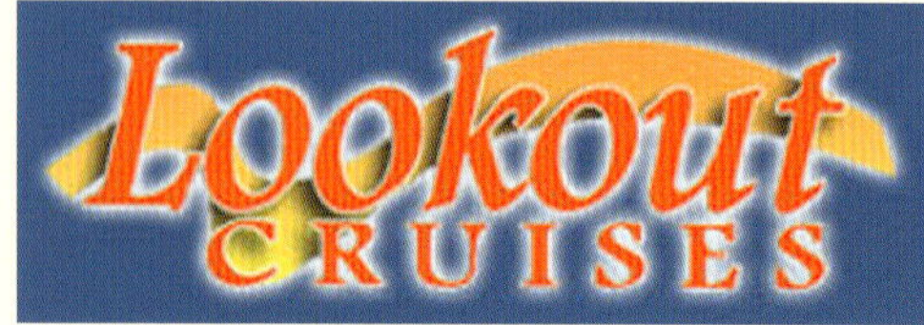

Scott Taylor
PHOTOGRAPHY

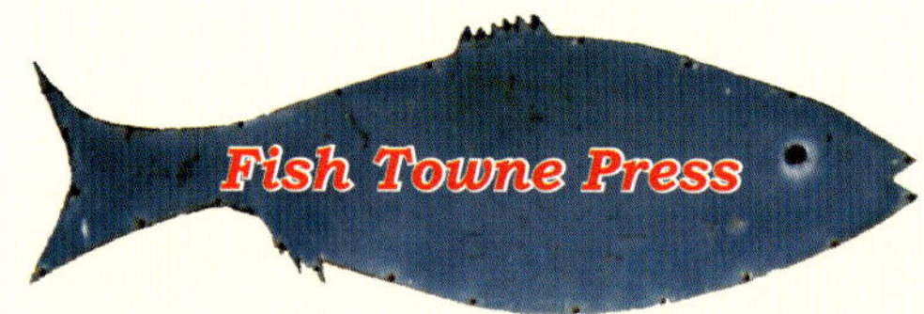

Richard & Elizabeth Olsen

Richard and Elizabeth Olsen
In Memory of Ken Tilley

EASTERN OFFSET
PRINTING
COMPANY

$500 Level

John & Sonda Warrington
(Beaufort Yacht Sales)
Bruce and Gwynne Chadwick
John and Terry Hines
Bucky and Wendi Oliver
Ham and Ann Sloan

Patrons
(\$200)

Bill & Fran Abbruzzese
Gene & Helen Aman
Richard H. Bierly
Doug & Caroline Brady
Ed & Claire Burdett
Watts & Betsy Carr
R. Hunter Chadwick Jr.
John & Ginny Costlow
Brent & Kelli Creelman
Dr. Douglas Creelman
Hugh & Nan Cullman
David & Allison DuBuisson
George & Sallie Ellinwood
Pete & Mei Evans
Billy Green & Vivian Tilley
Norman Greisen
Larry & Joyce Gross
Z. Bryan Haislip
Steve & Chasie Harris
Carol Bessent Hayman
Joe & Marianna Hollinshed
Pete & Tracy Huley
Bob & Susan Hunter
Dave & Clara Inscoe
Christopher Jamkauskas
Tommy & Julie Lee
Sandy & Bet McClamroch
Tom & Peg Midyette
Vick & Pat Moore
Eddy & Barbara Myers
Bert & Sharon Owens
George & Dell Paschal
Charles & Patricia Phillips
Jimmy & Jo Piver
Randy & Sally Christine Repass
Robert & Virginia Santucci
Robin Schonberger
Joseph & Melanie Schwarzer
Dana & Mary Smith
Jim & Susan Smitherman
Jim & Amy Thullen
Emily M. Vaughan
Jose & Elian Vecina

INTRODUCTION

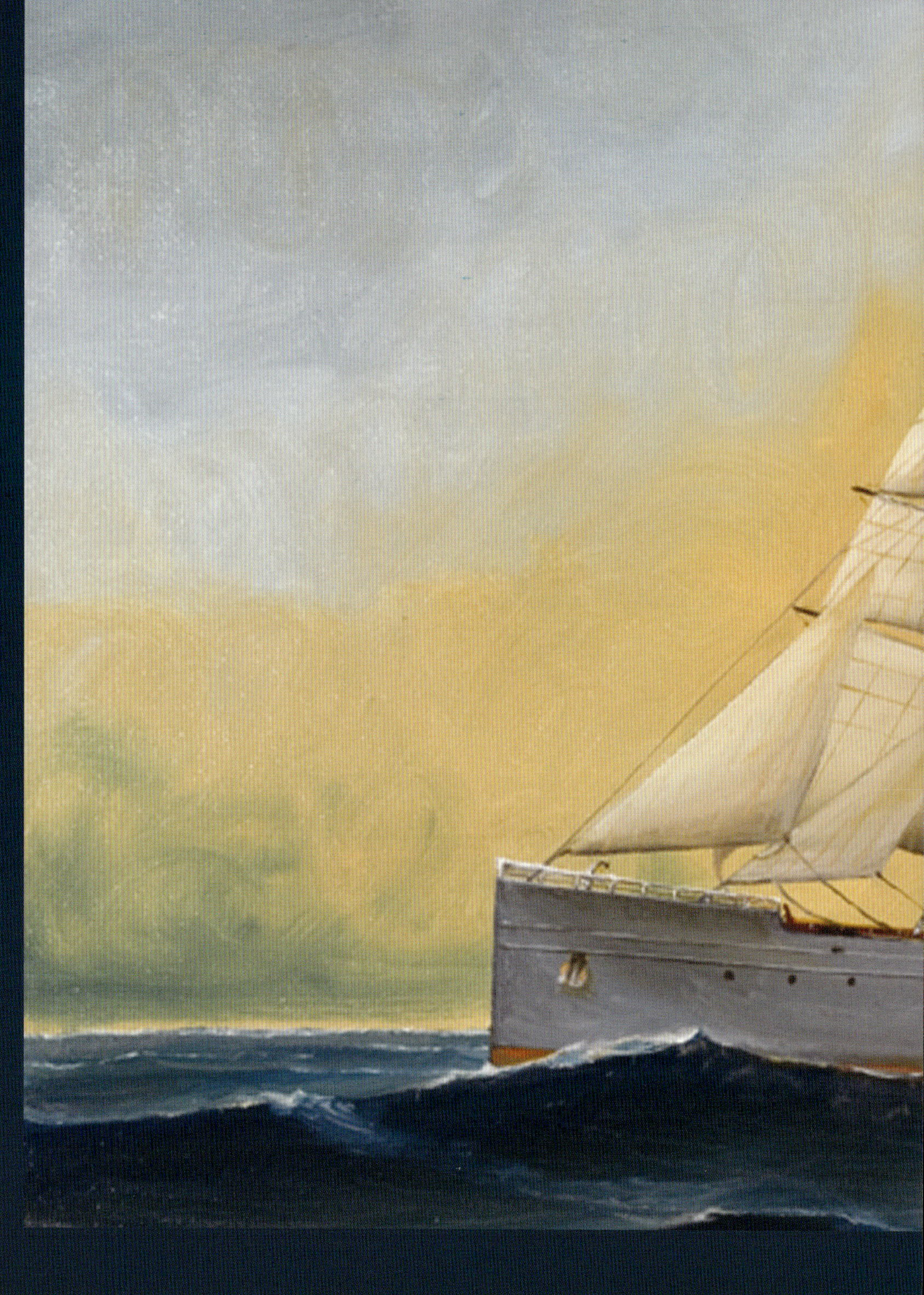

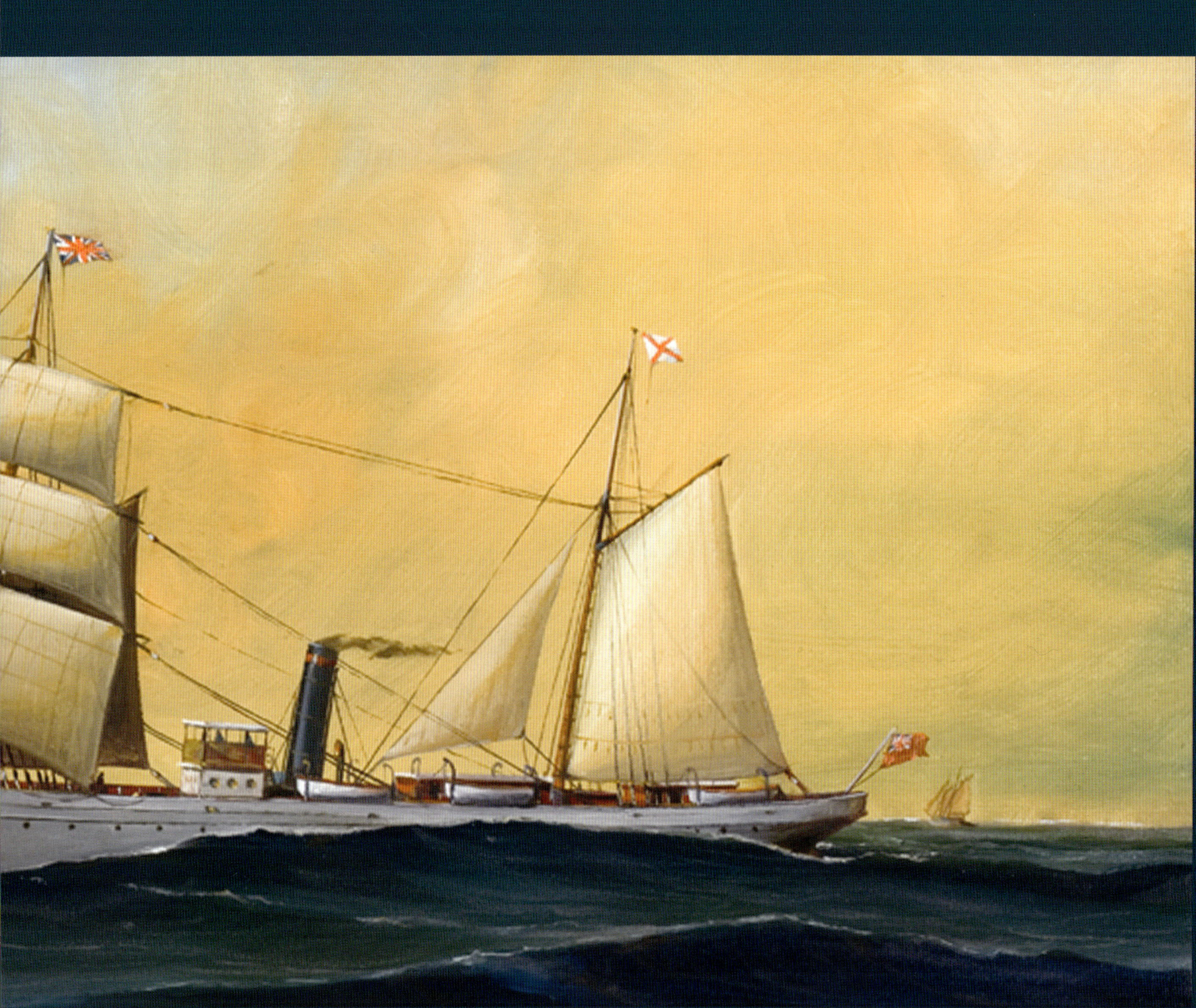

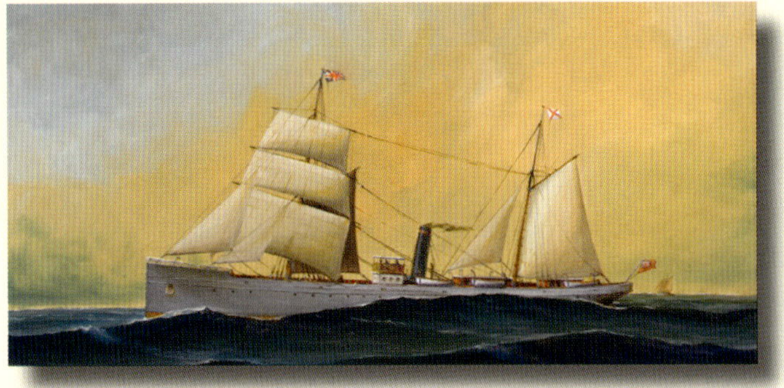

Merionethshire

Paul Hee's work has an international reputation. He has carved out an individual niche in the field of contemporary maritime art. His paintings, while accurately portraying their historical prototypes, also carefully reproduce the styles of contemporary maritime artists. This combination of realism and stylistic fidelity adds an extra level of interest to his work, which both general and specialist audiences appreciate and enjoy.

Why have artists, especially since the 17th Century, found ships and the sea such compelling subjects for their work? Why have collectors responded so enthusiastically to this genre? No writer has better responded than John Ruskin, in the fifty pages of *The Harbors of England* (1856):

> Of all things, living or lifeless, upon this strange earth, there is but one which, having reached the mid-term of appointed human endurance on it, I still regard with unmitigated amazement...and that is the bow of a Boat. There is not, except the very loveliest creatures of the living world, anything in nature so absolutely notable, bewitching, and, according to its means and measure, heart-occupying, as a well-handled ship under sail in a stormy day...Take it all in all, a Ship of the Line is the most honorable thing that man, as a gregarious animal, has ever produced.

Maritime art, inspired by the compelling combination of aesthetic elegance and technological sophistication embodied in contemporary shipping, flourished in the western world from the 17th Century until the late 1800s. Its popularity declined during the first half of the 20th Century, although this same period saw some of the most exciting exploitation of contemporary fine art movements into work produced for advertising and other commercial applications. Since World War II we have witnessed a relentless resurgence of interest in maritime work, both from earlier masters and from contemporary artists, possibly fueled, initially at least, by the visual power of the stunning canvases war artists produced during the conflict.

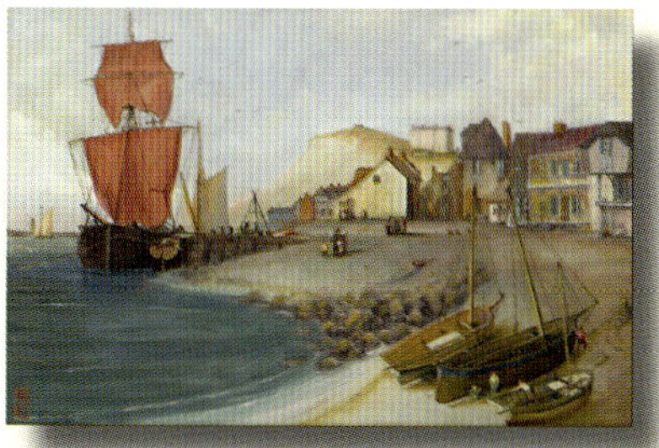

Low Water at Folkestone

Until recently, maritime artists have worked within the broad parameters of their contemporaries' schools of thought, and this is hardly surprising, since few practitioners confined their work wholly to a single genre, nor conceived of themselves as specialists. The 17th Century Dutch maritime canvases fit wholly within the prevailing aesthetic that governed Dutch landscape painting of the era; English maritime and landscape art from the later 1700s display similar attention to "rusticity," quality of light, and subtly formal composition; the Neo-classicism of French studio art around 1800 also pervades contemporary maritime work of all kinds—seascapes, battles, or ship portraits.

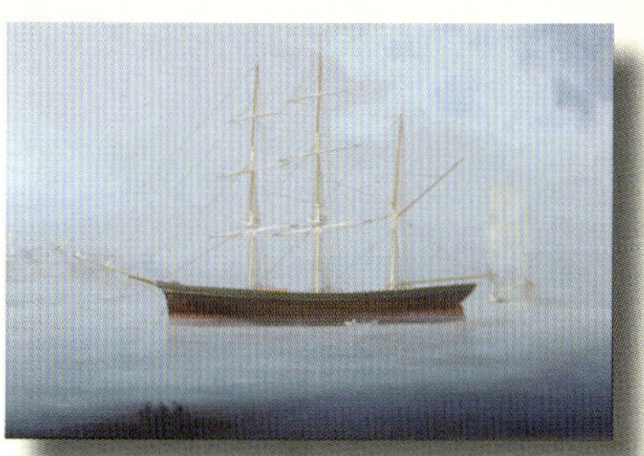

Moored in Fog on Connecticut River

The Romanticism of studio artists, like that of their fellow writers and composers, was a reaction to a world of industrialization. It generated some of the most powerful examples of maritime art from any era—Géricault's *The Raft of the Medusa* and Turner's *The Slave Ship* or *The Fighting Téméraire*, for example. Then, from the mid-1800s, artists began moving away from the studio towards painting directly from nature, in a search for beauty and truth derived from the very experience of immersion in the environment they observed and then explored and exposed.

The Hudson River School in the eastern United States and Impressionism (and its aesthetic successors) in France, for example, emerged from this paradigm, and such influences again made their mark on the form and presentation of contemporary maritime art. Impressionism and Post-Impressionism, infused with strong elements of the American Naïve and Realist schools, subsequently dominated the style of maritime art produced in the first half of the 20th Century (and much of the often remarkable work created during two world wars and the conflicts that followed them).

The paradigm that has dominated the world of maritime art since the end of the Second World War, most probably a reaction against the dominance of abstractionism during the 20th Century, might best be termed "superrealism." Its practitioners set themselves multiple simultaneous objectives: to generate evocative images that engage their viewers, to recreate scenes – such as *Dauntless* Defeats *Sappho* on page 127 – or events from the past (sometimes specific but at other times more general), to convey the "truth and beauty" of the maritime experience. In addition to deploying all the traditional tools of artistic composition, these recent generations of maritime painters have elevated the importance of historical research, meticulous reconstruction, and fidelity of depiction to a central position within the creative process and the final product. (In this they are not alone, since an identical approach prevails within the field of aviation art.)

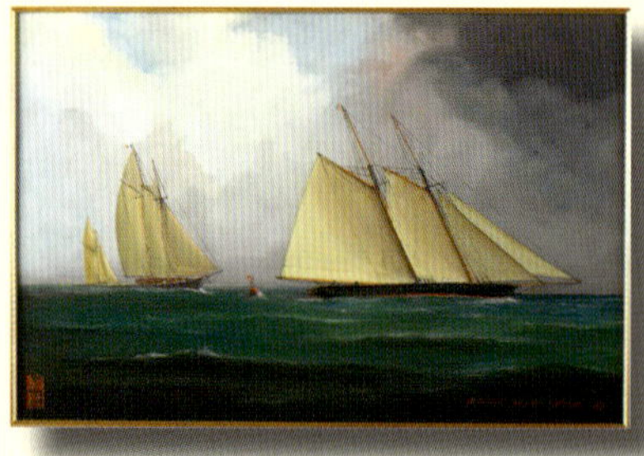

DAUNTLESS DEFEATS *SAPPHO*

Earlier generations of painters have demonstrated that attention to accuracy of presentation and fidelity to detail need be no obstacle to the creation of powerful art. The works of the Willem Van de Veldes (Elder and Younger) and twin brothers John and James Bard in the late 17th Century serve as important documents recording the shipping of that era while maintaining their compelling artistic integrity. Antonio Jacobsen's ship portraits are both technical records and gorgeous artworks. Even the rigidly stylized broadside views (meticulously accurate in their depiction) of the Bard brothers never allow their formulaic character and prototypical fidelity to diminish the exuberance of their painting.

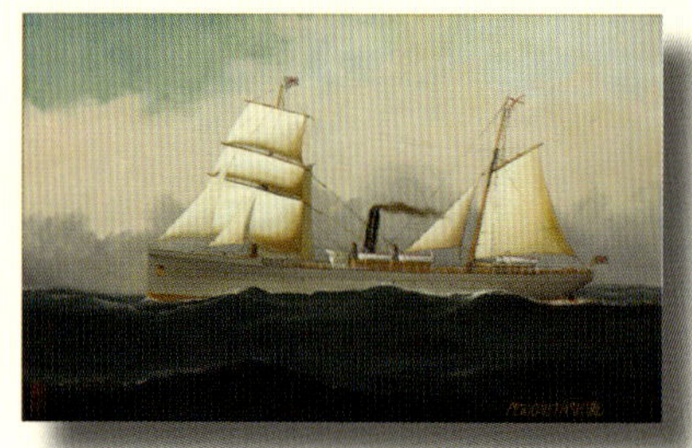

MERIONETHSHIRE

Contemporary maritime artists' devotion to accuracy has also resulted in some remarkable paintings (the work of the late Thomas Hoyne immediately comes to mind). In less talented hands, however, it can render the finished canvas sterile, stripping the image of vitality, precluding viewer involvement, and generating a tour-de-force of technical illustration rather than a compelling work of art.

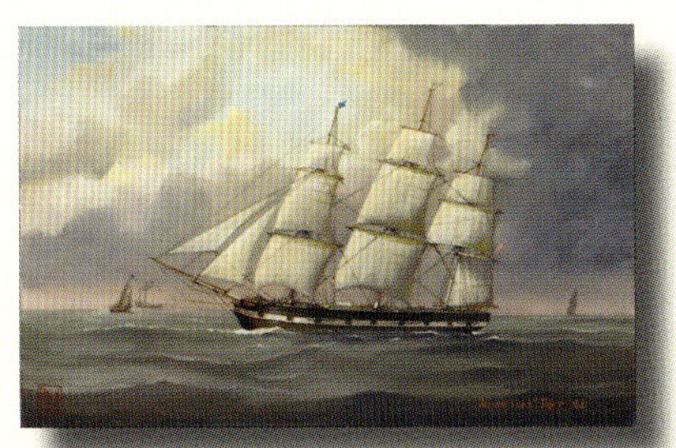

Tiger 1841

Paul Hee has taken a different approach, one that has garnered him an international reputation for his work. He eschews the current dedication to "superrealism" in his work, preferring to carefully reproduce the styles of maritime artists contemporary with the vessels and scenes that fill his canvases, while still accurately and realistically portraying their historical prototypes.

His work displays very noticeable differences between the styles he deploys to portray a late 17th Century vessel in a storm, an early 19th Century fleet action, or a late 19th Century steamer. The presentations of each vessel, the ocean, the background and sky, the lighting, and the color palette all correspond with the practices of leading maritime artists of the period.

Within the very large body of his work, there are some particular examples that stand out, both as works in their own right and as embodiments of Paul Hee's particular approach to maritime art. The beautiful composite painting of several vessels at one time commanded by Horatio Nelson that appears on page 141 (and also on the book cover) owes much of the basis for its concept and composition to a fine contemporary work by Nicholas Pocock; yet Paul Hee's treatment of light and color, while faithful to the norms of the period, enriches the viewer's experience with the drama of a glorious sunset that both provides a dramatic background and highlights the vessels themselves.

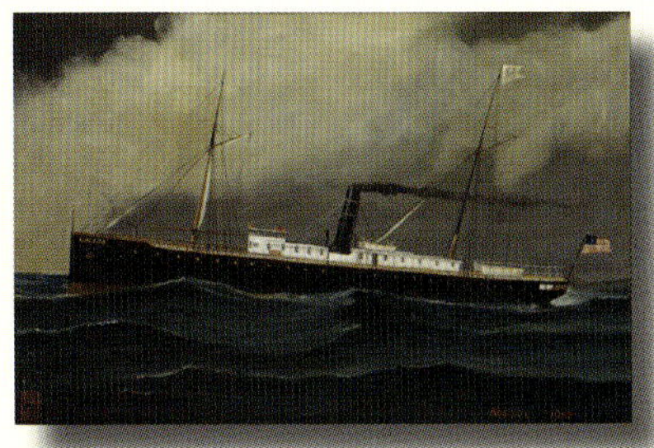

Niagara

Contrast this work with the paintings of the liner *Merionethshire* of 1885 on the cover of this chapter or the steamer *Niagara* of 1902 on page 59. Here are splendid examples of classic ship's portraits in the style of Antonio Jacobsen, but, once again, Paul Hee's approach to depicting ocean and sky, still in accord with contemporary conventions, is clearly his own.

Hee demonstrates his versatility and his deep understanding of the various stylistic strands of maritime art, especially in the 19th Century, with some unusual works. His depictions of the steamboats *Norwich* and *Harlem* (pages 112 and 113) and the painting of the bugeye *Edna G. Lockwood* (page 136) clearly are inspired by portraits of similar vessels by the Bard brothers.

Their settings and the almost draftsman-like presentation of the steamboats are typical of such works. Nevertheless, Hee's especial concern for depicting the interplay of light and water make these paintings distinctly his own. Two other highly individual works are his portrait of Olaudah Equiano (page 25), and *The White Squadron* (below and page 40).

Olaudah Equiano looks out at us from a classically stereotypical late 18th Century frame, yet Hee's care to maintain stylistic integrity never obstructs access to the vitality of this remarkable sitter.

The White Squadron (below and page 40) has its roots in yet another artistic convention, the exuberant popular illustrative work of the late 19th Century, but Hee's dramatic use of light and line transcends the boundaries of meticulous attention to stylistic limitations.

After viewing his *oeuvre* as a whole, it is readily apparent that Paul Hee, for all his versatility, finds the soul of his art in the transcendent luminescence so dominant in 19th Century maritime painting. Light—dazzlingly exuberant, tranquilly evocative, or menacingly looming—dominated the most compelling maritime art of this era, and Paul Hee has drawn deep from the well of its artistic experience.

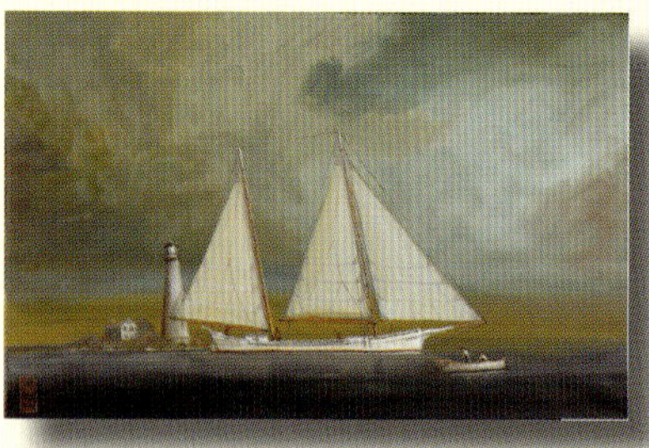

Edna E. Lockwood

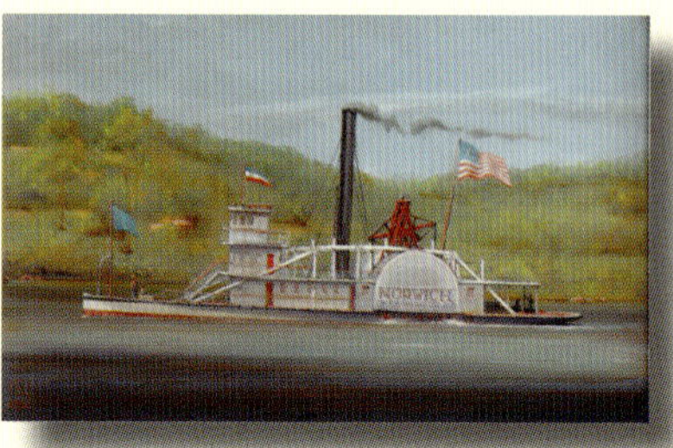

Norwich

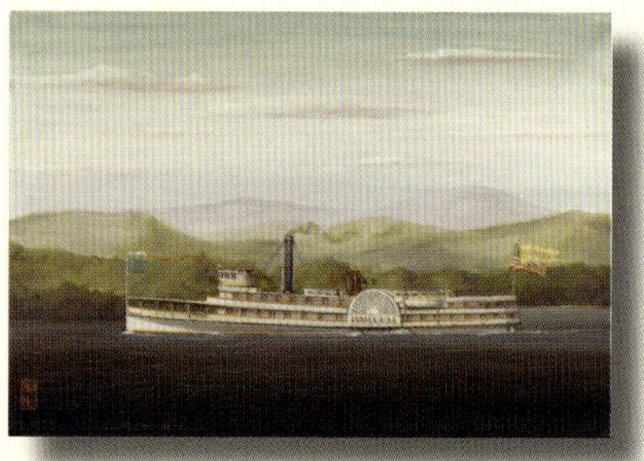

Harlem

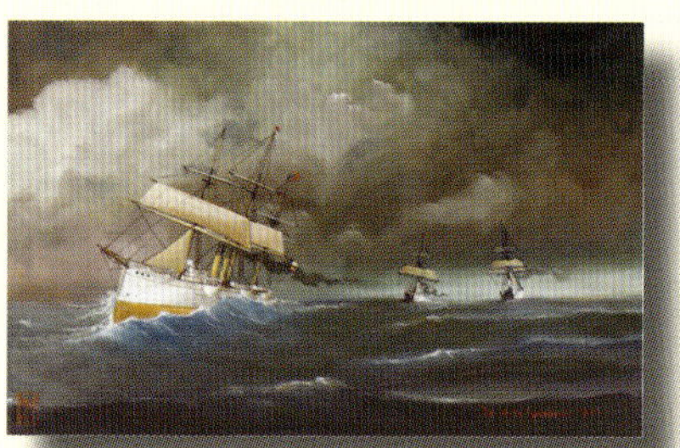

The White Squadron

His paintings are suffused with the world view of masters such as Nicholas Pocock, Thomas Buttersworth, Francis Sartorius, Thomas Luny, Thomas Dutton, and the incomparable J.M.W. Turner from England, and similar American luminaries, especially Antonio Jacobsen and Samuel Walters. Paul Hee's works depicting 19th Century vessels incorporate the same sensibilities and sensitivities particularly well.

It is unusual among current maritime artists to find this combination of concern for historical accuracy and for stylistic fidelity that is central to Hee's work. The greatest danger of this approach is that it can be all too easy for an artist, in his concern for historic stylistic fidelity, simply to replicate the work of the painters who inspire him. Fortunately, Paul Hee has succeeded in steering clear of this trap. Like any practitioner of the arts, he cheerfully and gratefully acknowledges the debt he owes to earlier masters, but his work remains clearly and identifiably his own.

Paul Fontenoy
Curator
Maritime Research & Technology
North Carolina Maritime Museum

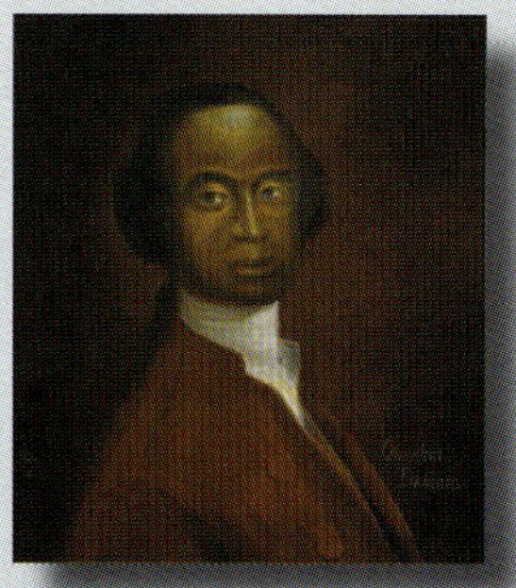

Olaudah Equiano

Abducted at 11 in western Africa and sold into slavery in the Royal Navy, Olaudah Equiano sailed the world on slave and merchant ships. In 1776, he bought his freedom from a Philadelphia Quaker. Equiano settled in London, became a scientist's assistant, married into English society, and wrote the first known published work by a black man. His autobiography, *The Interesting Narrative of The Life of Olaudah Equiano* or *Gustavas Vasa, the African, by Himself*, first published in 1789, gave voice to the popular movement to repeal slavery. Called "the father of black literature," Equiano wrote the book "to excite in august assemblies a sense of compassion of the miseries which the slave trade has entailed on my unfortunate countrymen." His book became a best seller, and he, a rich man. A decade after Equiano's death in London in 1797, England abolished the slave trade.

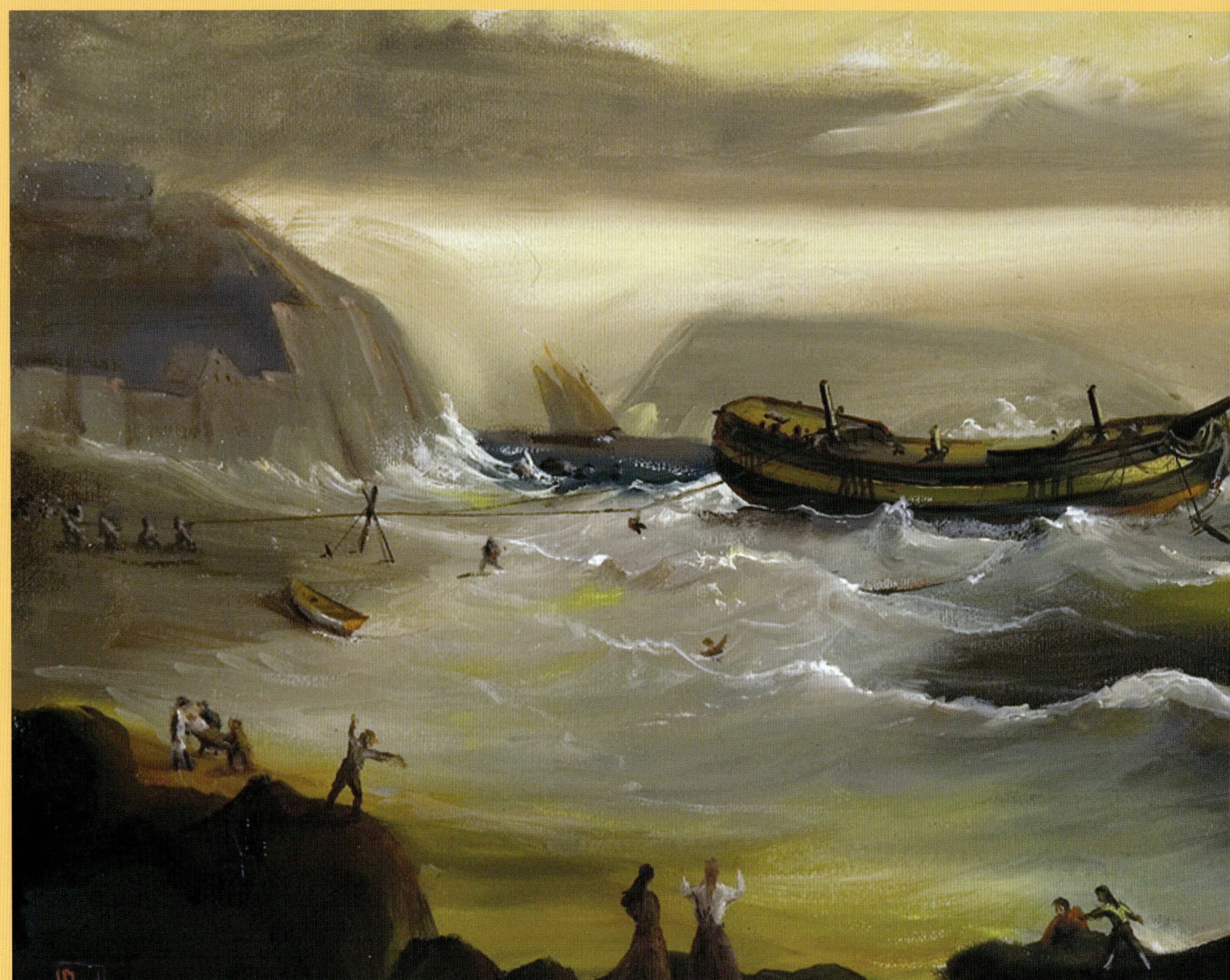

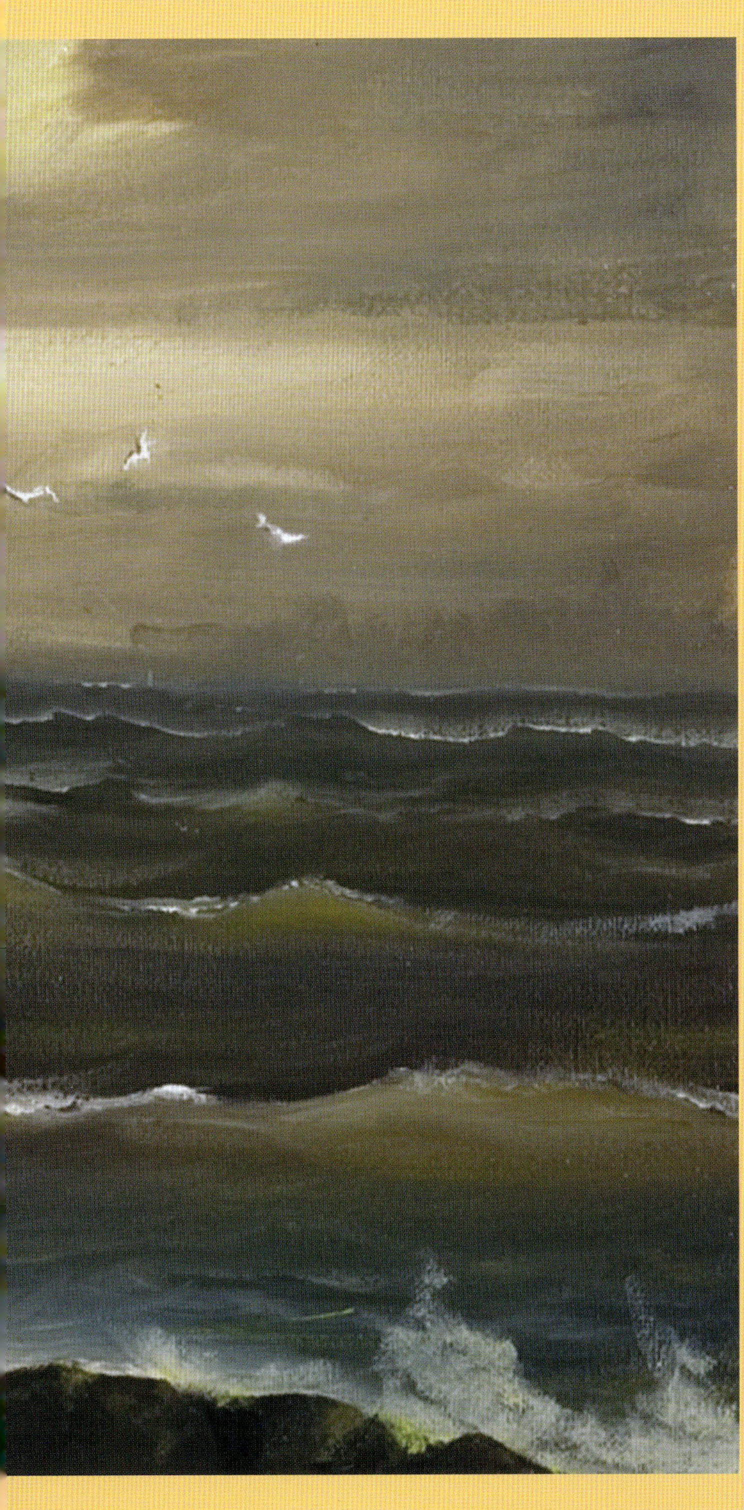

CHAPTER I

ADVENTURES

Wreck of the Dutton

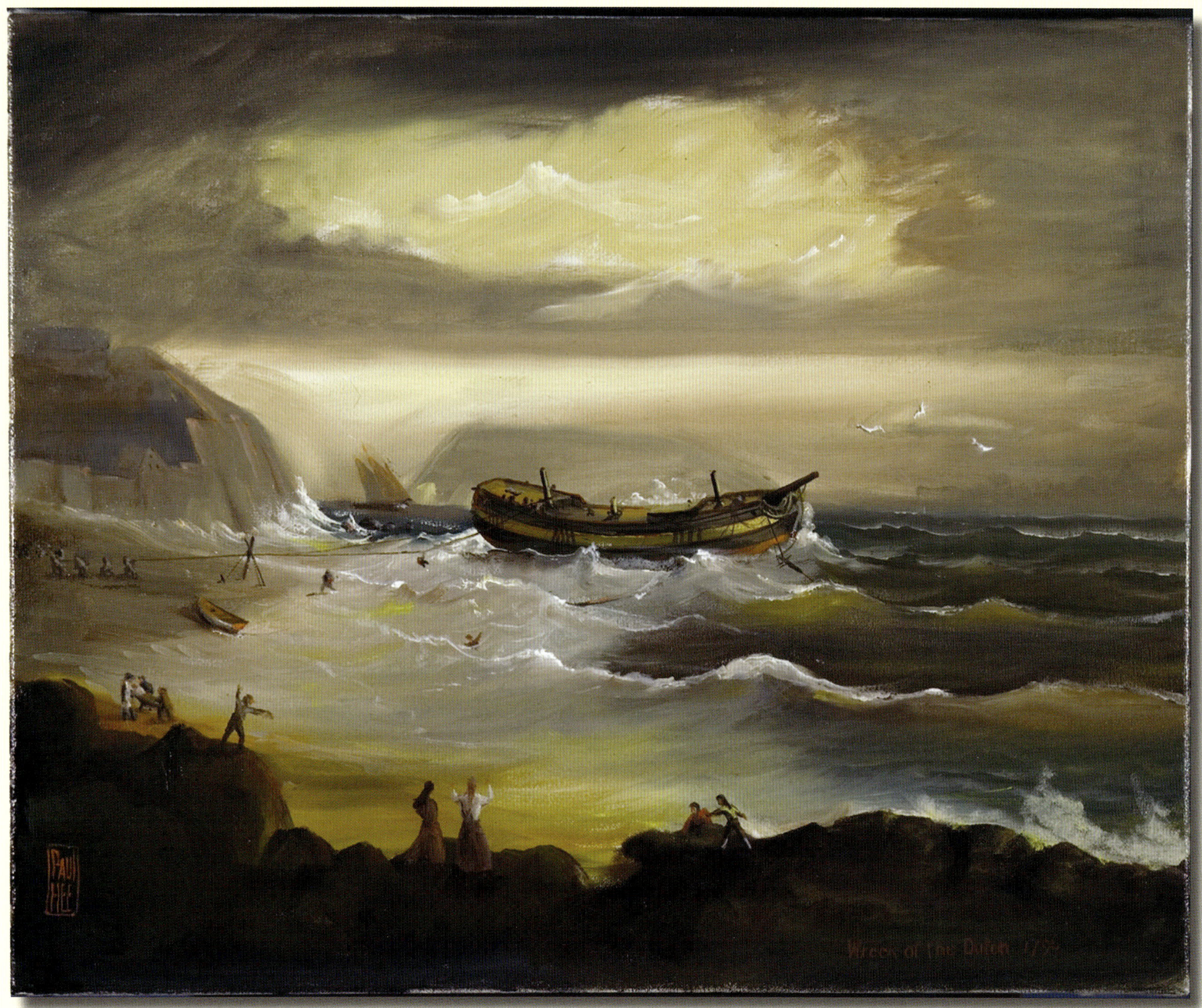
Wreck of the Dutton

Wreck of the Dutton
18" x 28"

The East Indiaman *Dutton* wrecked in a gale at Plymouth Sound off the coast of Devon on January 16, 1796. Built on the Thames in 1781, the troop transport was bound for the West Indies with 400 men and a number of women and children when *Dutton* struck shoals, lost the rudder, and was swept onto the rocky shore below the Citadel. A passerby, Captain Edward Pellew, who lived in Devon, saw the ship strike the rocks broadside on. With his men, Pellew swam out to the sinking vessel in heavy surf, rigged a lifeline, and risked his life to save all but four aboard. For his heroism, the young captain was made a baron and, after a long, distinguished Naval career, became Admiral Sir Edward Pellew 1st Viscount Exmouth (1757-1833). His statue stands today at the National Maritime Museum, Greenwich, London.

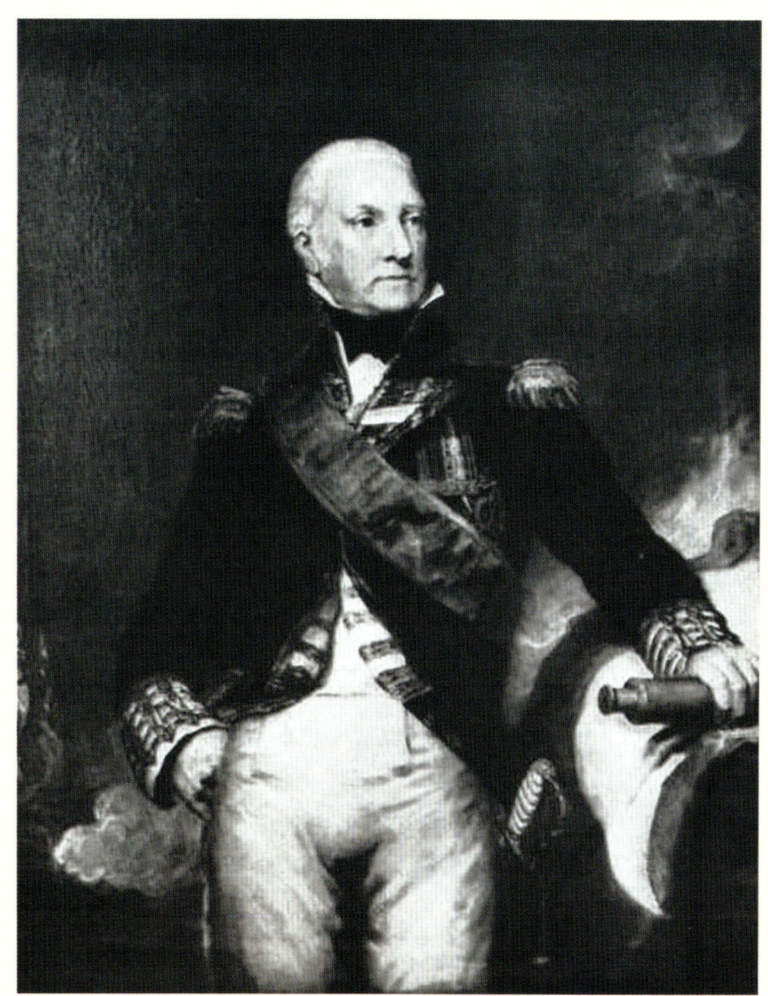

Admiral Sir Edward Pellew

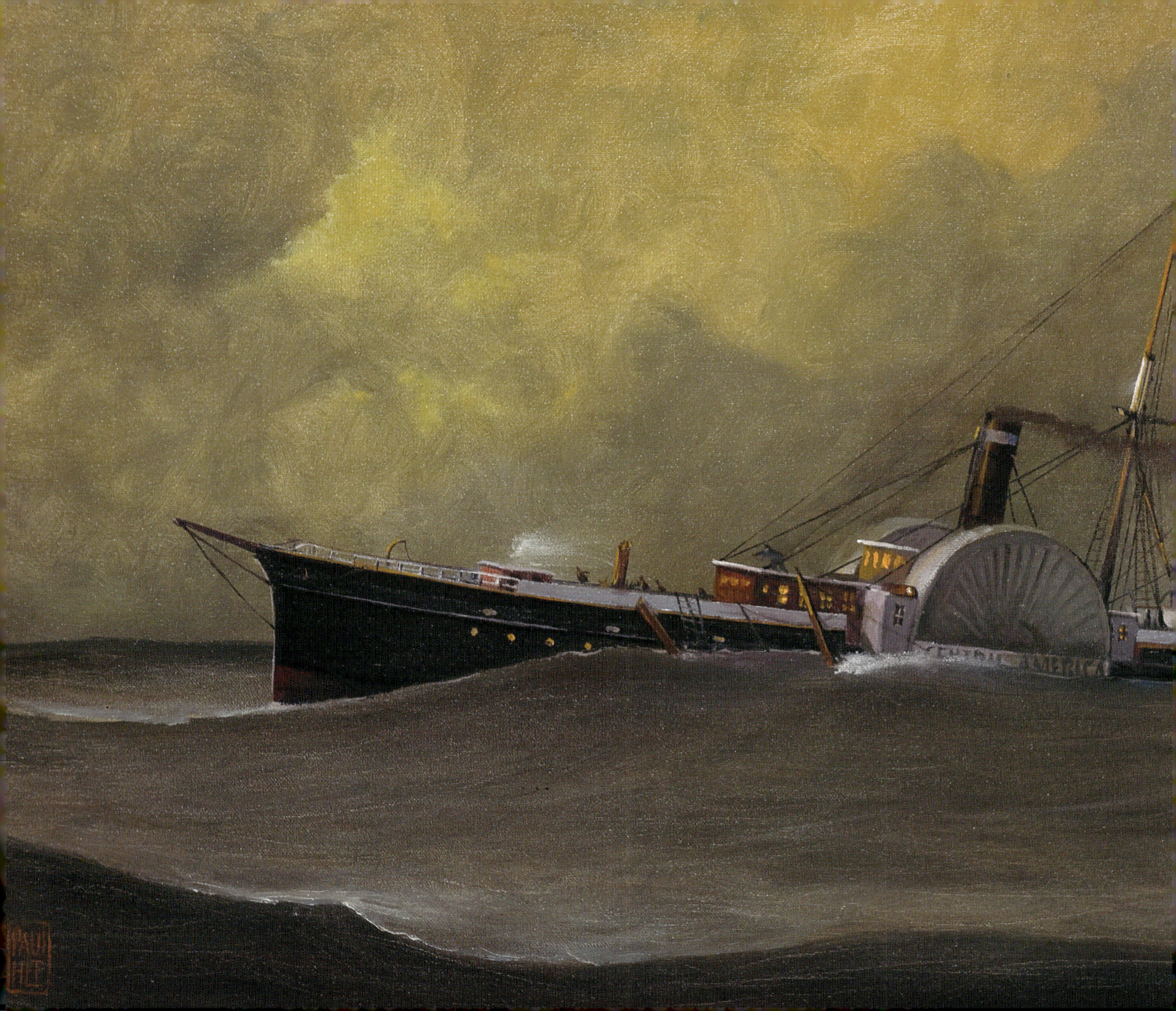
CENTRAL AMERICA

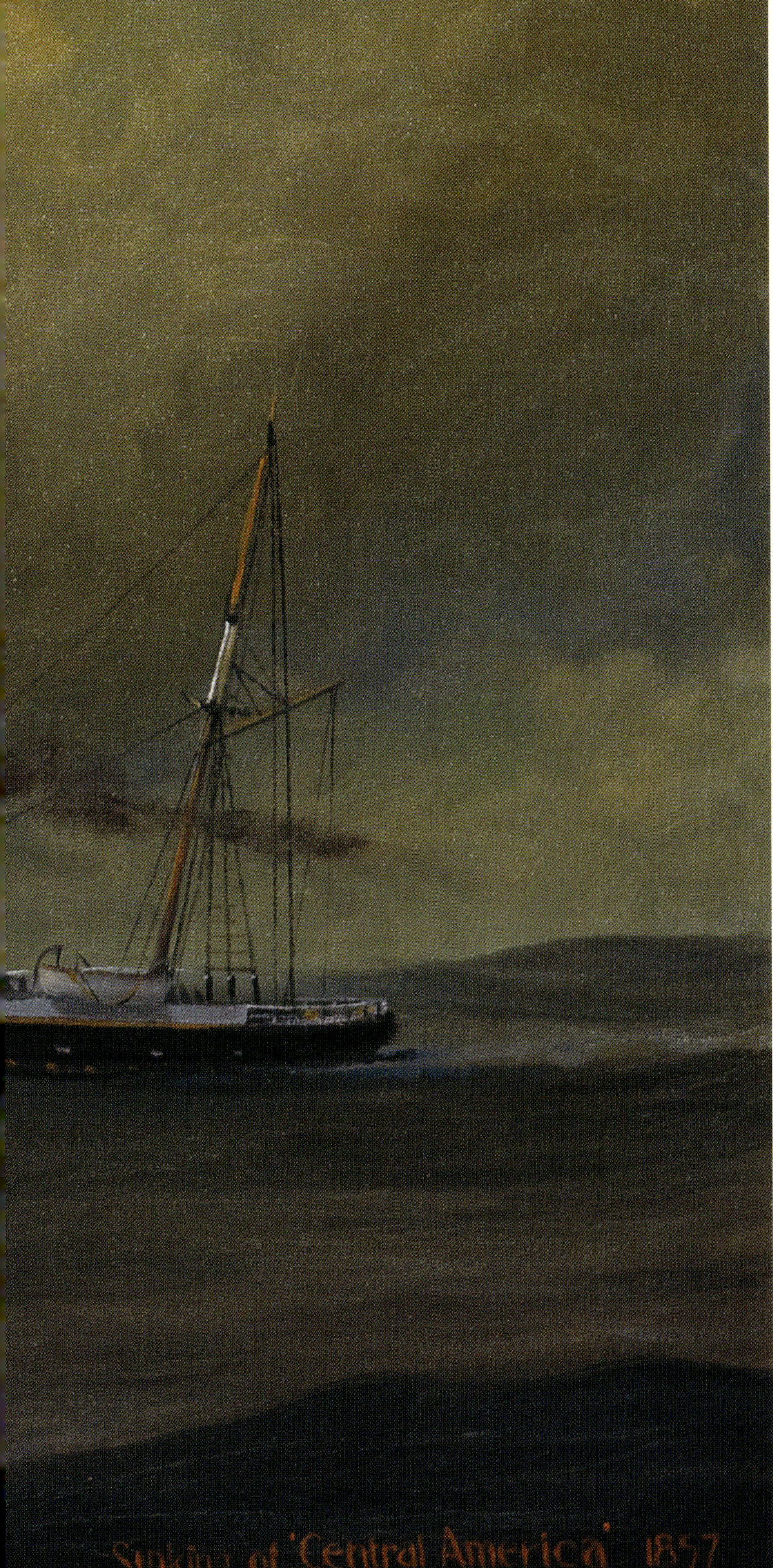

SS Central America (Ship of Gold)

20" x 30"

Bound for New York, *SS Central America,* a 280-foot side-wheel steamer loaded with gold, got caught in a 105-mph hurricane off the Carolina coast on September 11, 1857. The ship went down with 477 passengers and 101 crew and 15 tons of gold from the California Gold Rush. More than 200 passengers, mostly women and children, were rescued by two passing vessels. The lost gold, then worth $2 million, contributed to The Panic of 1857, a sudden downturn in the U.S. economy that did not end until the Civil War. On Sept. 11, 1987, Tommy Thompson's salvagers recovered $150 million in gold at 8000-foot depths. One 80-pound gold brick, nicknamed *Eureka*, sold at auction for a record $8 million.

The Panic of 1857

In early 1857, the storm clouds of recession had gathered. Led by agriculture, individual sectors of the economy began to draw against their bank deposits, putting greater and greater pressure on the gold reserves that banks relied upon to back their privately issued notes. In August 1857, the bubble burst. The New York office of the Ohio Life Insurance and Trust Company closed its doors. Most New York banks were creditors of Ohio Life, and, as prices fell and the values vanished, several of those banking firms failed. A concurrent delay of gold shipments from California contributed to the despair. This was compounded by the sinking of the *Central America*, which sent its huge load of gold – historian Bray Hammond estimates a value equal to one-fifth of the gold then in Wall Street coffers – to the bottom of the sea. With that gold, it had been hoped that banks could withstand any run; without it, they were at grave risk of failure. General William Tecumseh Sherman, a New York banker at the time of the sinking, wrote in his memoirs that the "absolute loss of this treasure went to swell the confusion and panic of the day."

—*America's Lost Treasure*, by Tommy Thompson

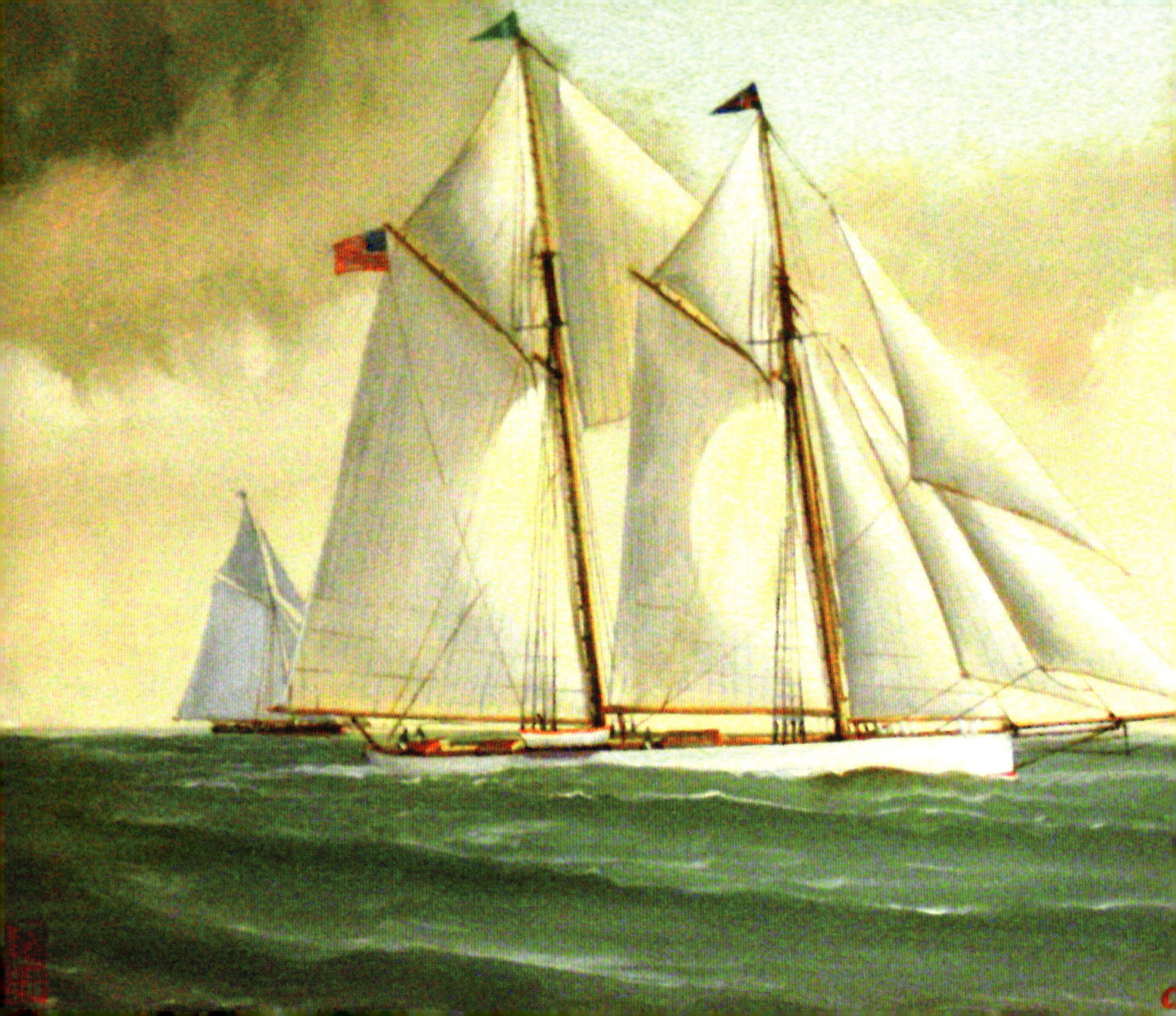

Coronet

20" x 30"

Sleek, swift and stylish, the 133-foot schooner *Coronet* is a surviving 19th century luxury yacht that recalls an extravagant nautical era. Built in 1885 for New York millionaire Rufus T. Bush to cruise the world in comfort, *Coronet* was a pilot schooner gilded to the hilt. She has been called the "oldest, largest and most original grand yacht in the world." *Coronet* sported mahogany-paneled staterooms, marble-treaded staircase, cloisonné chandelier, stained glass doors and a piano. No harbor queen, *Coronet* won a trans-Atlantic race in 1887, circumnavigated the globe, and in 1896, sailed from San Francisco to Japan with Amherst astronomer David Peck Todd to observe a total solar eclipse. The 40,000-mile round-trip voyage inspired Mabel Loomis Todd's 1898 book, *Corona & Coronet.* Restoration of *Coronet's* elegant appointments is underway at the International Yacht Restoration School in Newport, Rhode Island.

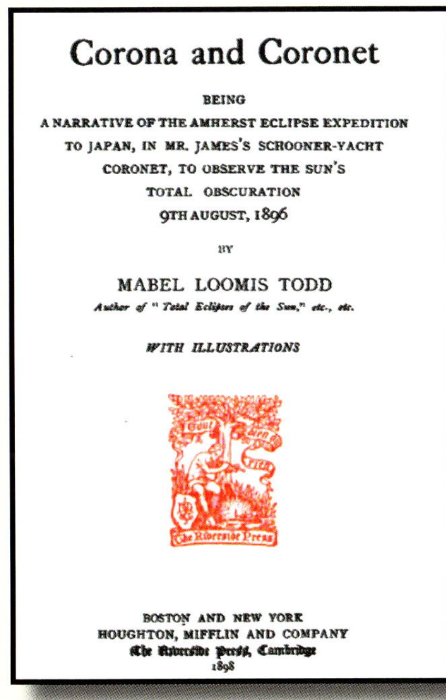

Corona and Coronet

BEING
A NARRATIVE OF THE AMHERST ECLIPSE EXPEDITION
TO JAPAN, IN MR. JAMES'S SCHOONER-YACHT
CORONET, TO OBSERVE THE SUN'S
TOTAL OBSCURATION
9TH AUGUST, 1896

BY

MABEL LOOMIS TODD

Author of "Total Eclipses of the Sun," etc., etc.

WITH ILLUSTRATIONS

BOSTON AND NEW YORK
HOUGHTON, MIFFLIN AND COMPANY
The Riverside Press, Cambridge
1898

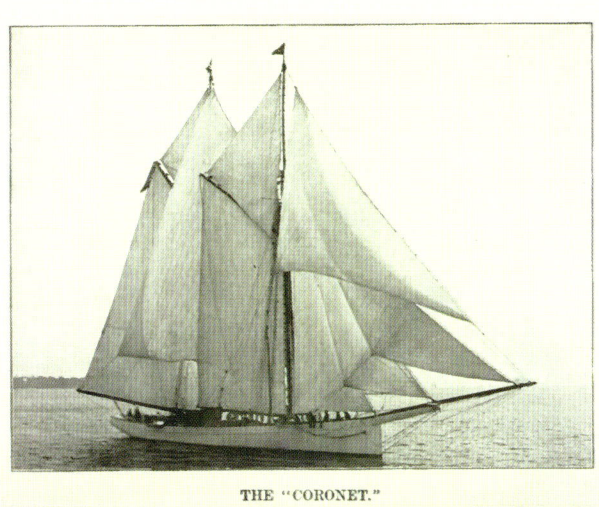

THE "CORONET."

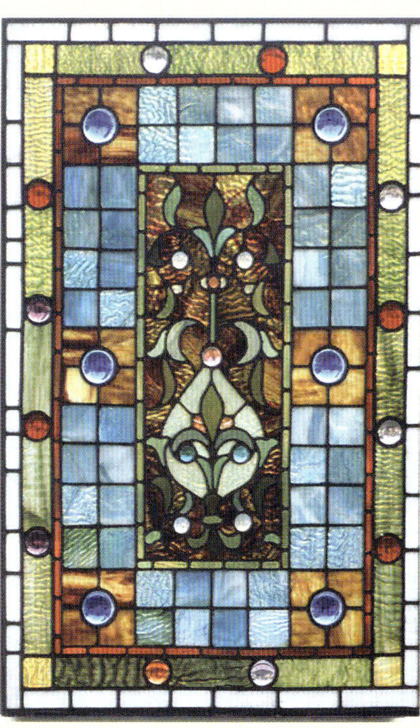

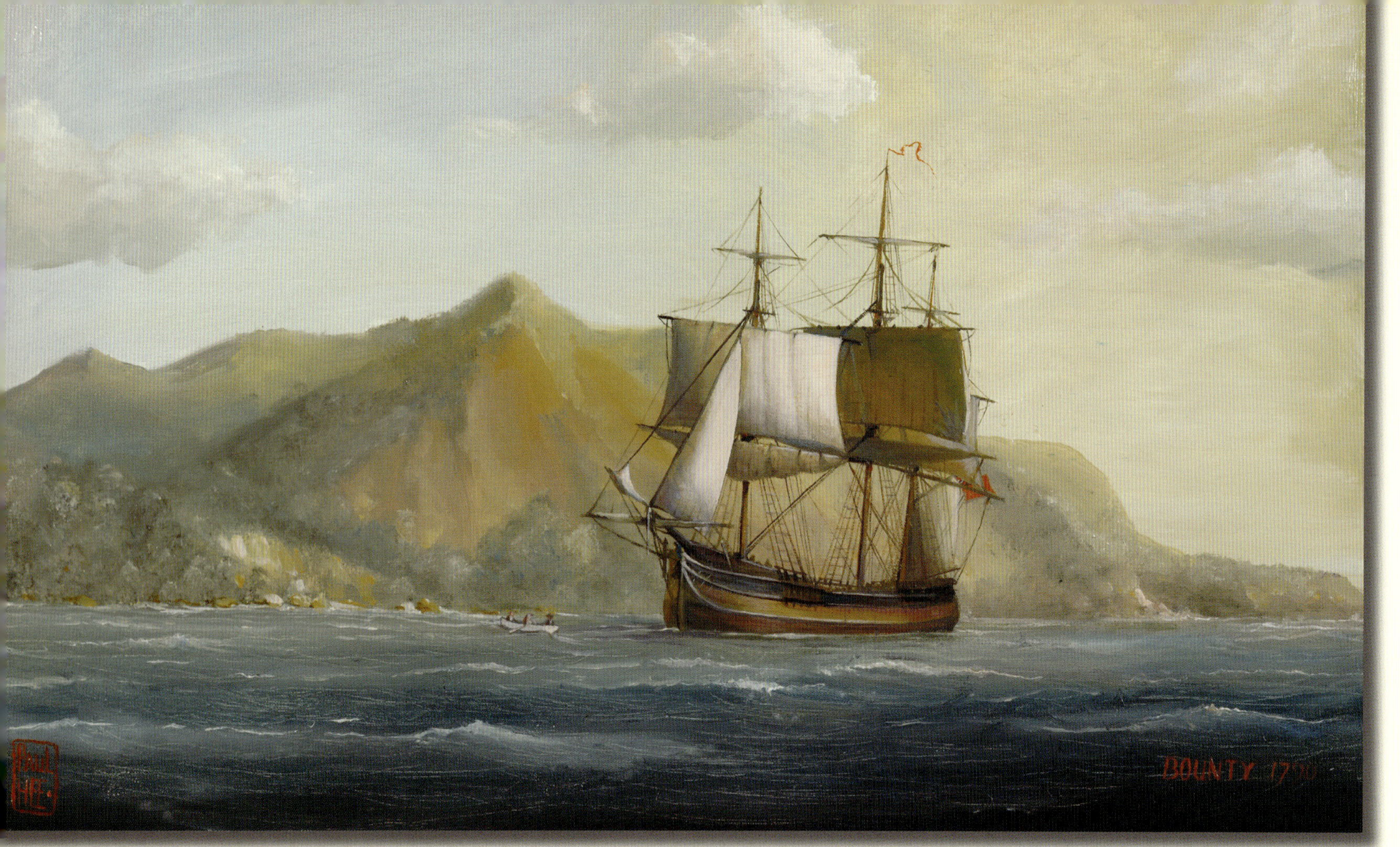

HMS Bounty 1787

18" x 28"

Originally named *Bethia*, the three-masted, 215-ton, 90-foot-10-inch collier, built in 1784, was refitted and renamed *HMS Bounty* in 1787. Under Lt. William Bligh's command, Bounty left England December 23, 1787, with 45 volunteers on a 10-month voyage to Tahiti to gather breadfruit. Sailors, mostly young and single, spent five months ashore and fell in love with the women, island, and Polynesian life-style. On the reluctant return voyage to England, Fletcher Christian mutinied, put Bligh and 18 loyalists in a 23-foot lifeboat, and sailed on. Christian sailed to Tahiti and the Cook Islands, but discovered Pitcairn misplaced on British charts and sailed east. To avoid detection, he burned and sank *Bounty* on January 23, 1790 in what now is Bounty Bay.

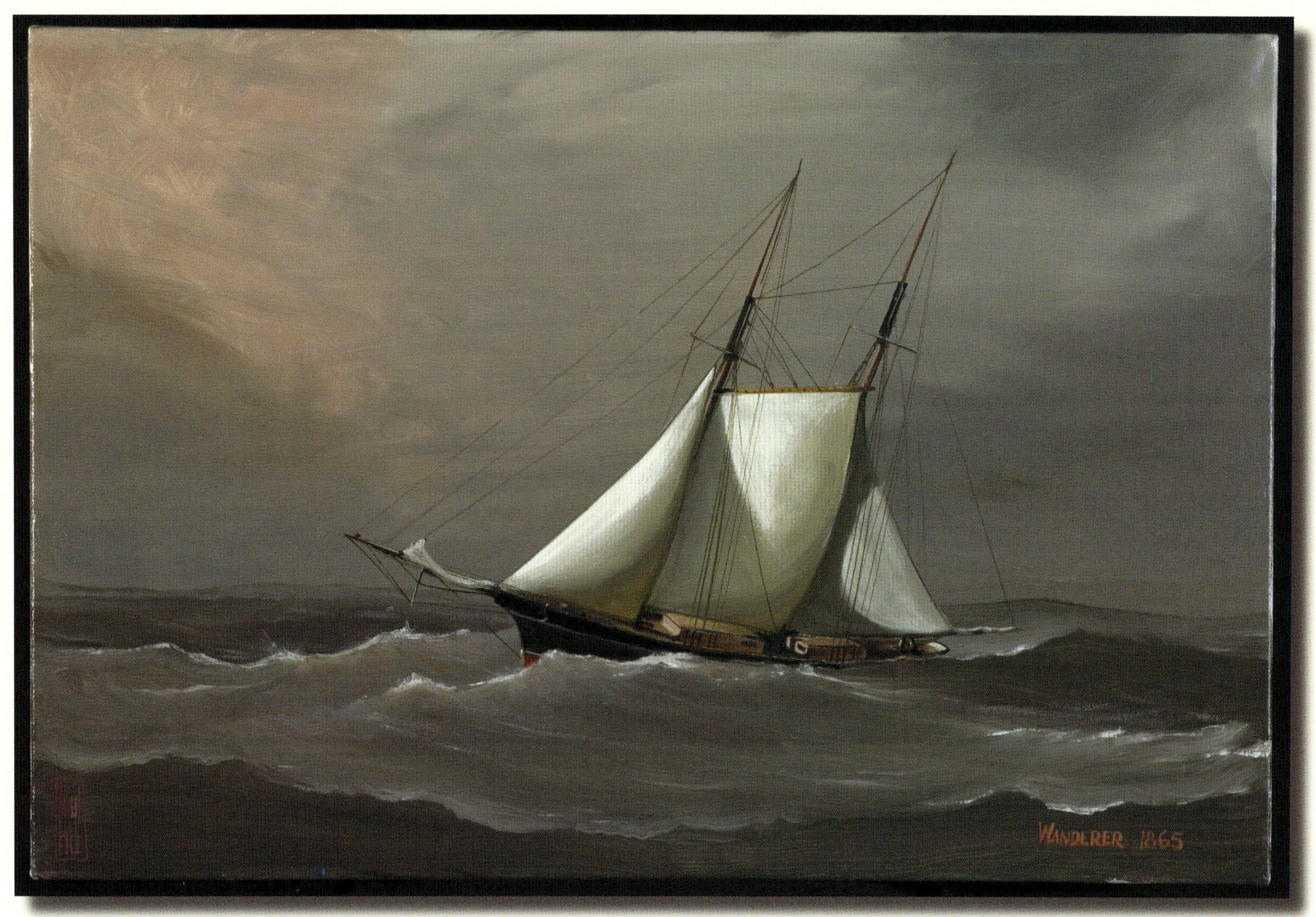

WANDERER

20" x 30"

In 1858, William C. Corrie took *Wanderer* on a successful clandestine voyage, illegally transporting slaves from the Congo River to Jekyll Island, Georgia. Built by Thomas B. Hawkins at Setauket, New York in 1857, this extreme schooner was seized by the U.S. Navy at Key West at the outbreak of the Civil War and used as a cruiser until 1865. *Wanderer* wrecked off the coast of Cuba on January 21, 1871.

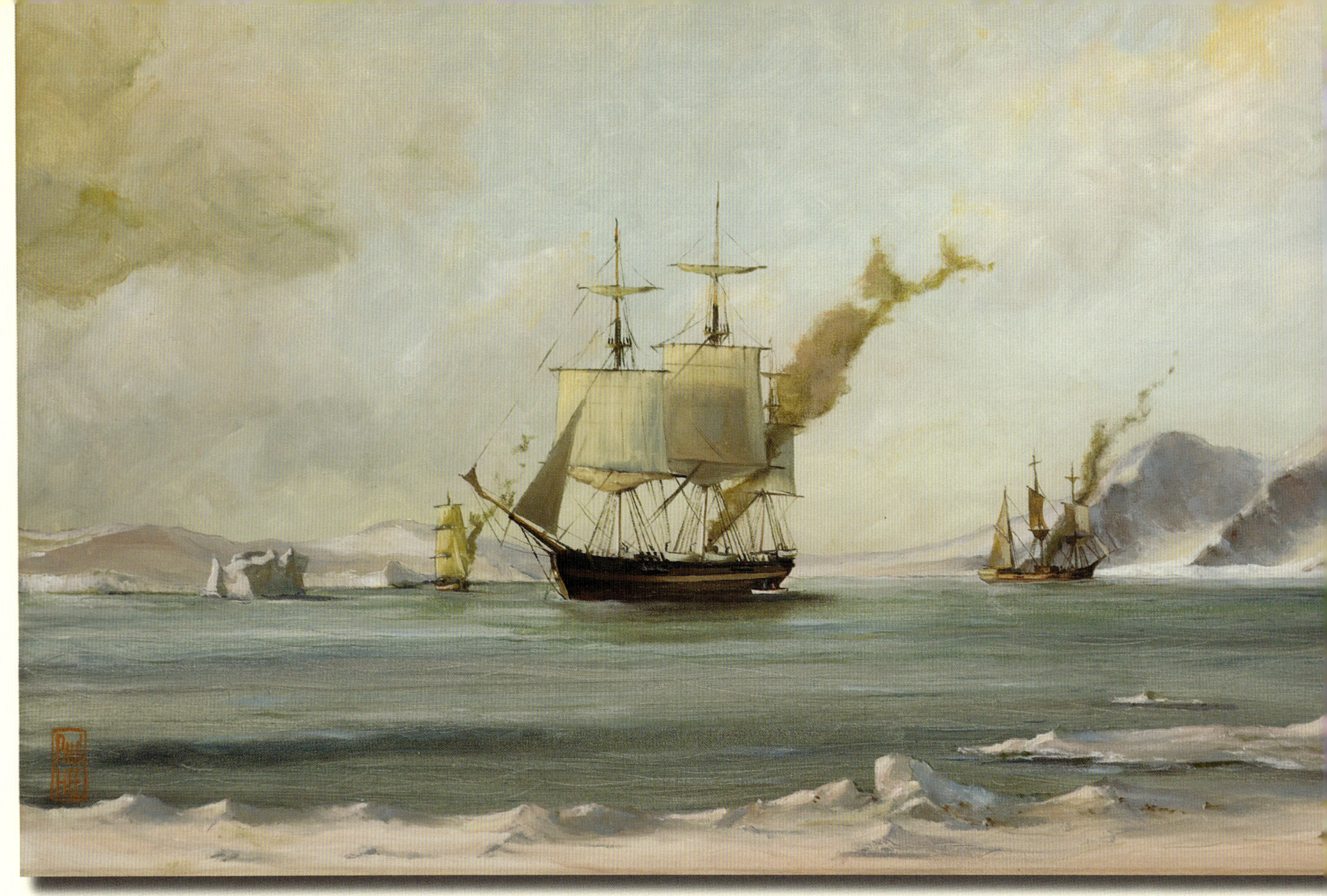

Arctic Whalers 1857

20" x 30"

Smoke rises from three 19th Century New England whale ships anchored amid glaciers in the Arctic Ocean as crews cook whale blubber in large vats to separate the oil. New Bedford whalers sailed schooners and barques around Cape Horn and on to Hawaii for a 15-day layover. After replenishing stores, whalers, mostly young men, ventured north to Alaska through the Bering Strait to hunt whales, often spending nine months at sea in the Arctic.

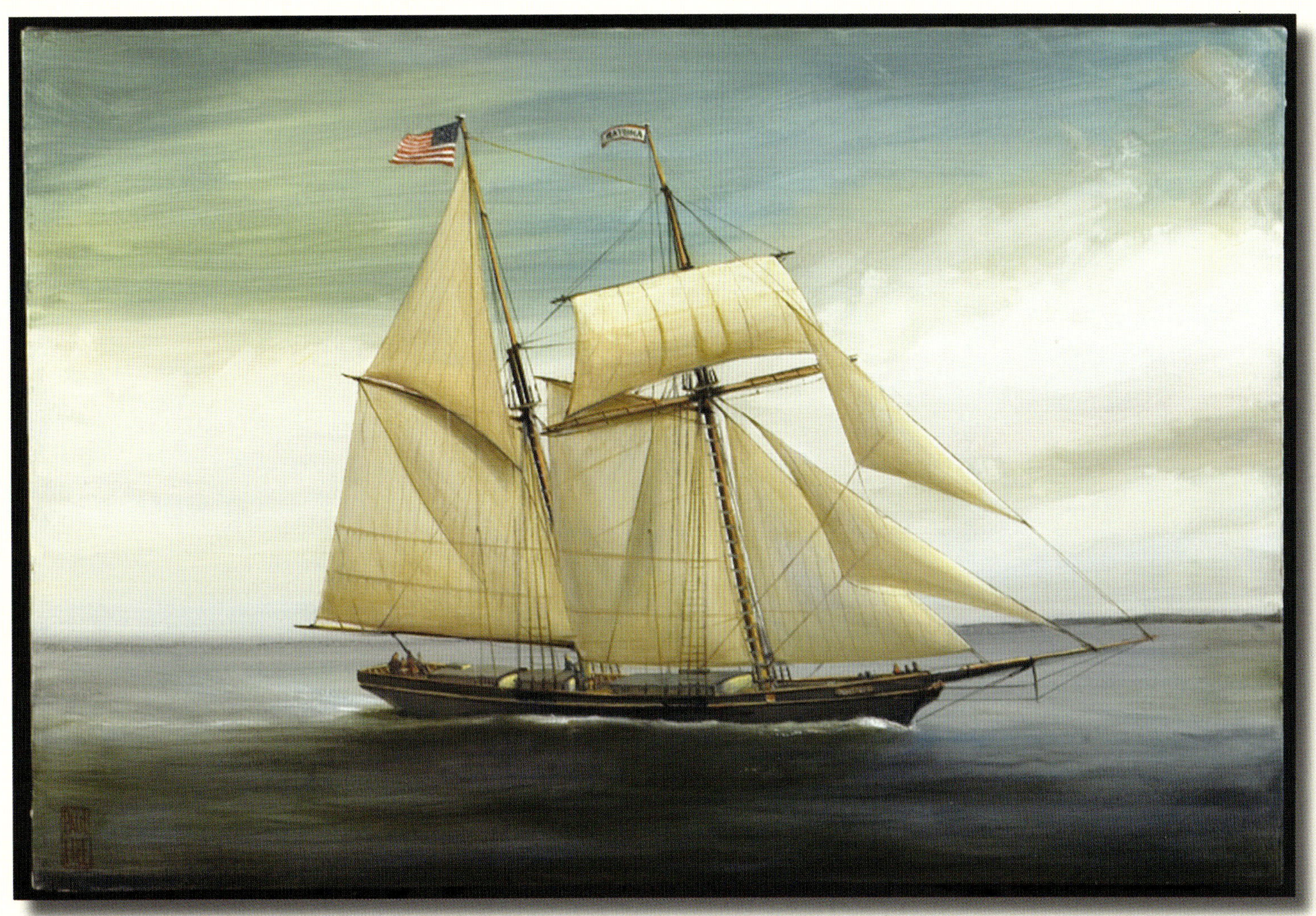

Amistad

18" x 28"

The original schooner *Amistad* was a slaver seized off the coast of Cuba in 1839 by the slaves aboard. They brought the ship into U.S. waters and successfully rebuffed efforts by the Spanish government to extradite them to Cuba to face murder and piracy charges. This painting depicts a reproduction of the schooner *Amistad*, built at Mystic Seaport in 1998. The ship serves as an educational and training vessel.

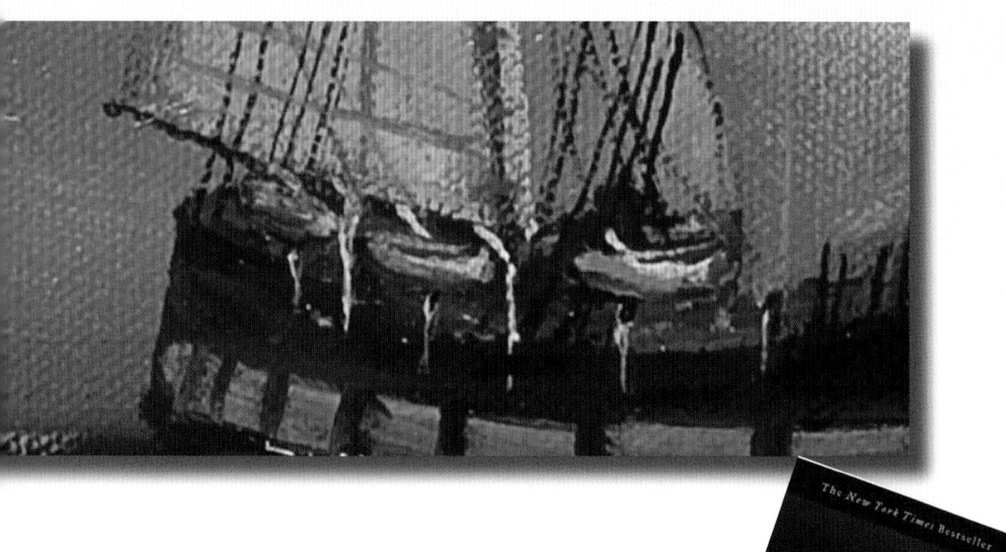

Essex 1820

18" x 20"

Essex enters Windward Passage, the 50-mile strait between Cuba and Haiti, which links the Caribbean Sea with the Atlantic Ocean. On November 20, 1820, the Nantucket whaler was struck by an 80-ton whale in the middle of the Pacific Ocean. The 20-man crew took to three open boats as the *Essex* sank. Adrift at sea 95 days, only eight men survived, seven were eaten, the others lost. Finally, whalers aboard the *Dauphin* and sailors on the British brig *Indian* came to their rescue. Survivor Owen Chase wrote the *Narrative of the Most Extraordinary and Distressing Shipwreck of the Whale-Ship Essex,* which inspired Herman Melville's novel *Moby Dick*. *In the Heart of the Sea: The Tragedy of the Whaleship Essex* by Nathaniel Philbrick is a recent bestseller.

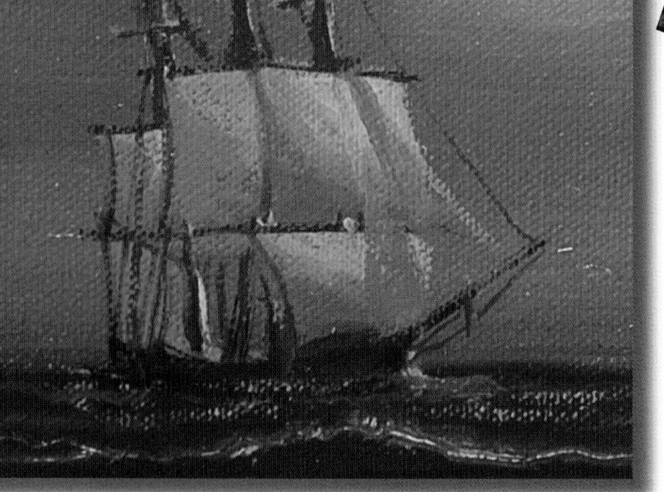

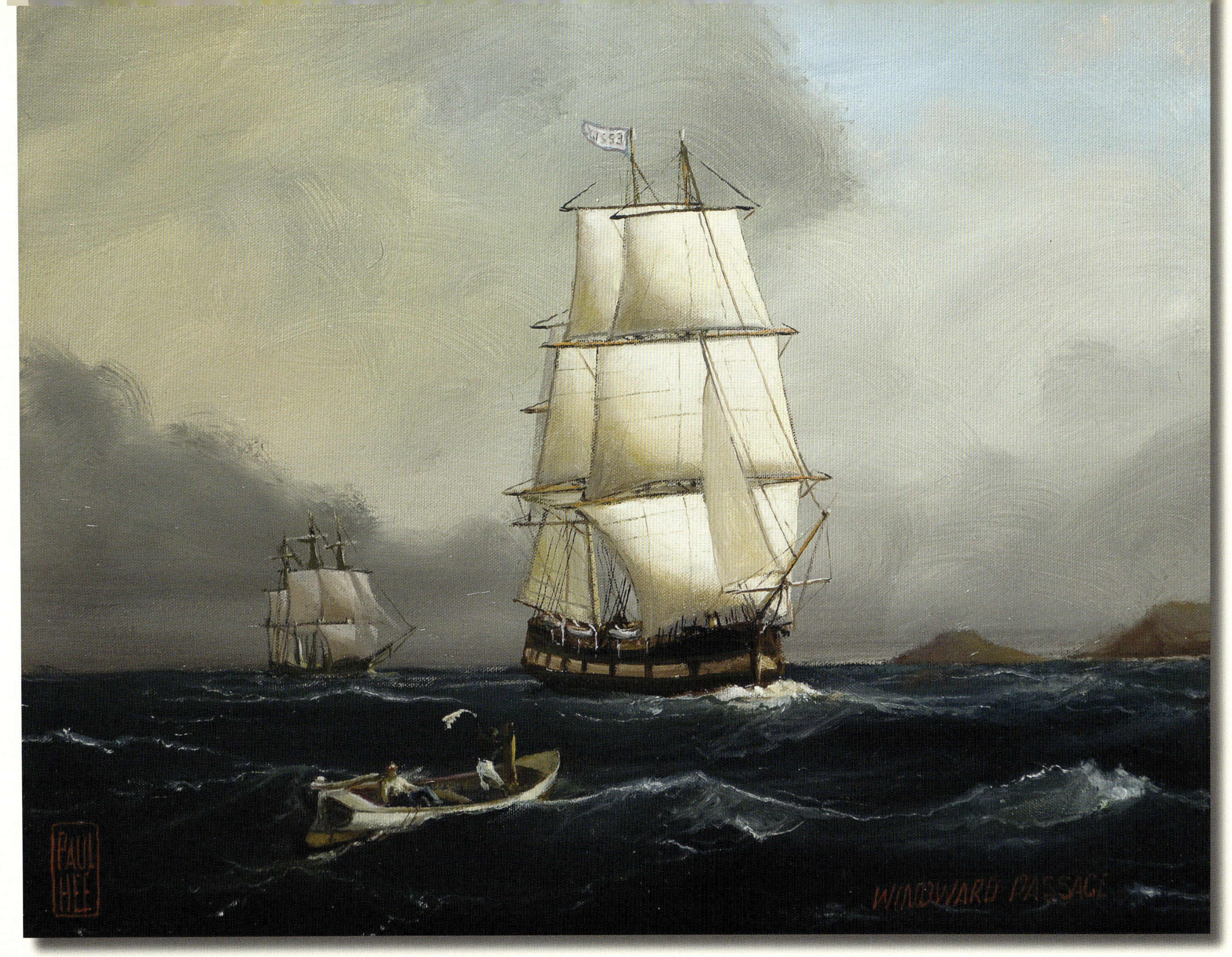

Essex 1820

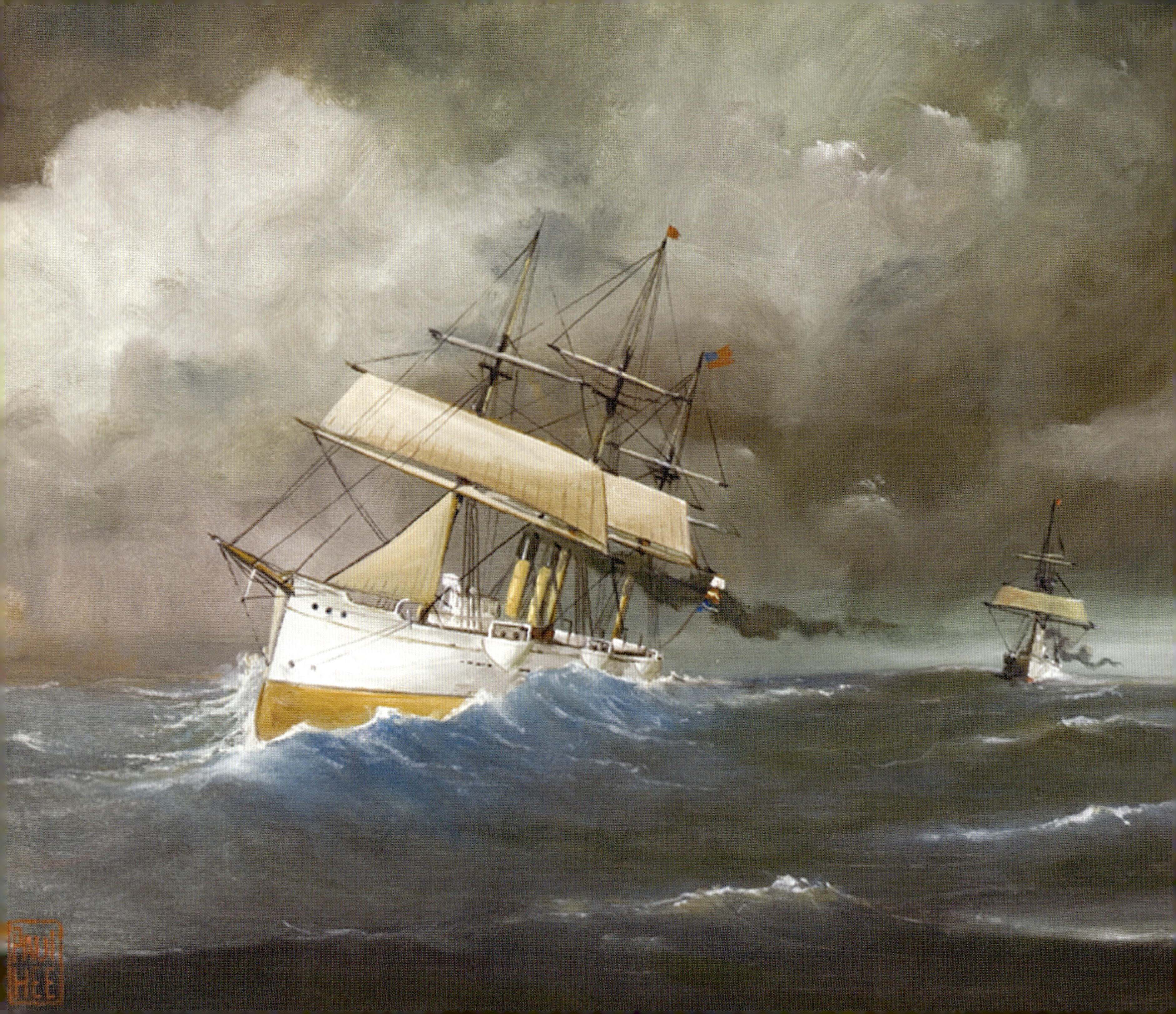
PAUL
HEE

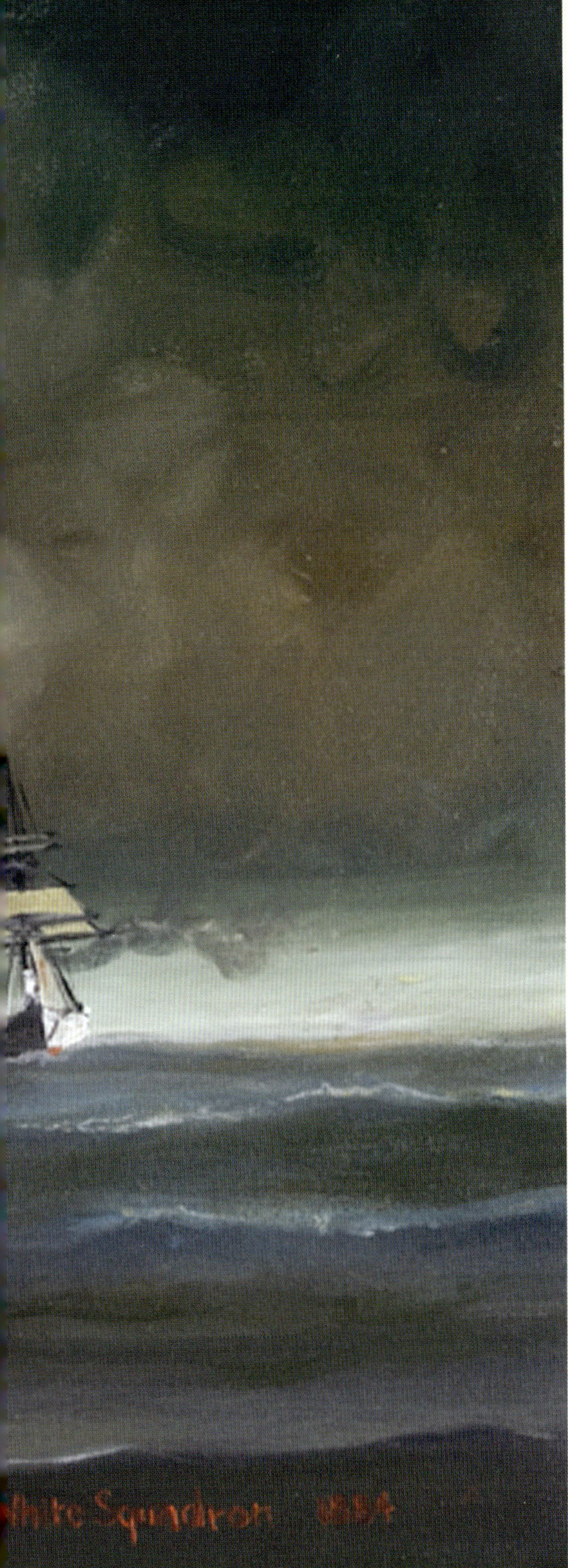

The White Squadron 1889

18" x 28"

To build a U.S. navy of steel, President Chester A. Arthur signed the 1883 act authorizing $1.3 million to build four ships known as The White Squadron. Six years later USS *Atlanta, Boston* and *Chicago*, and a dispatch vessel, *Dolphin,* were launched. Named for their white painted hulls, the full-rigged steam ships of steel marked the start of the "New Navy." *Boston* joined the fleet that fought the Battle of Manila Bay in 1898 which ended the Spanish-American War.

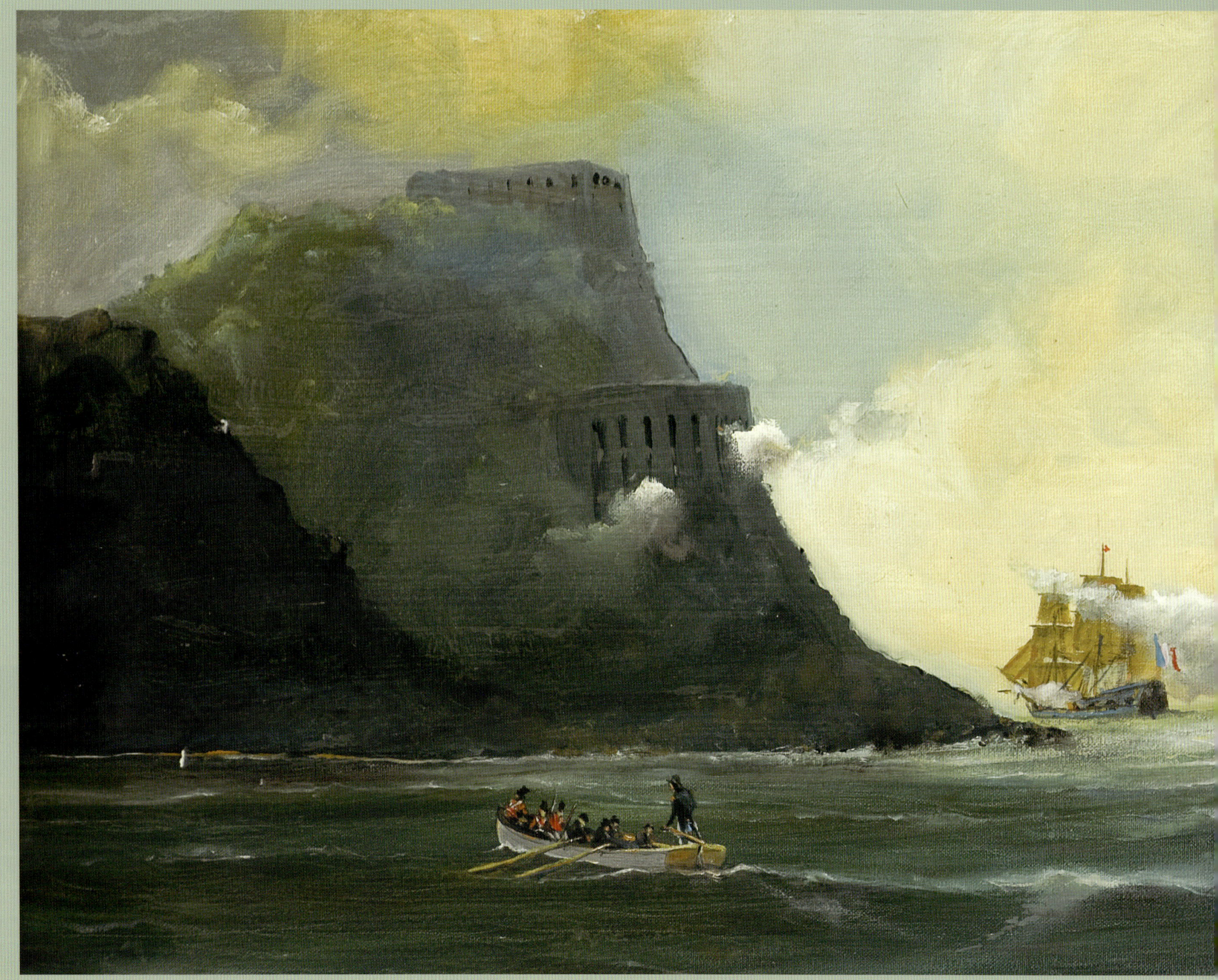

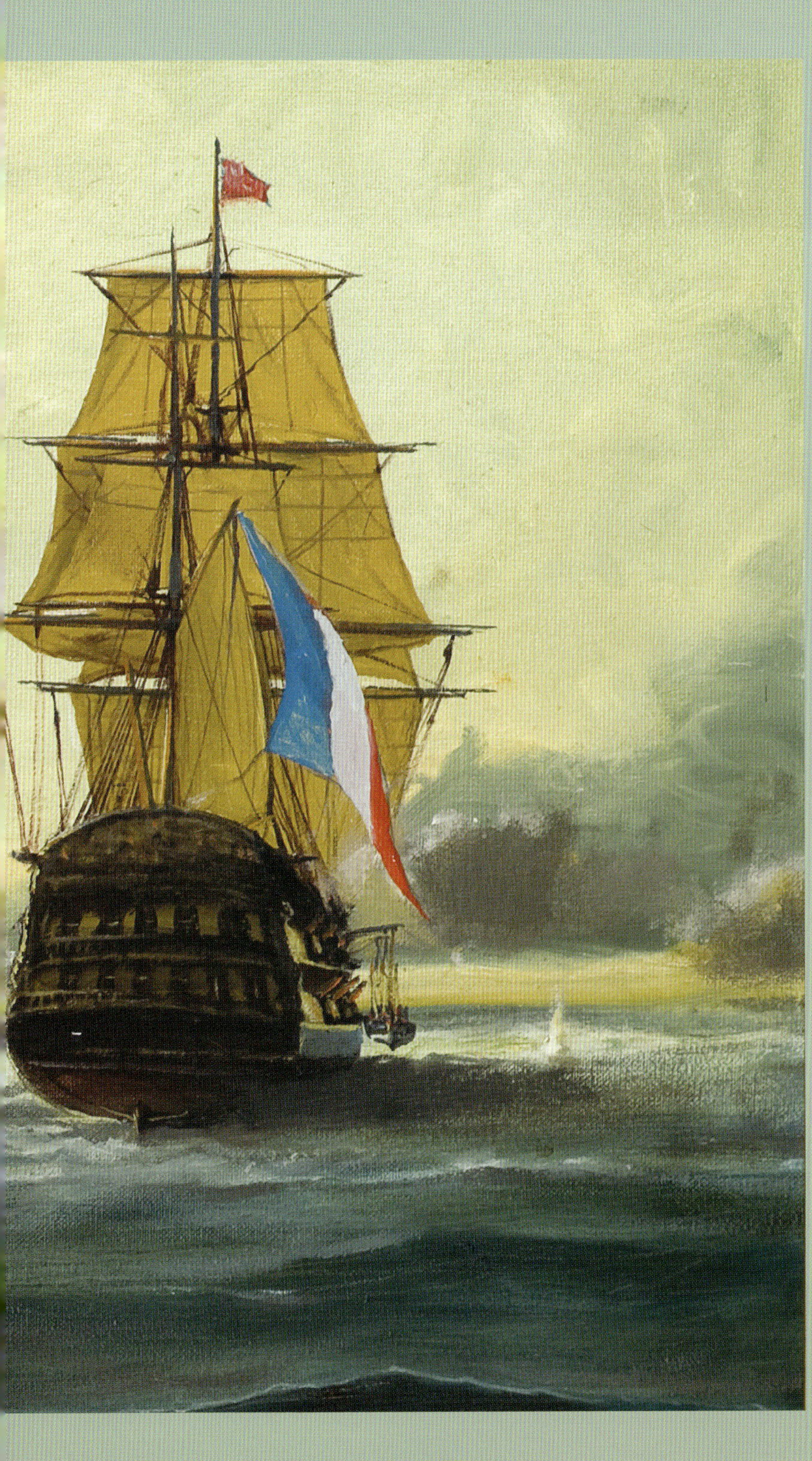

CHAPTER II

BATTLES

Bombardment of Haiti

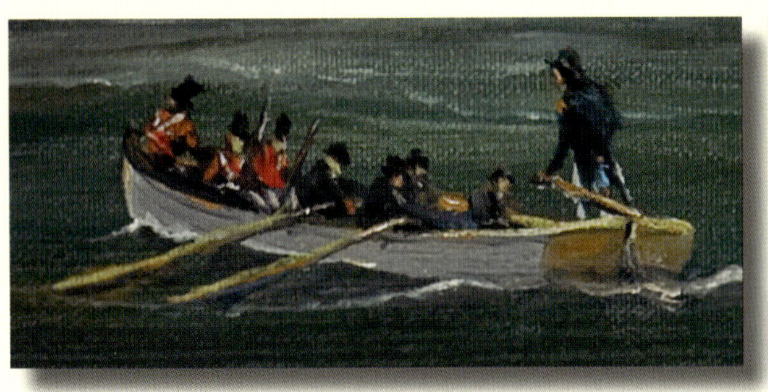

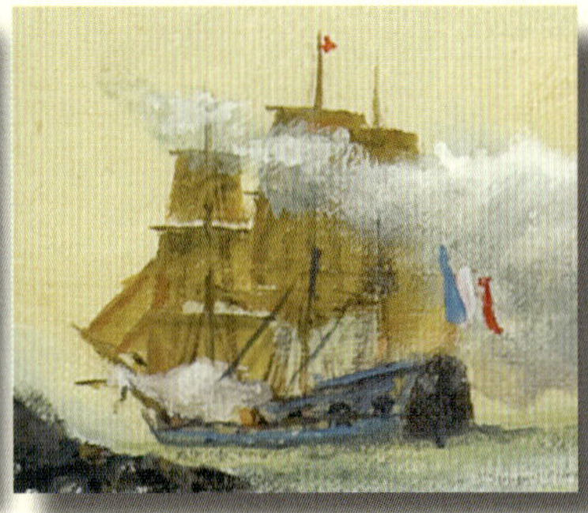

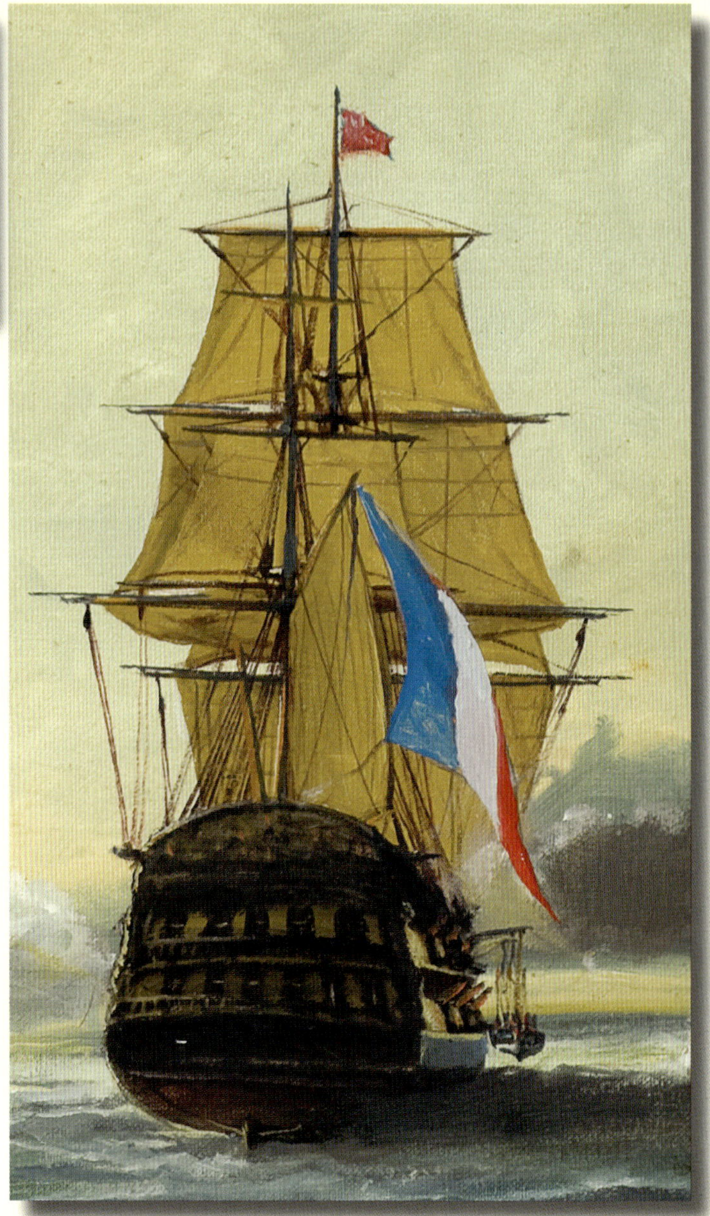

Bombardment of Haiti

18" x 28"

The crushing defeat of the French at Haiti by the black revolutionary slave Toussaint L'Ouverture, changed history. The Haitian victory halted Napoleon's North America campaign and led to independence for the island nation. Of great importance to young America, the French defeat forced the cash-strapped Napoleon to quit the port of New Orleans and sell the Louisiana territory "for a song" to the United States. The 1803 purchase, at a price of $15 million, doubled the size of the country, taking in territory that became 14 states and two Canadian provinces.

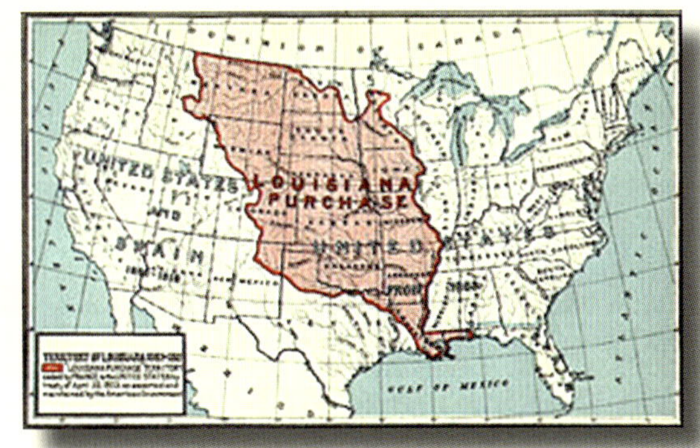

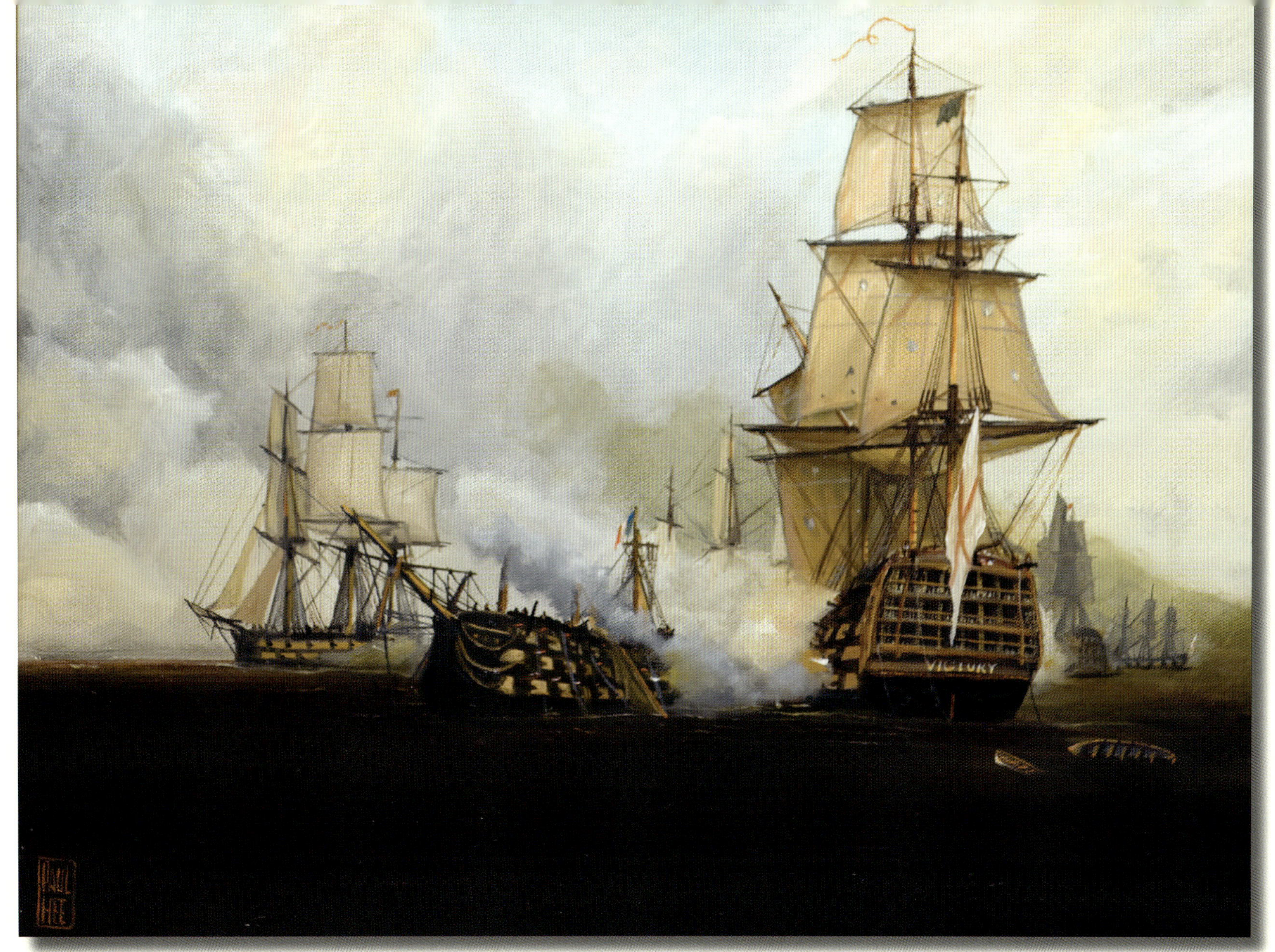

Victory & Amazon

20" x 30"

Two flagships of Admiral Lord Nelson are shown off Dover, England: the 100-gun *Victory* (Battle of Trafalgar 1805) and the 38-gun frigate *Amazon* (Boulogne, France 1801). This painting was inspired by British marine artist Thomas Luny (1759-1837).

Bayonnaise Captures Ambuscade

18" x 24"

In a four-hour battle on the Bay of Biscay, the French 24-gun corvette *Bayonnaise* captured the *32*-gun British frigate *HMS Ambuscade* on December 13, 1798. The French captain rammed *Bayonnaise's* bowsprit though *Ambuscade's* mizzen shrouds. When the mast fell, 200 French marines boarded, firing muskets. British losses were 10 dead, including Captain Henry Jenkins, and 36 seamen wounded. The French lost 11 seamen and a colonel. *Ambuscade* was taken into the French Navy but was recaptured by the British in the Atlantic on May 28, 1803. *Bayonnaise* was beached and set afire in 1803, to avoid capture by *HMS Ardent.*

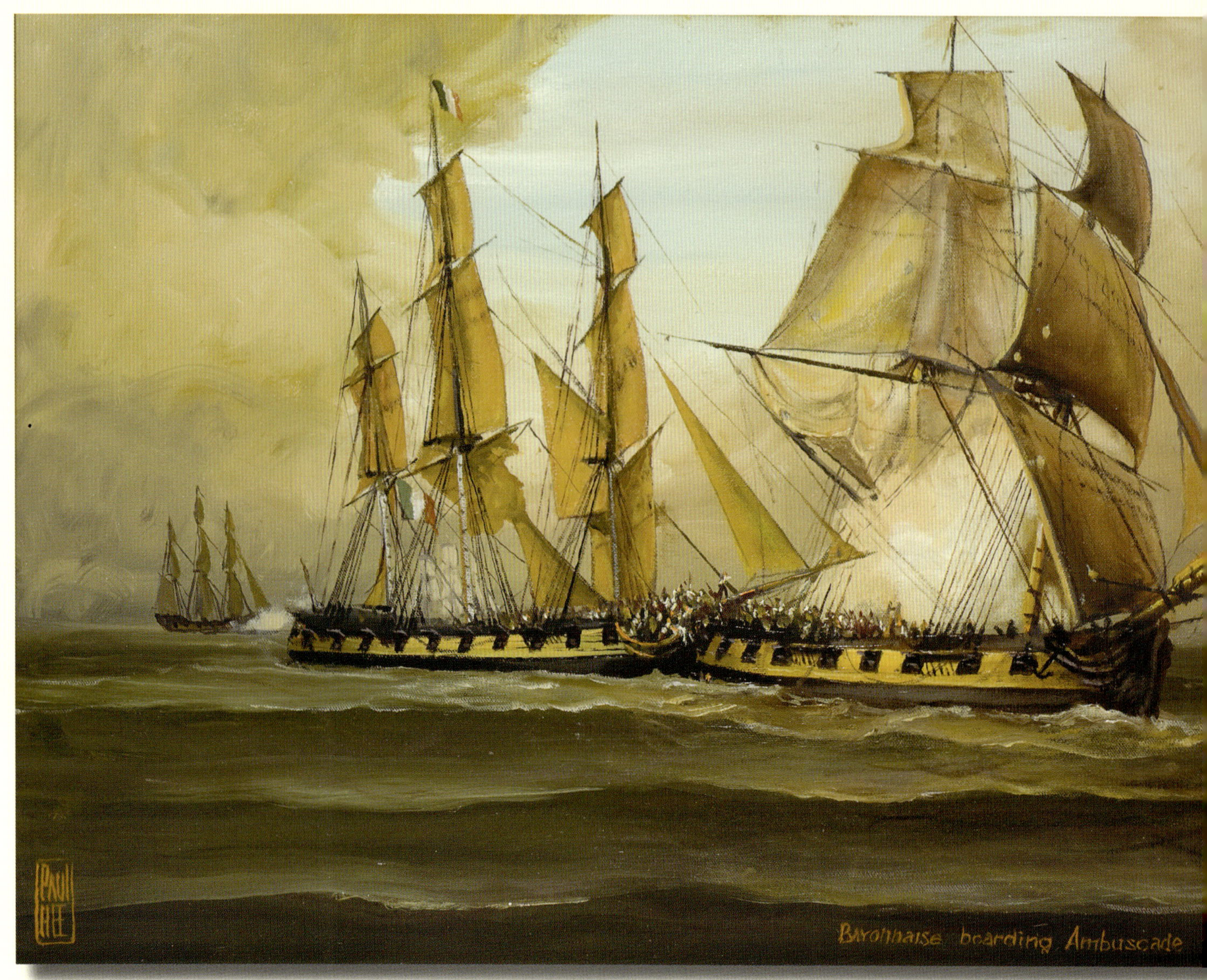

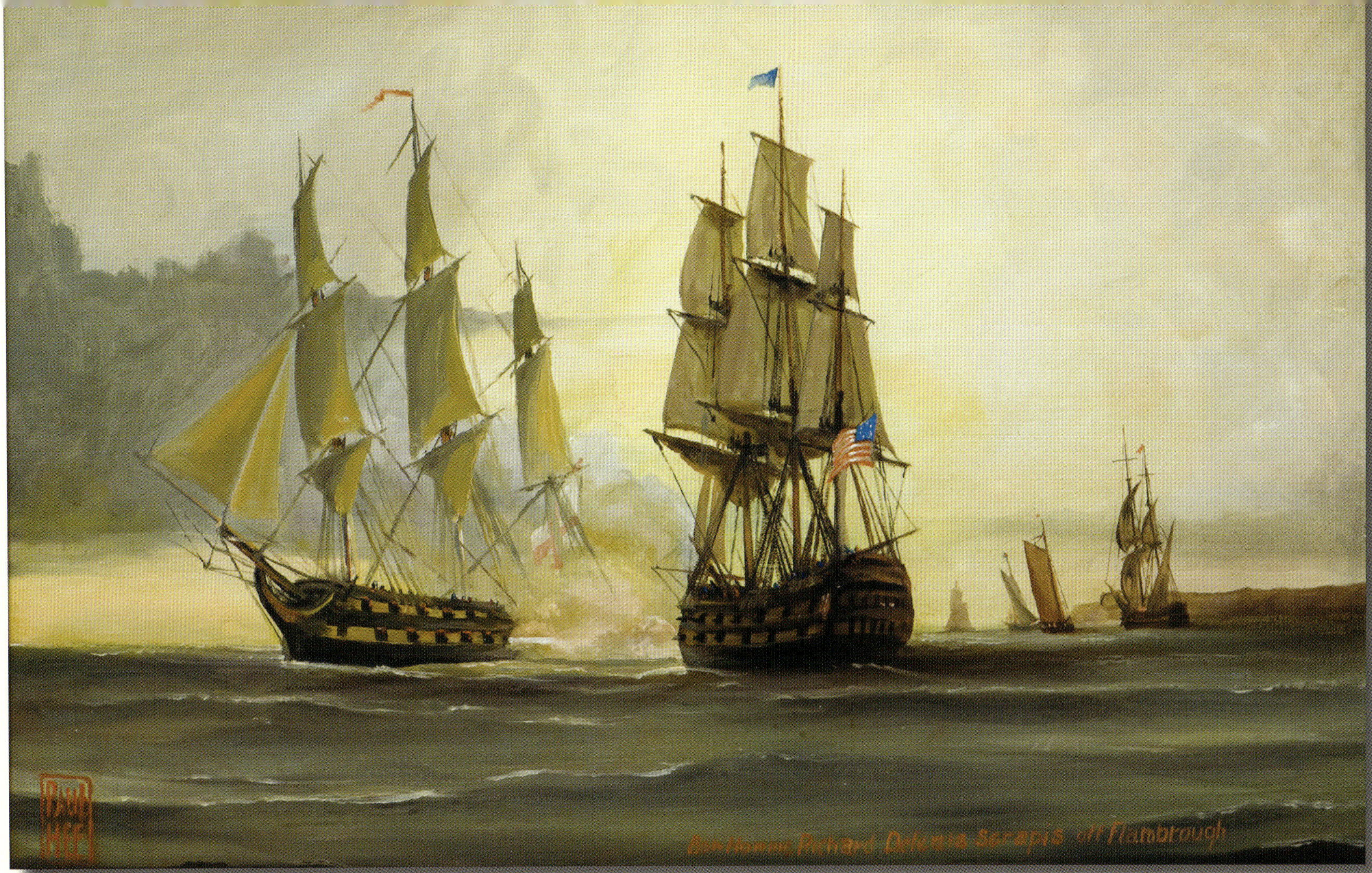

Bonhomme Richard defeats *Serapis* 1779

18" x 24"

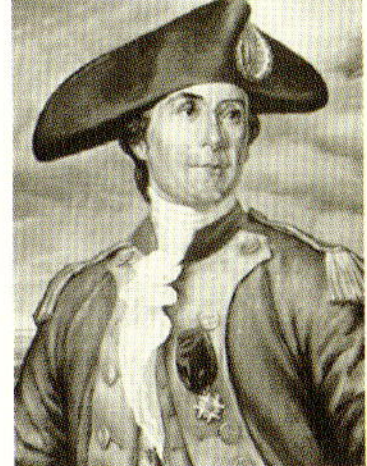

John Paul Jones

"I have not yet begun to fight," John Paul Jones declared from his broken ship on September 25, 1779, off the Yorkshire coast at Flamborough Head. In one of the fiercest Revolutionary War battles, the British 50-gun ship *Serapis* set *Bonhomme Richard* ablaze and she began sinking. Jones and crew fought nearly four hours to capture *Serapis,* just as his 40-gun, 152-foot frigate sank into the North Sea. It was the first American defeat of a British ship in British waters, a victory that earned John Paul Jones, then only 33, the title of "father of the American Navy."

HMS Royal George at Quiberon Bay

18" x 28"

Royal George was the flagship of Admiral Sir Edward Hawke at the Battle of Quiberon Bay, on the west coast of France, on November 20, 1759. Hawke astonished the French fleet, commanded by Marshal Conflans, by hotly pursuing it into a bay during a gale. His fleet destroyed seven French ships, including the flagship *Soleil Royale,* and drove eleven other ships ashore, for the loss of two ships that ran aground after the action.

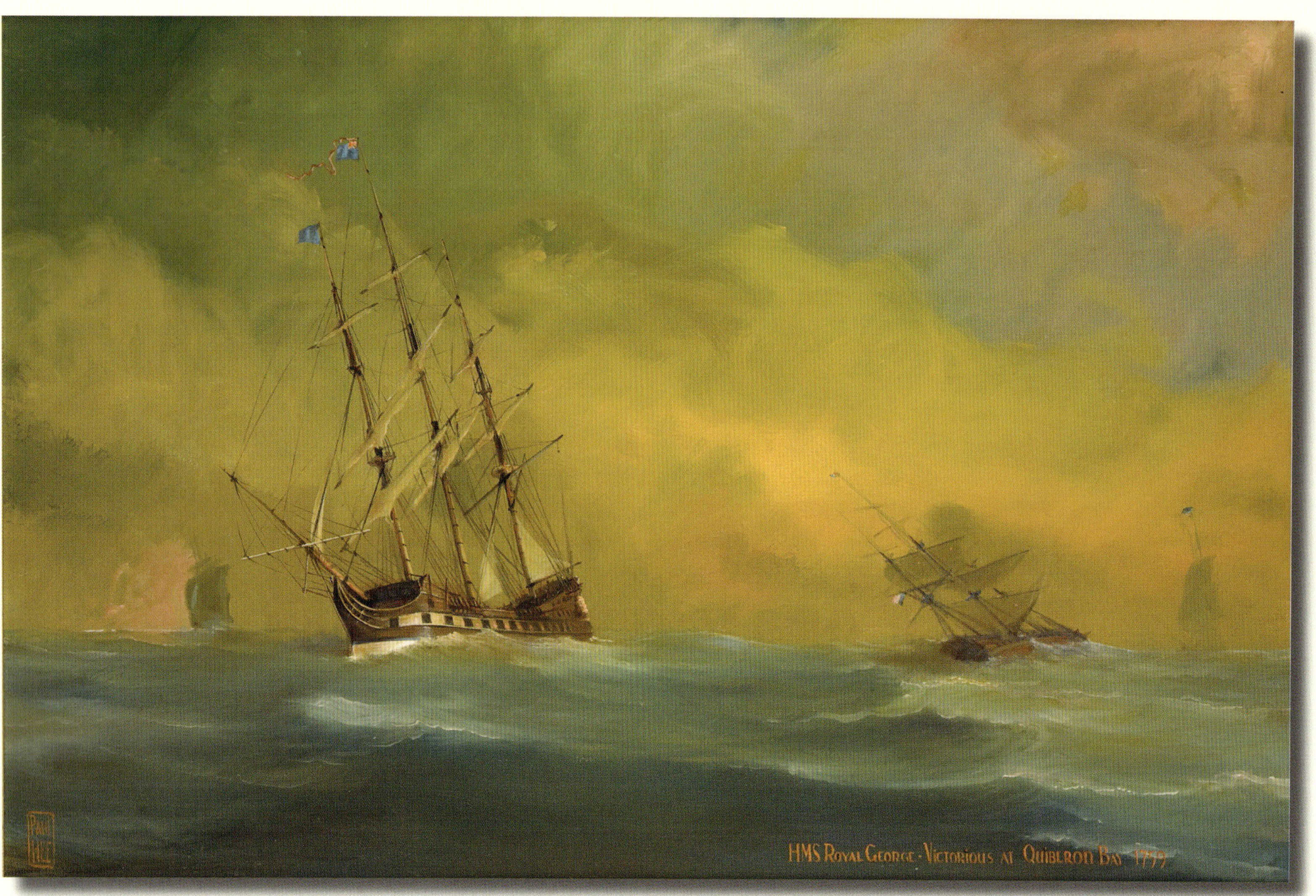

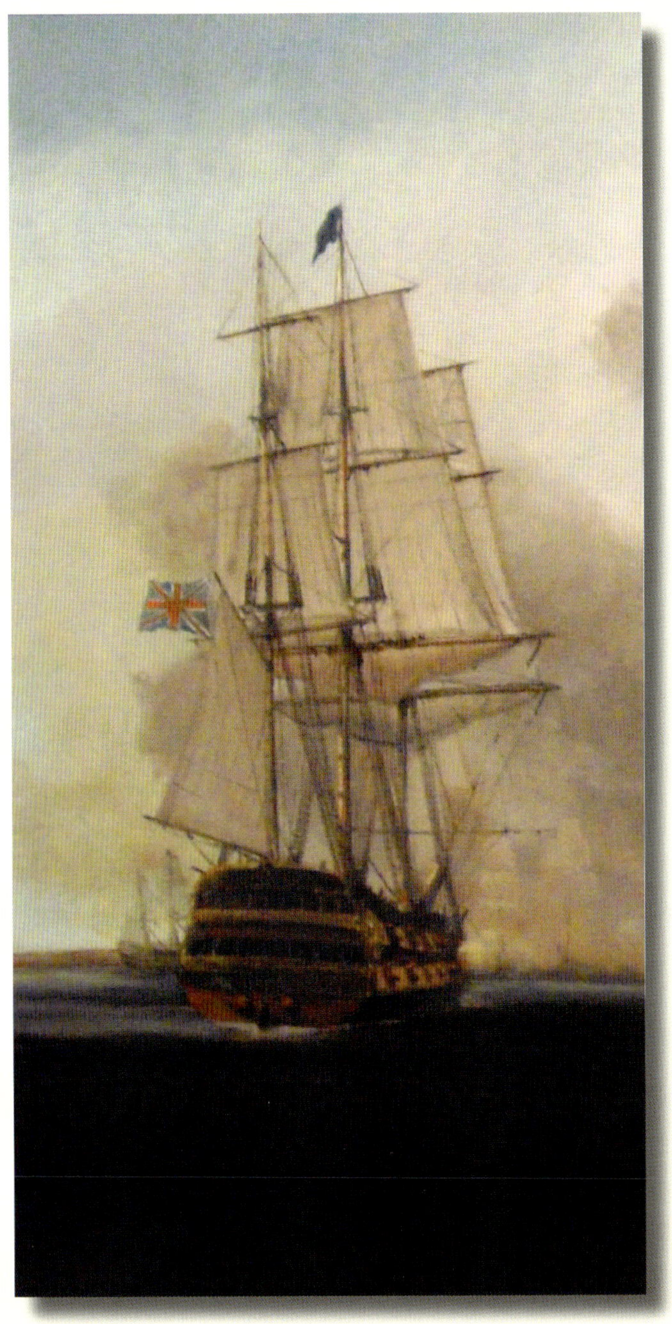

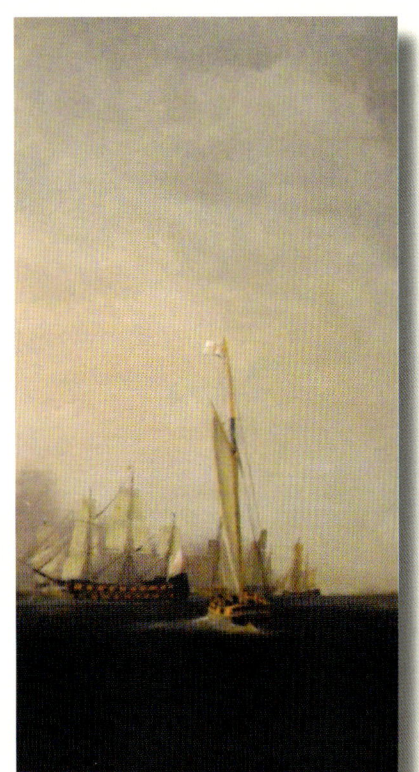

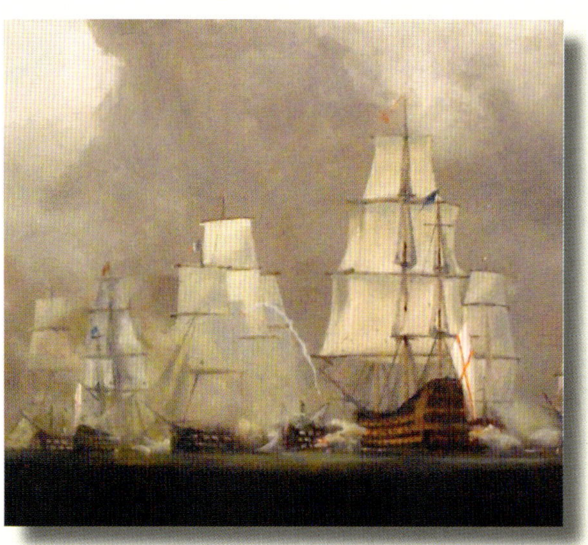

Battle of Trafalgar

24" x 58.5"

The 1805 battle off Cape Trafalgar between the Royal Navy and the combined fleets of Spain and France involved 27 British ships against 33 Spanish and French ships. No British ship was lost, but the Spanish-French fleet lost 22 ships. Admiral Lord Horatio Nelson fell mortally wounded aboard *HMS Victory* but the last great sea battle of the period established British supremacy on the high seas in the 19th century.

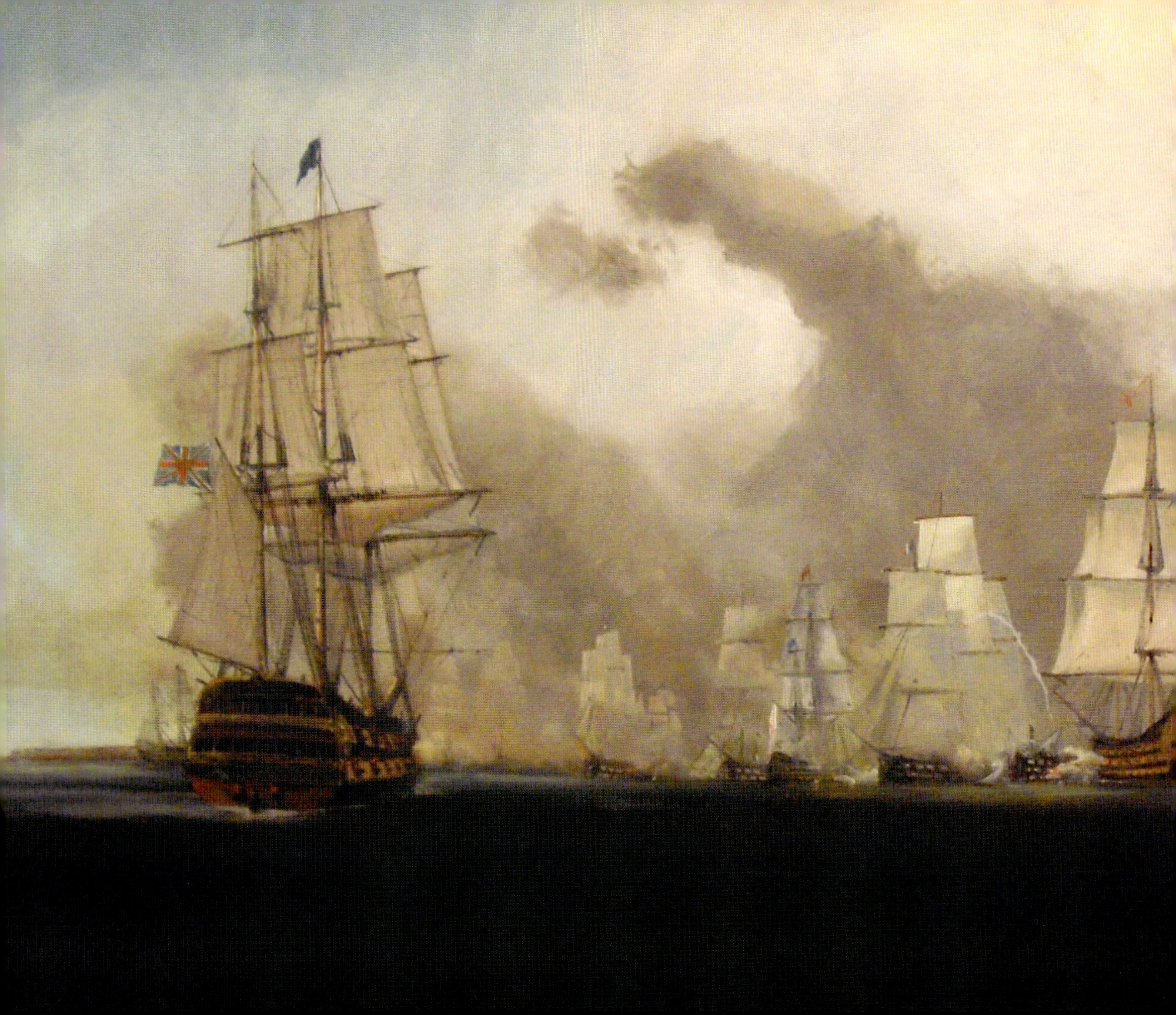

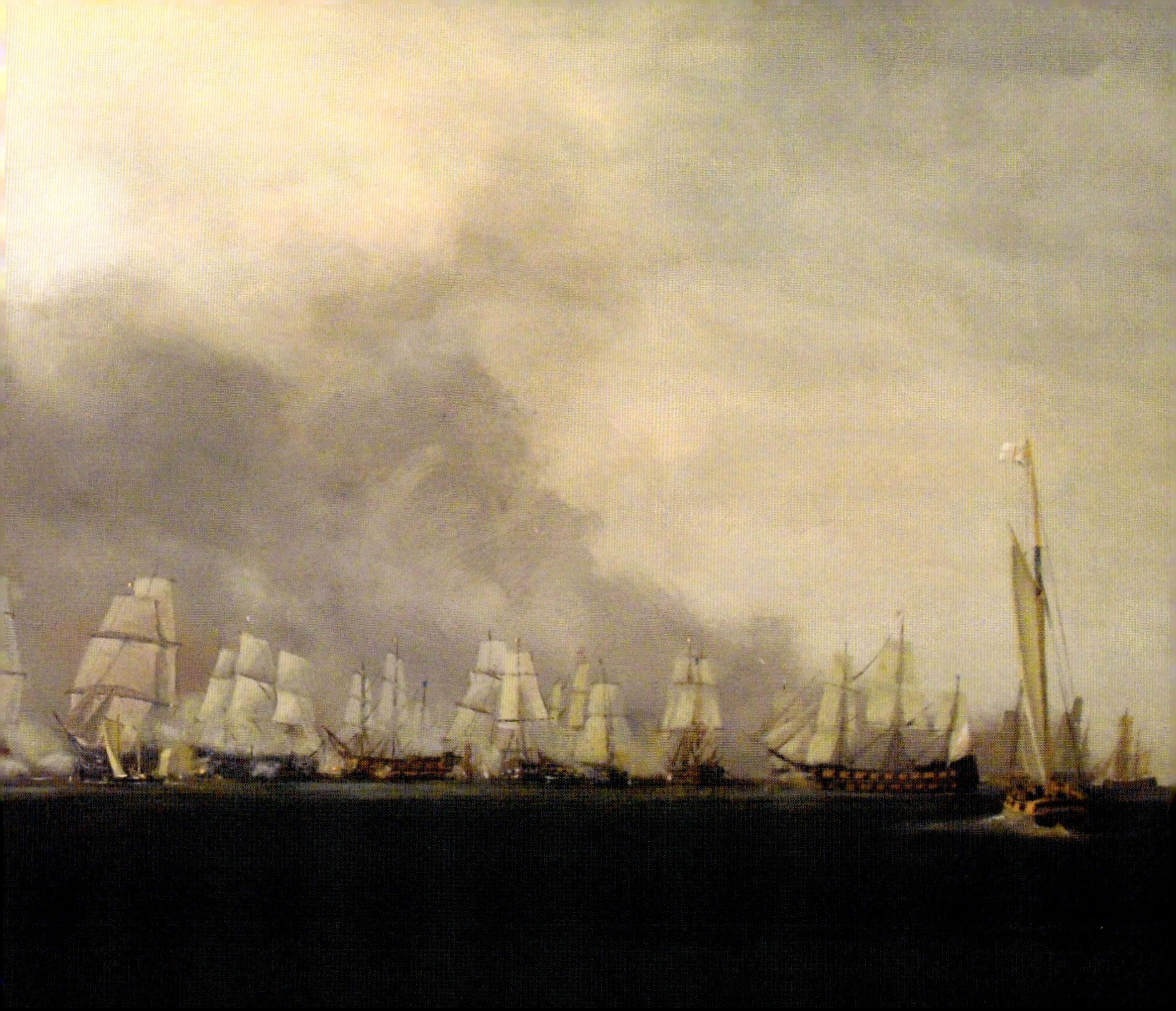

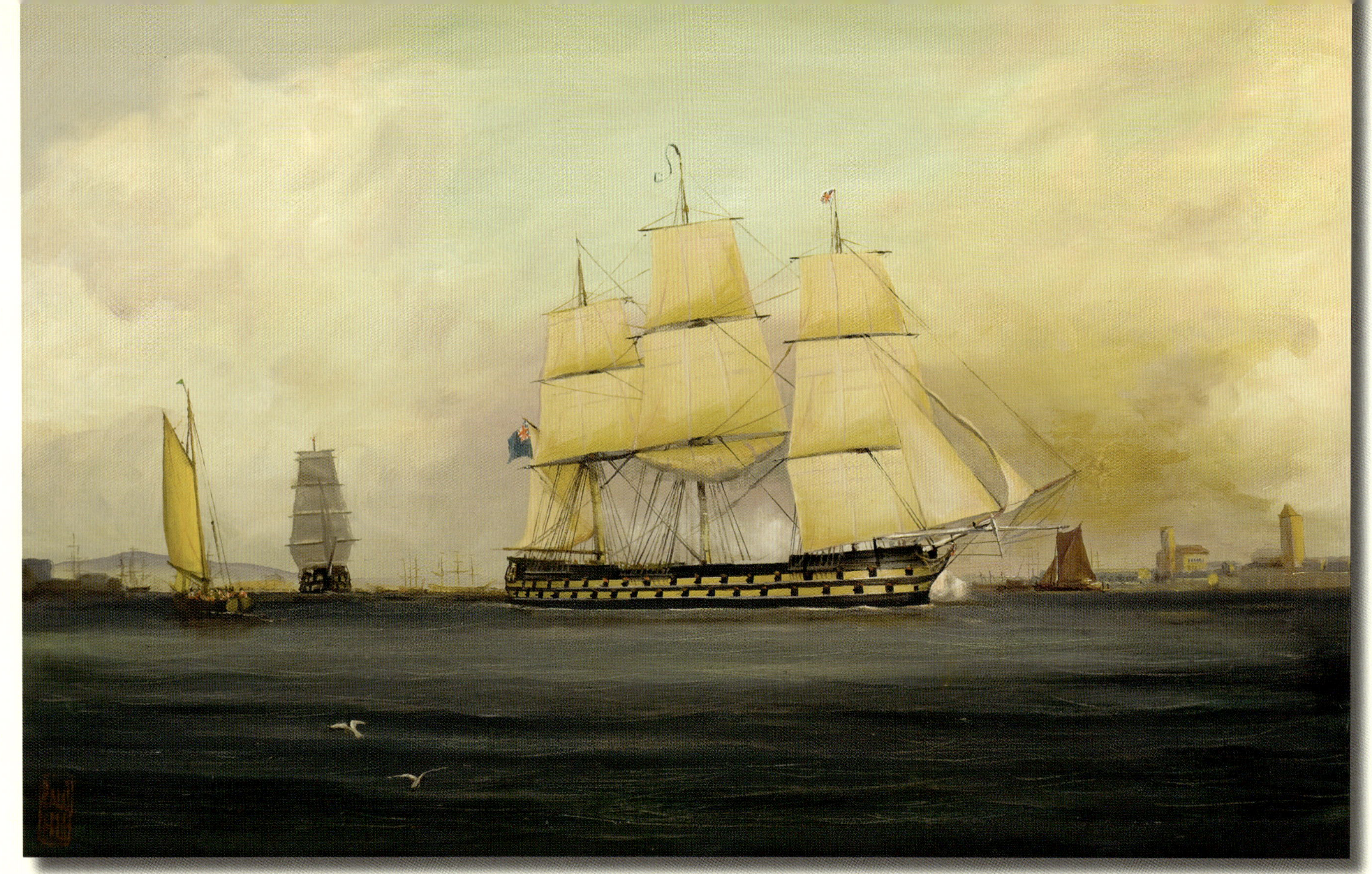

HMS Revenge

18" x 28"

The 74-gun ship *HMS Revenge* is shown sailing from Portsmouth, England, after repairing heavy damage sustained at the Battle of Trafalgar, October 21, 1805. Launched on April 13, 1805, she was broken up in 1849.

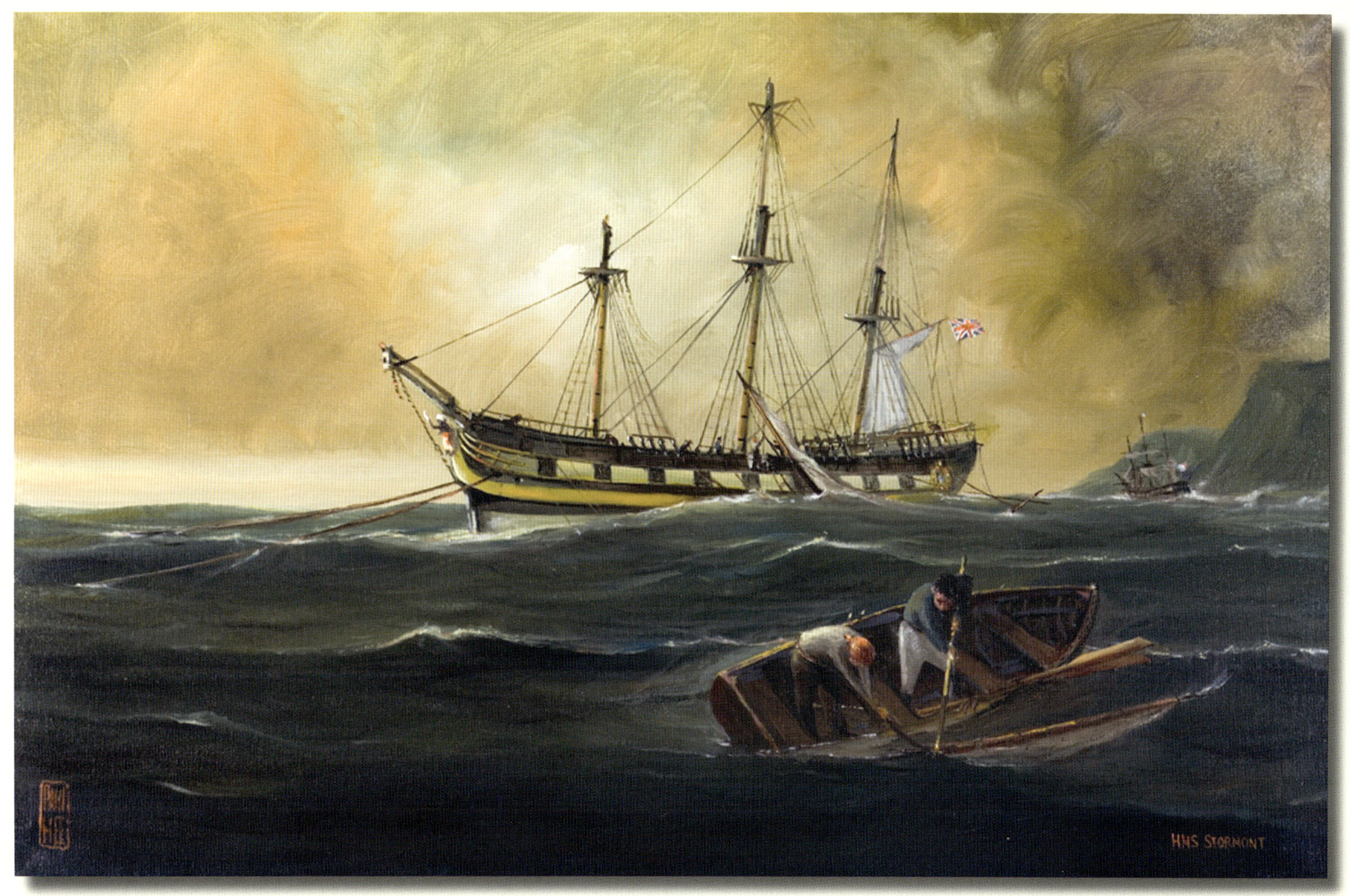

HMS Stormont

18" x 28"

The 16-gun sloop *HMS Stormont*, purchased by the Royal Navy in 1781, was captured by the French on January 23, 1782 off the Demerara River, near the seaport of Georgetown, Guyana. Sailors, foreground, recover a spar so they can re-rig sails and press on.

HMS Neptune

18" x 28"

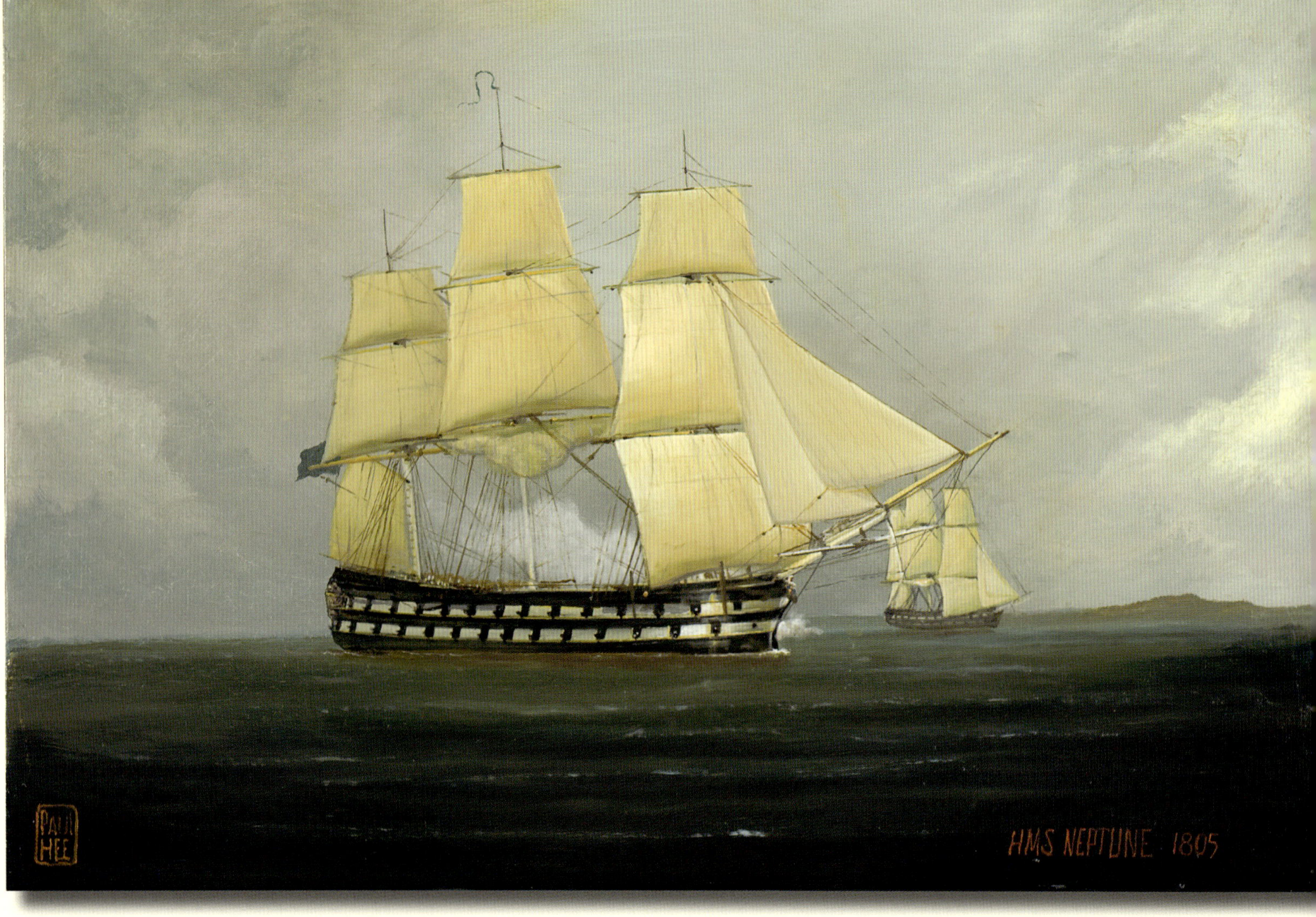

Neptune was built as a 98-gun three-deck 2nd-rate ship of the line in the Royal Dockyard at Deptford in 1797. She was the second ship of the Royal Navy named for the King of the Sea. *Neptune* fought in the line at the Battle of Trafalgar (October 21, 1805) under the command of Captain Thomas Fremantle, one of Lord Nelson's close personal friends. She was the third ship of the weather line that broke the Franco-Spanish line, following behind Admiral Nelson's flagship, *Victory*, and the famous *Temeraire*. After the battle, *Neptune* towed the crippled *Victory*, bearing the body of Horatio Nelson, back to Gibraltar. *Neptune* saw considerable action over the next five years and was laid up in 1810. She was broken up in 1818.

USS Spark

18" x 20"

The first of three United States Navy ships named *Spark* was a bold pirate hunter on the Barbary Coast and Caribbean Sea. The 103-foot privateer was built in 1813 at Sag Harbor, Long Island, New York. *Spark* signed up for US Navy duty to fight the British in 1814, but war ended before she went to sea. The 12-gun brig then joined the hunt for Algerian pirates in the Mediterranean under Lt. Thomas Gable. On June 19, 1815, *Spark* captured five ships, including the Algerian flagship *Mashuda*, near Cape de Gatt. In the Carribean, *Spark* chased buccaneers and seized their sloops from 1821 until she retired in 1825.

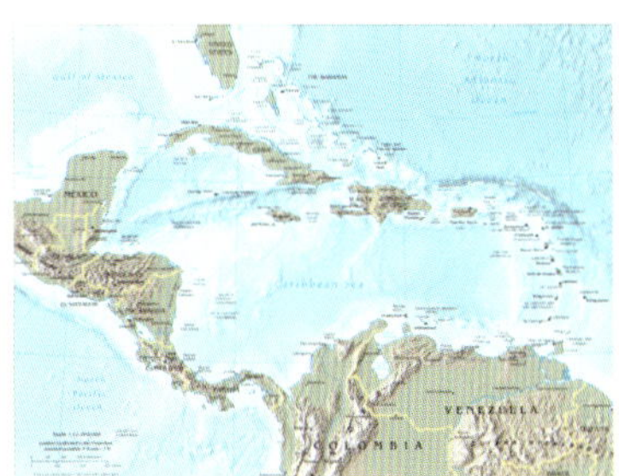

Caribbean Sea

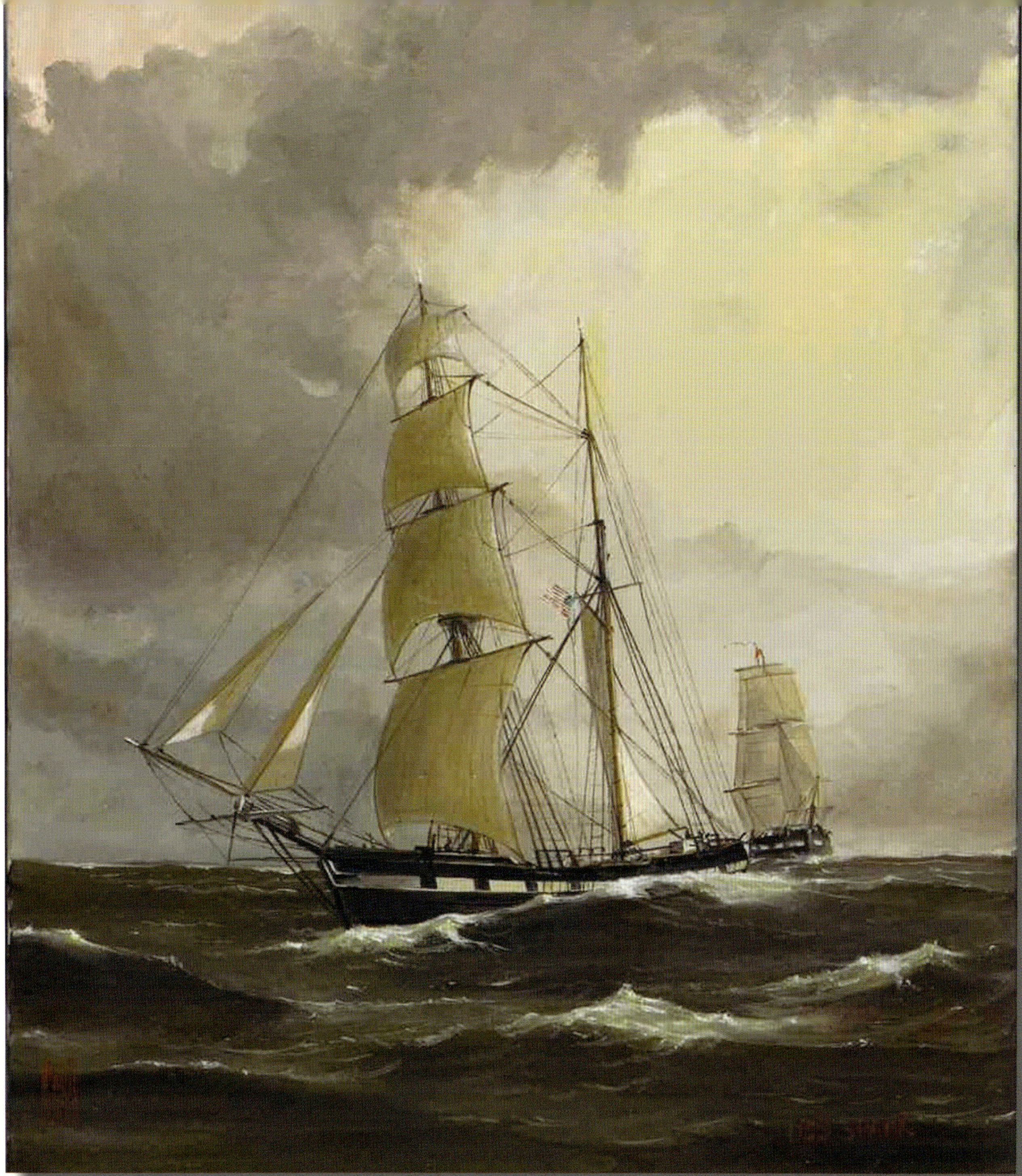

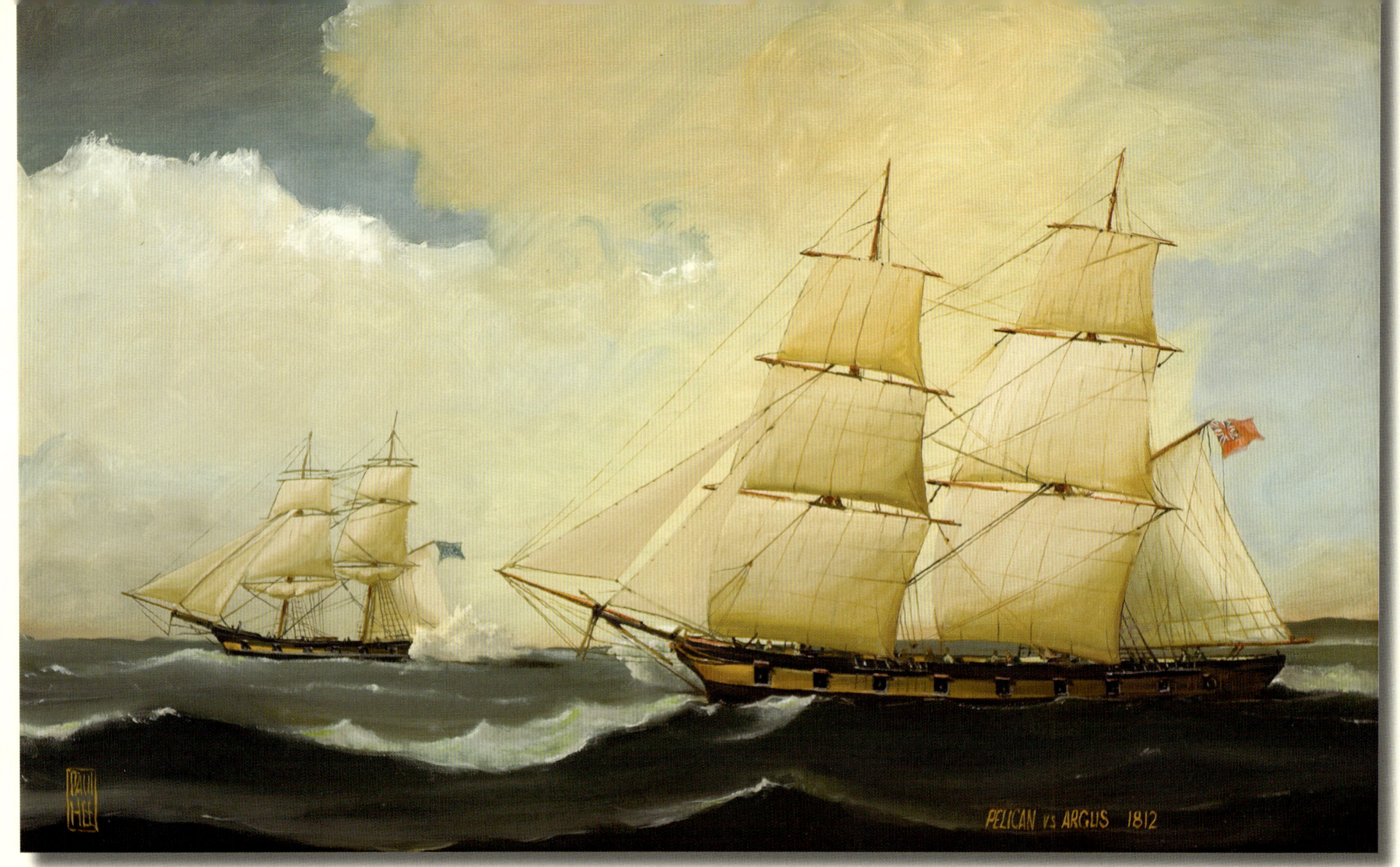

Pelican vs. Argus 1813

18" x 28"

During the War of 1812, the United States brig *Argus* cruised in British home waters for a month, raiding British merchant shipping. On August 14, 1813 the British brig-sloop *Pelican* intercepted her off St. David's Head, Pembrokeshire. After a 45 minute fight, which left Master Commandant William Henry Allen of the *Argus* mortally wounded, *Argus* surrendered. Ten of the American brig's crew were killed and 14 wounded. The English lost two men killed and five wounded.

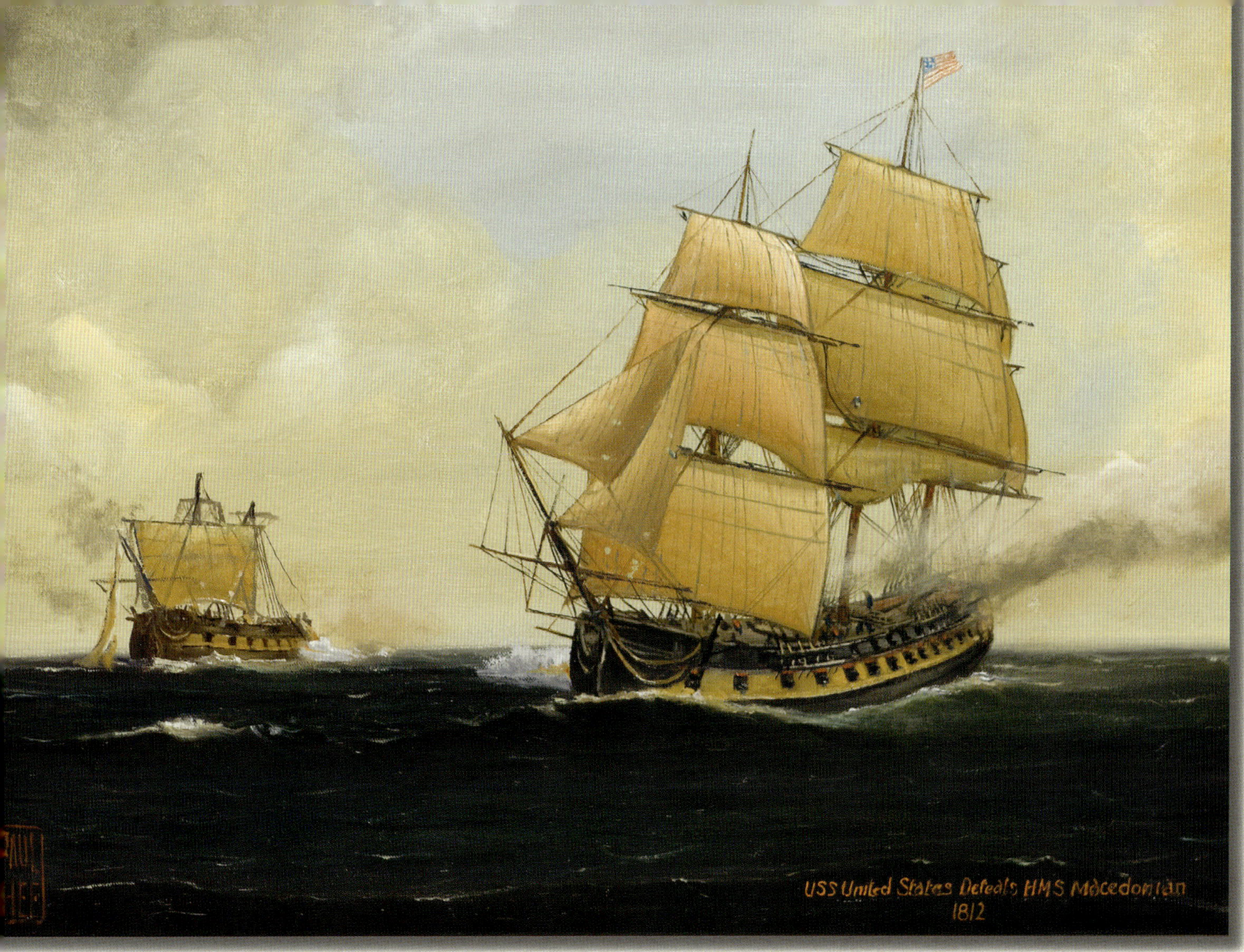

United States vs. Macedonian

18" x 28"

At dawn on October 25, 1812, 500 miles south of the Azores, the 44-gun US frigate *United States* spotted topsails on the horizon. Captain Stephen Decatur attacked the 38-gun British frigate *Macedonian* with 24-pounder cannons. His first shot, an errant broadside, drew return fire from Captain James Carden's 18-pounders, disabling a spar. Decatur's next broadside destroyed *Macedonian's* mizzen top mast and shattered the frigate. British losses were 36 dead and 68 wounded. American losses were 7 dead and 5 wounded. After a hero's welcome in New York, Decatur was honored by President James Madison and Congress. The British ship was renamed *USS Macedonian* and joined the United States Navy. In 1861, the *United States* was captured by Confederates at Norfolk Naval Yard but was sunk in 1862 when they fled.

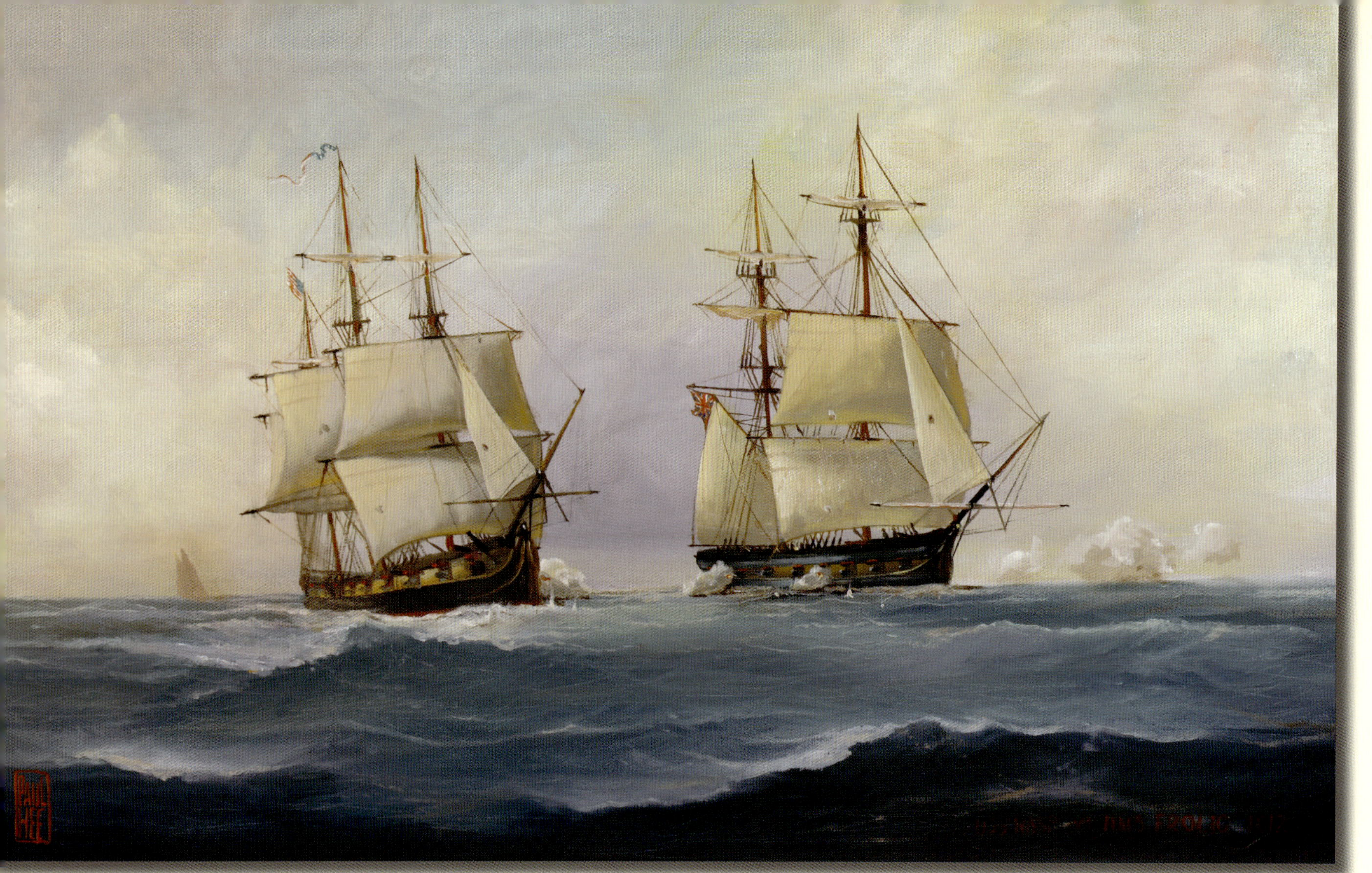

Wasp vs. Frolic

20" x 30"

The United States 28-gun sloop-of-war *Wasp* captured the British 22-gun sloop-of-war *Frolic* on October 18, 1812, while escorting a convoy from the West Indies. *Wasp's* casualties were five men killed, five wounded. *Frolic* had 30 killed, 50 wounded. Both vessels suffered heavy damage to spars and rigging. The hapless *Wasp* was captured a few hours later by the British 74-gun ship *Poictier.*

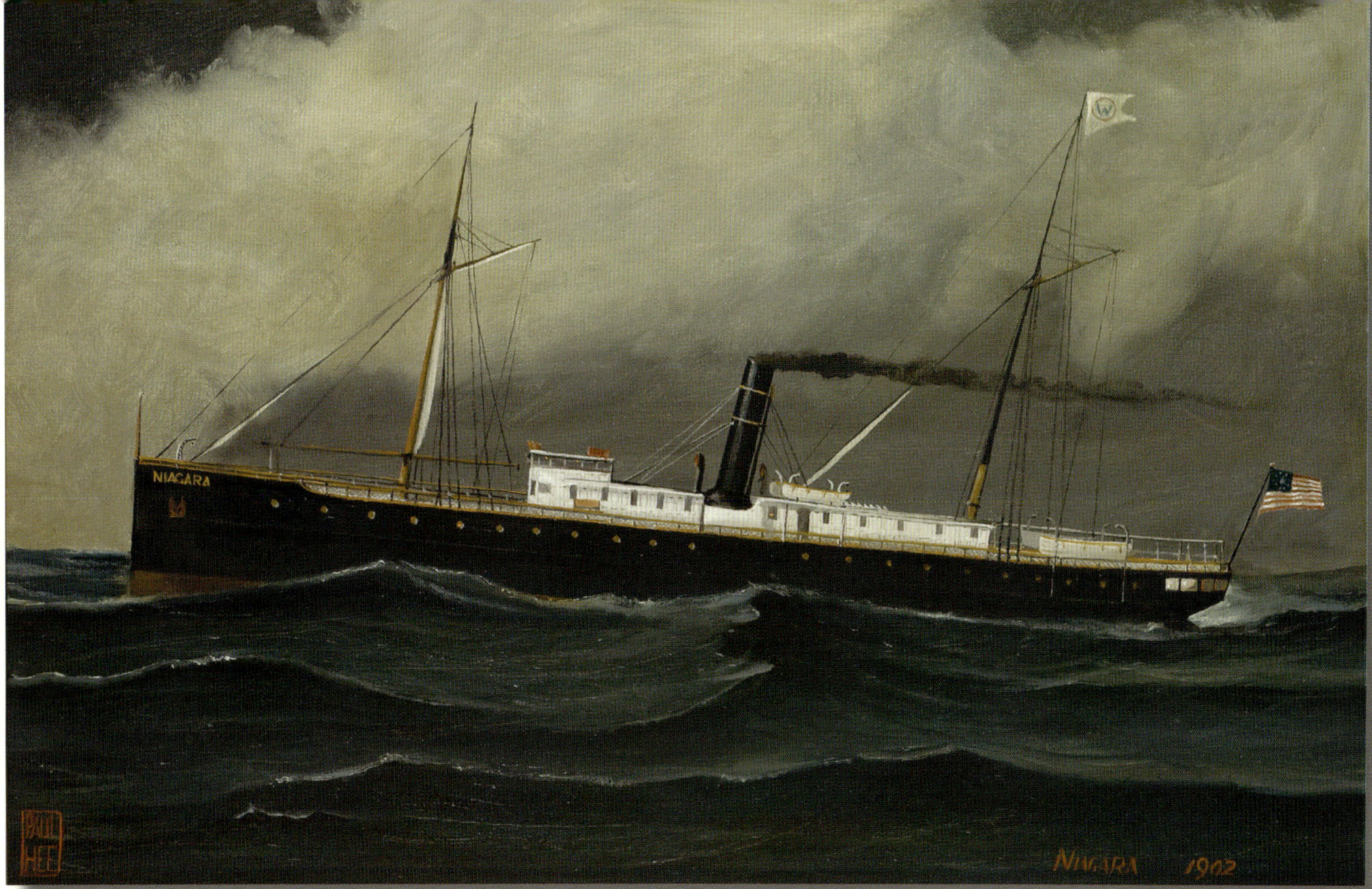

US Brig Niagara 1902

18" x 28"

Commodore Oliver Perry, aboard the US brig *Niagara*, and his nine-ship squadron, captured six British warships in the Battle of Lake Erie on September 10, 1813. "We have met the enemy and they are ours," Perry said. His victory reopened the upper Great Lakes supply lines for America in the War of 1812. Launched in 1813, the 198-foot warship was scuttled in 1820, raised and rebuilt in 1913, then made seaworthy for re-launch as a national historic vessel in 1990. *Niagara* sails today out of the Erie Maritime Museum.

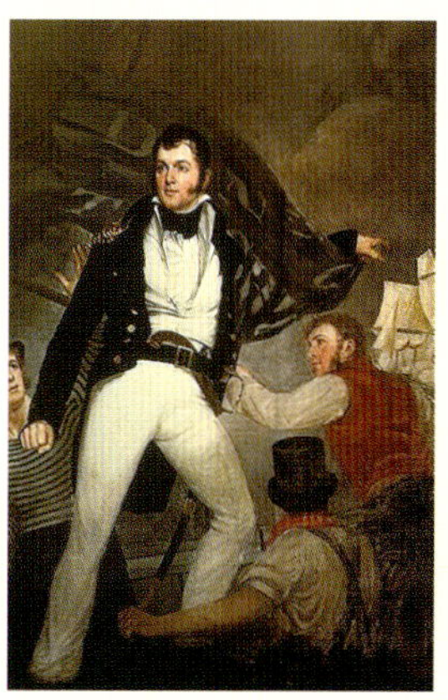

Oliver Perry

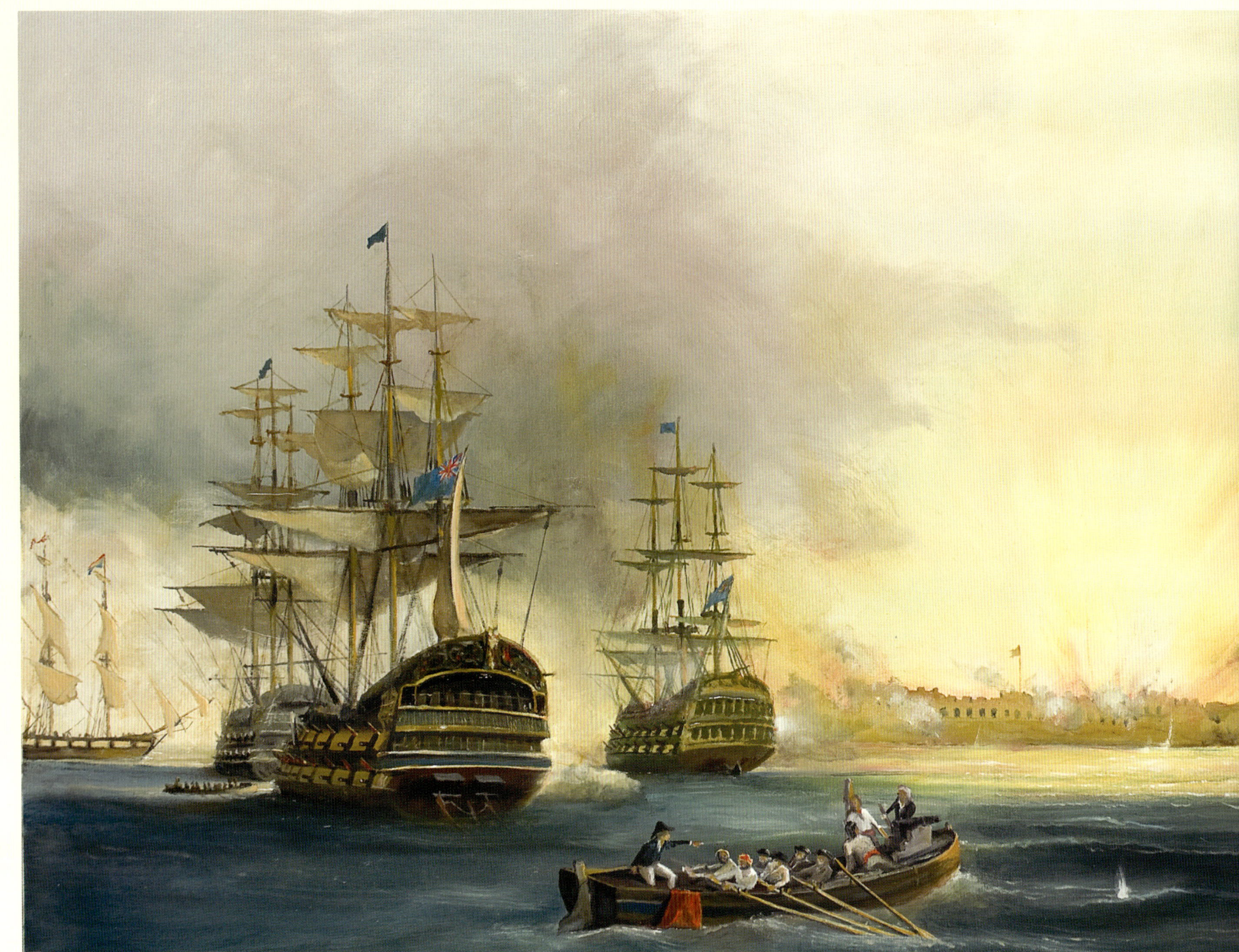

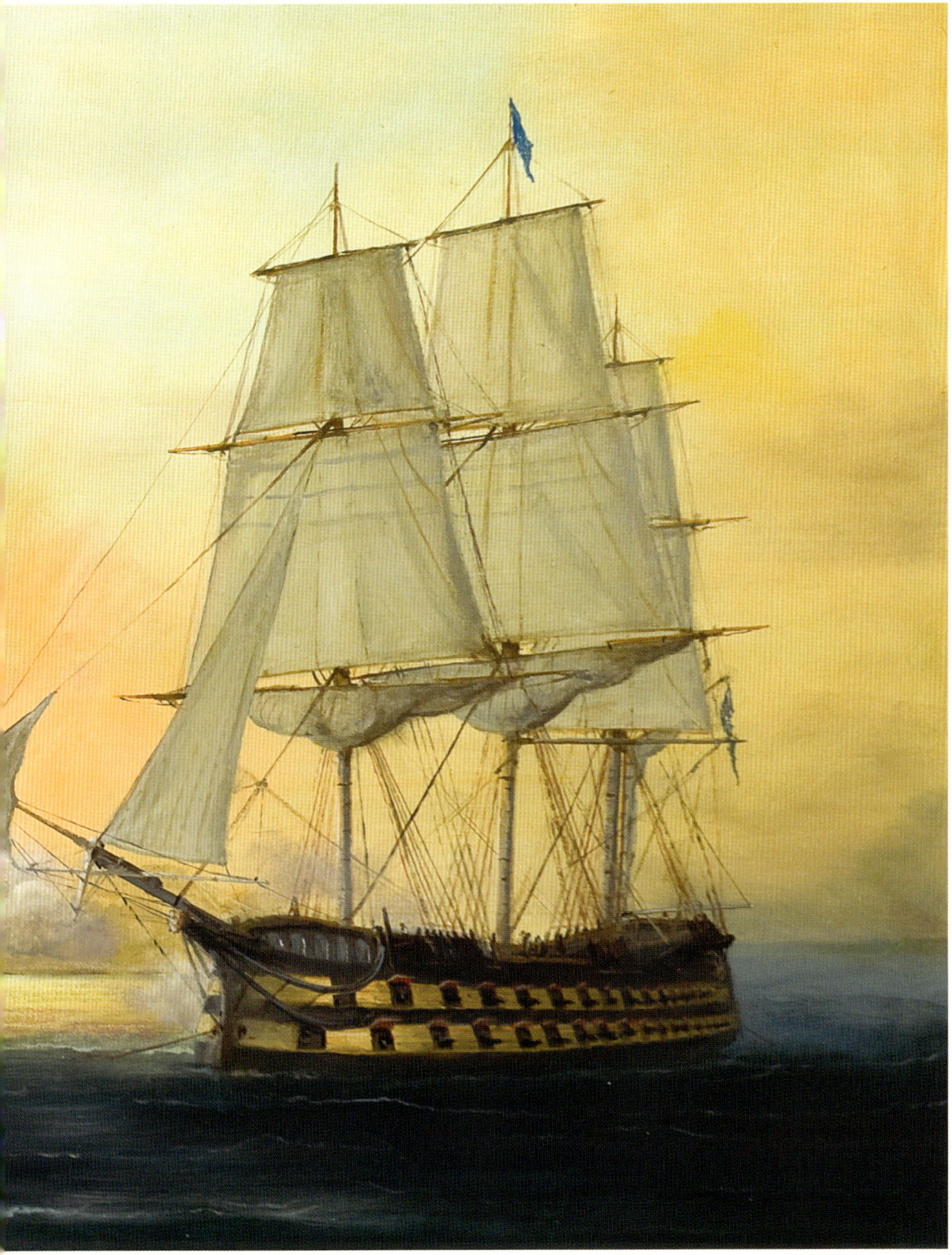

The Bombardment of Algiers 1816

18" x 28"

An Allied fleet bombarded Algiers for nine hours on August 27, 1816, after the Dey (governors) of Algiers imprisoned the British consul and massacred several hundred prisoners. Sir Edward Pellew, Viscount Exmouth, commanded the British squadron of five ships of the line, a 50-gun ship, four frigates, and additional small craft, assisted by a Dutch squadron of five frigates. The fleet sank thirty-three vessels after expending 50,000 rounds of ammunition, and suffered casualties of 150 men killed and 750 wounded. The British consul and 1,083 slaves were freed and the Dey of Algiers forced to pay a $385,000 indemnity.

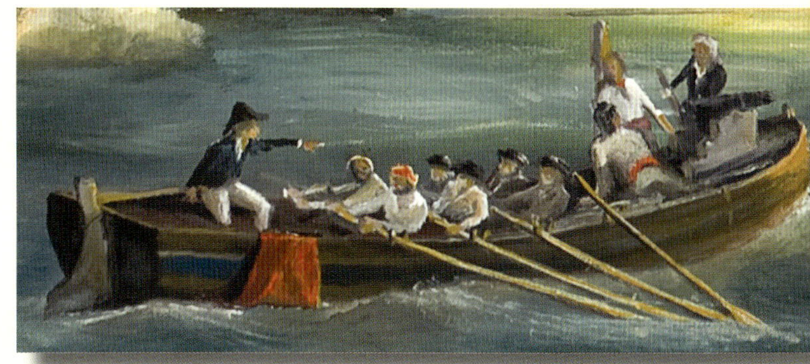

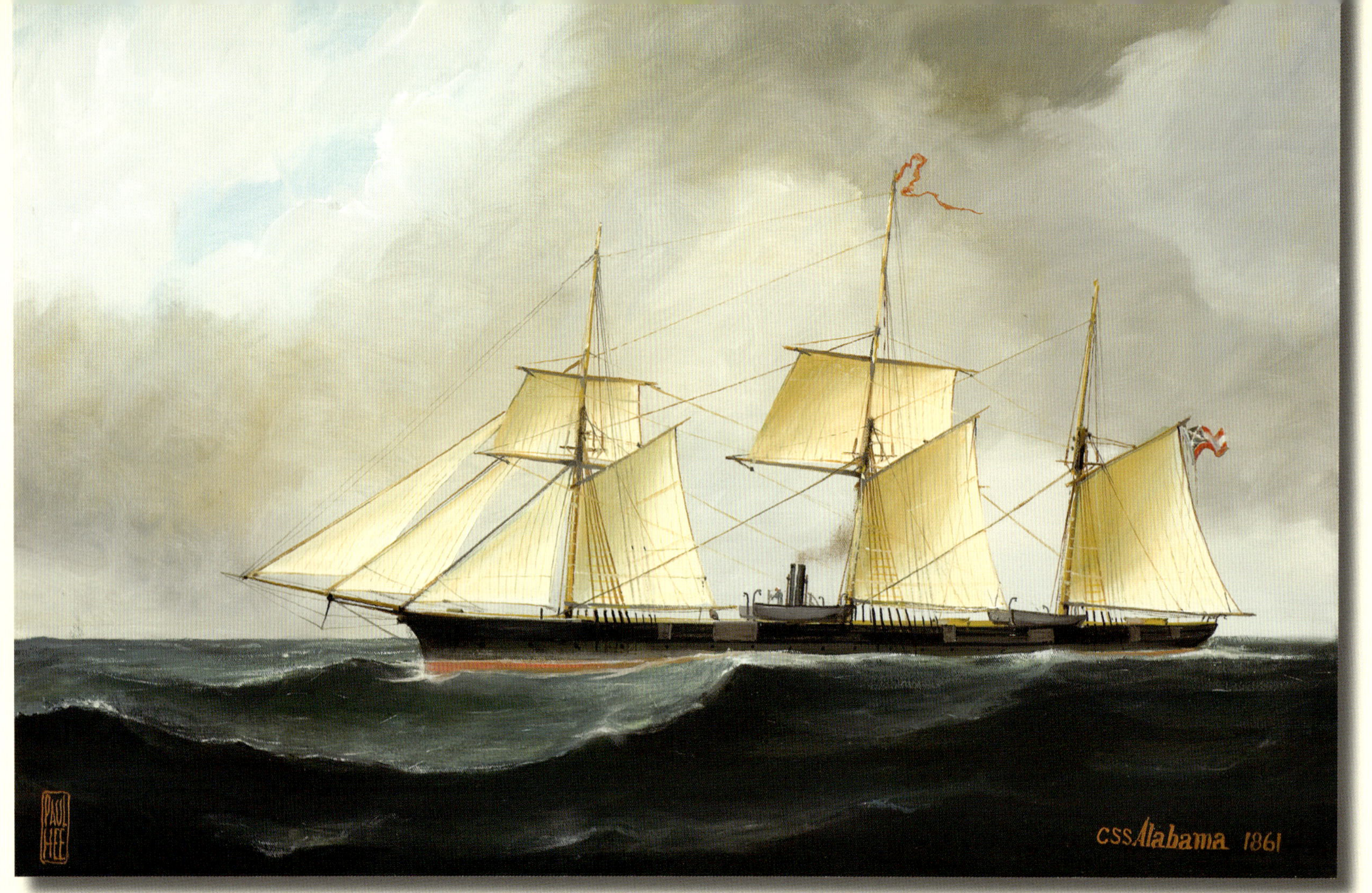

CSS Alabama

18" x 28"

A sloop of war commerce raider built by John Laird at Birkenhead in England, secretly for the Confederacy, *CSS Alabama* wreaked destruction on the United States merchant fleet during seven campaigns over a two-year period. She captured 447 Union merchant ships, burned vessels, and sank the Union blockader *Hatteras.* Powered by sail and steam, *Alabama's* top speed was 13.25 knots. At sea 534 of the 657 days of her life, she took 2,000 prisoners with no loss of life. On June 19, 1864 off Cherbourg, France, she was outgunned and sunk by the United States Navy sloop of war *Kearsage.* The wreck was discovered in 1984 in 200 feet of water, and her ship's bell and artifacts, including cannon, were raised in 2002.

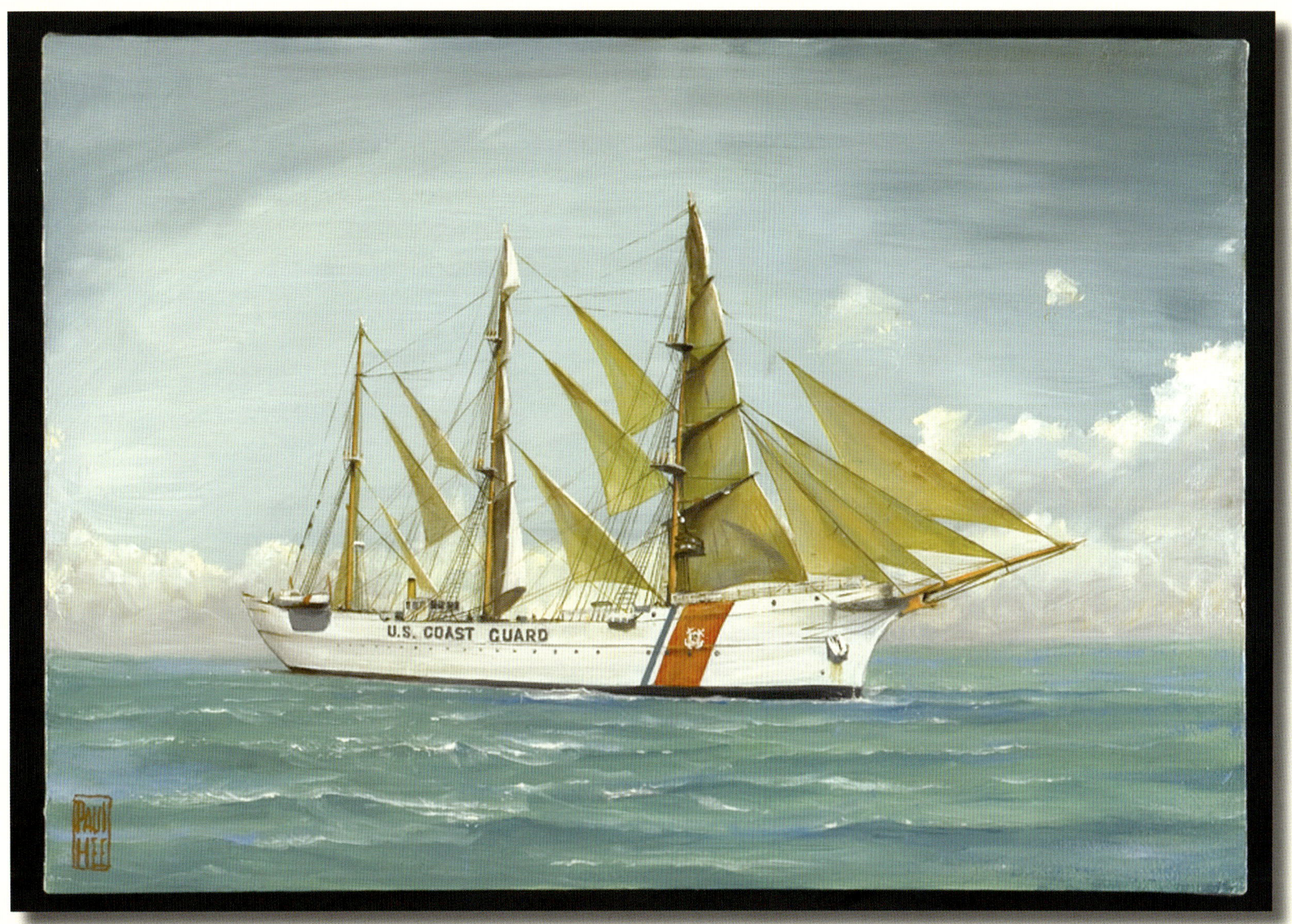

EAGLE
18" x 28"

Built by Blohm & Voss at Hamburg in 1936 as *Horst Wessel* for the Kriegsmarine, the United States seized the bark as war reparations at the end of World War II. Renamed *Eagle* in 1946, the US Coast Guard vessel operates as a training ship, based at the Coast Guard Academy at New London, Connecticut.

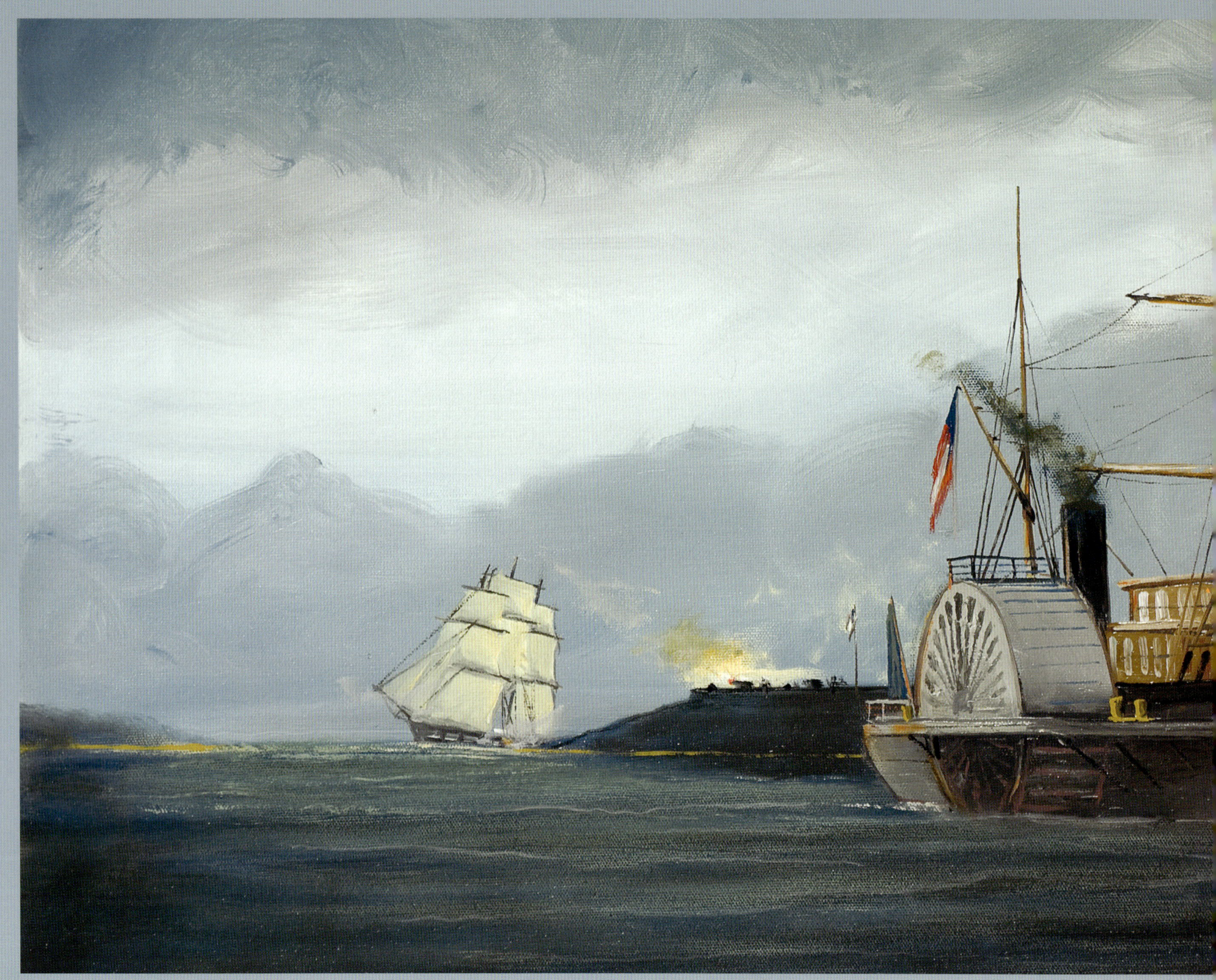

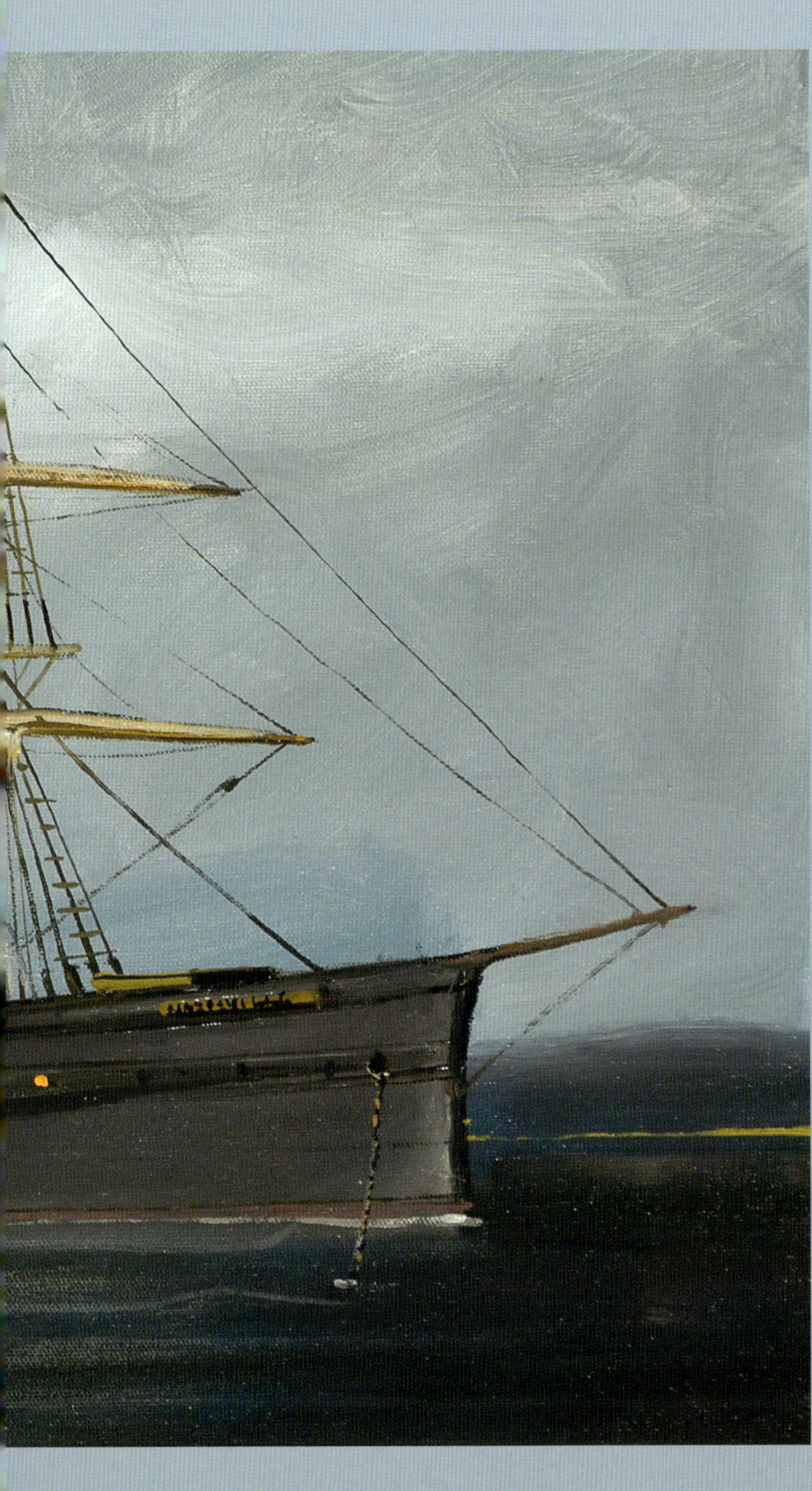

CHAPTER III

CAROLINAS

CSS Nashville 1862

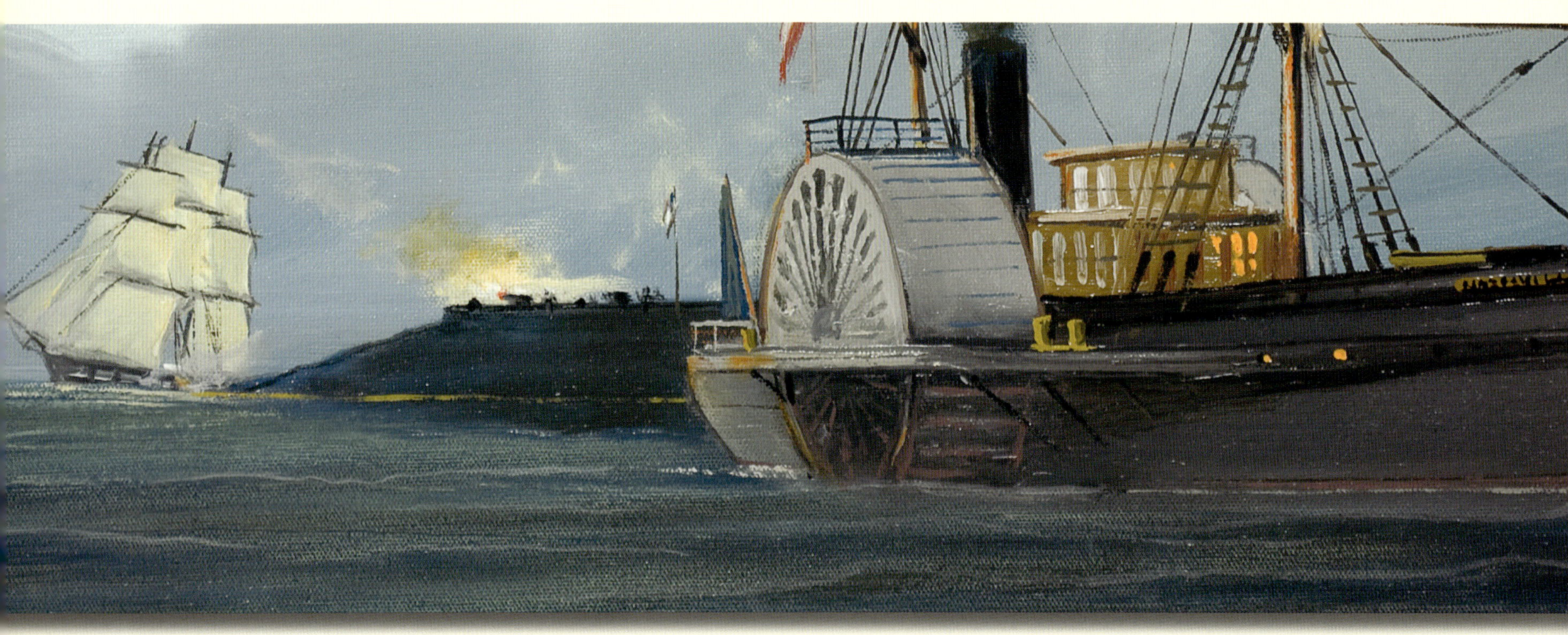

CSS Nashville 1862

18" x 28"

The Confederacy seized the 1853 side-wheel passenger steamer at Charleston, South Carolina, in 1861, and converted it to a lightly armed cruiser. On a combat cruise in the English Channel she captured and burned the sailing merchantman *Harvey Birch* on Nov. 19, 1861. Upon returning to American waters she captured and burned the schooner *Robert Gilfillan* on Feb. 26, 1862. Two days later, *CSS Nashville* ran the blockade into Beaufort, North Carolina, and, in November, became the privateer *Rattlesnake.* The monitor *USS Montauk* destroyed the *Rattlesnake* near Savannah, Georgia, on February 28, 1863.

Siege of Fort Macon 1862

18" x 24"

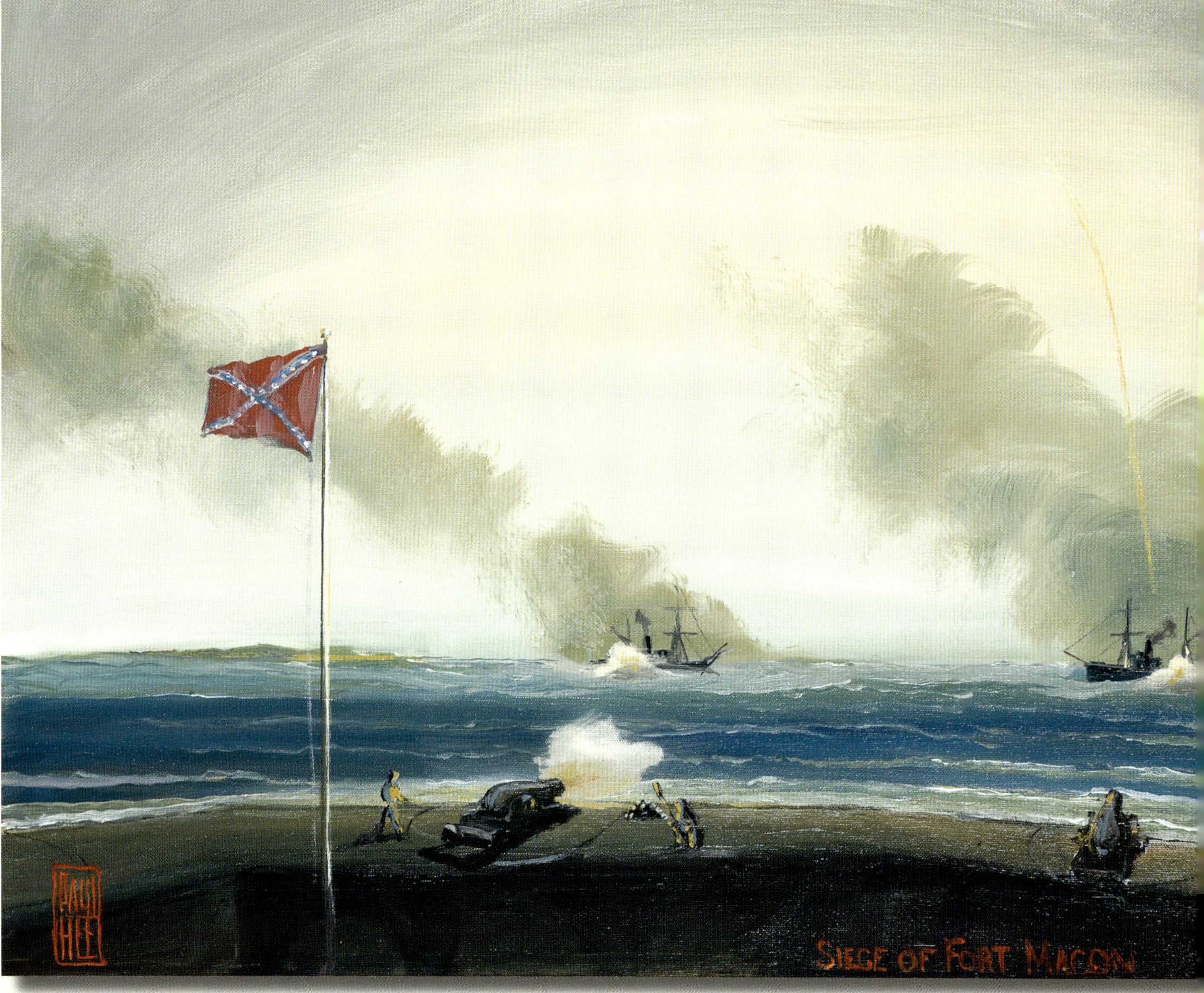

On the morning of April 26, 1862, US gunboats—*Daylight*, *State of Georgia*, and *Chippewa*, and the bark *Gemsbok*—advanced on Fort Macon. The ships fired "shot and shell" on the fort "for an hour and a quarter" in a wind-tossed sea that rolled the ships "so quick and deep as to render our guns almost unmanageable." A lucky shell from the fort passed through the rigging of the *Chippewa* with no injury to crew or damage to sail. Hoping the seas would subside, Commander Samuel Lockwood withdrew, but the wind and sea rose and he stood off. Toward evening a flag of truce waved from the fort. *Daylight* and *Gemsbok* stayed on in Beaufort, *State of Georgia* and *Chippewa* sailed on to Wilmington. Two British ships, *Alliance* and *Gondar,* were seized "as lawful prizes" at anchor in Morehead City.

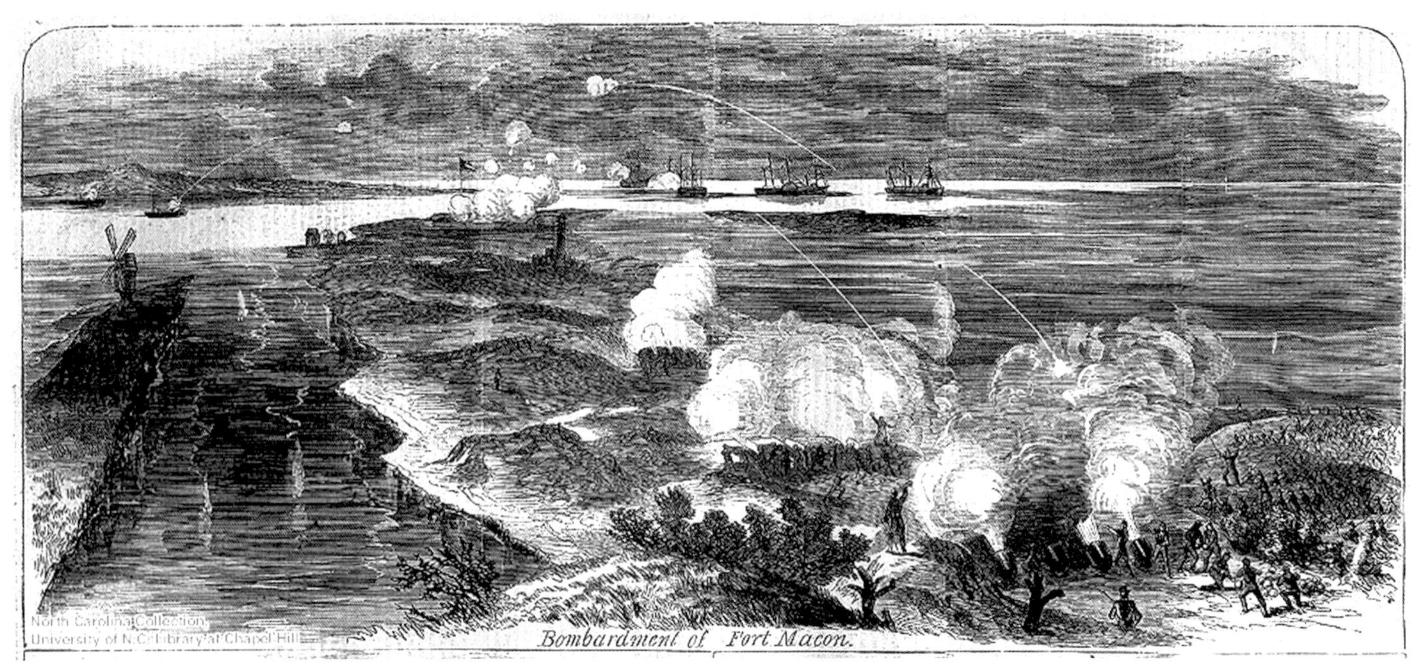
North Carolina Collection
University of N.C. Library at Chapel Hill
Bombardment of Fort Macon.

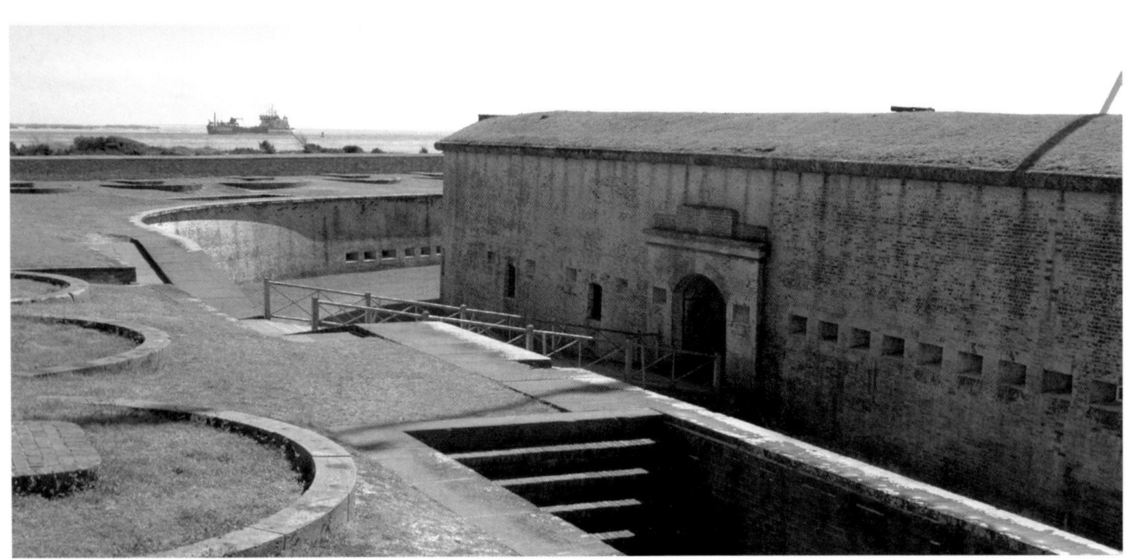

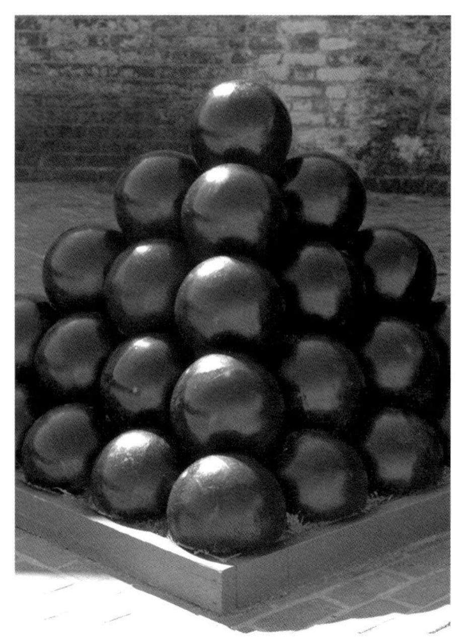

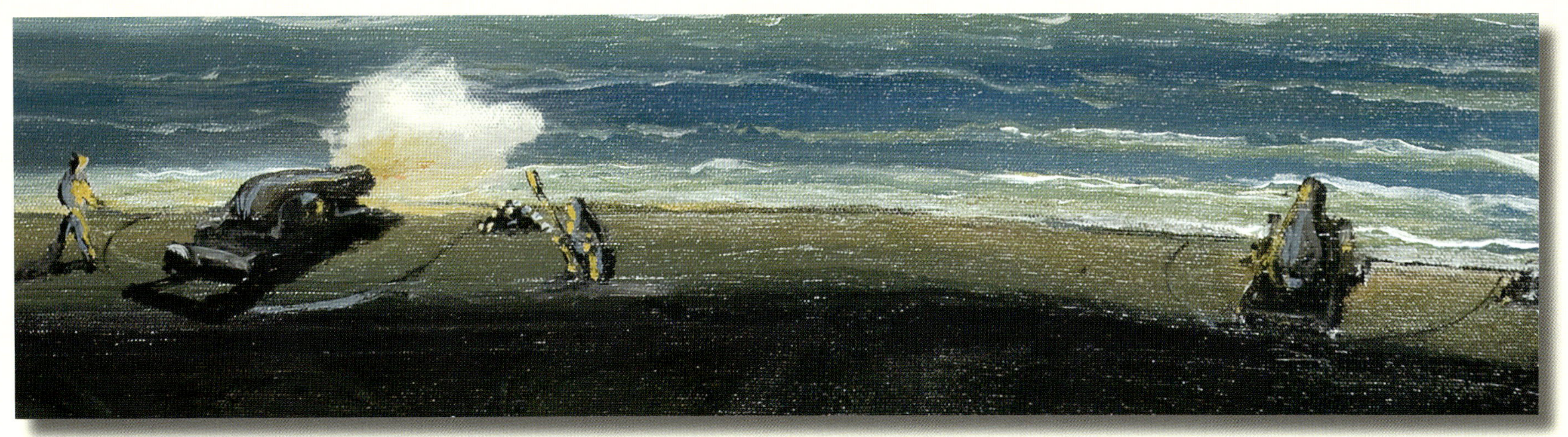

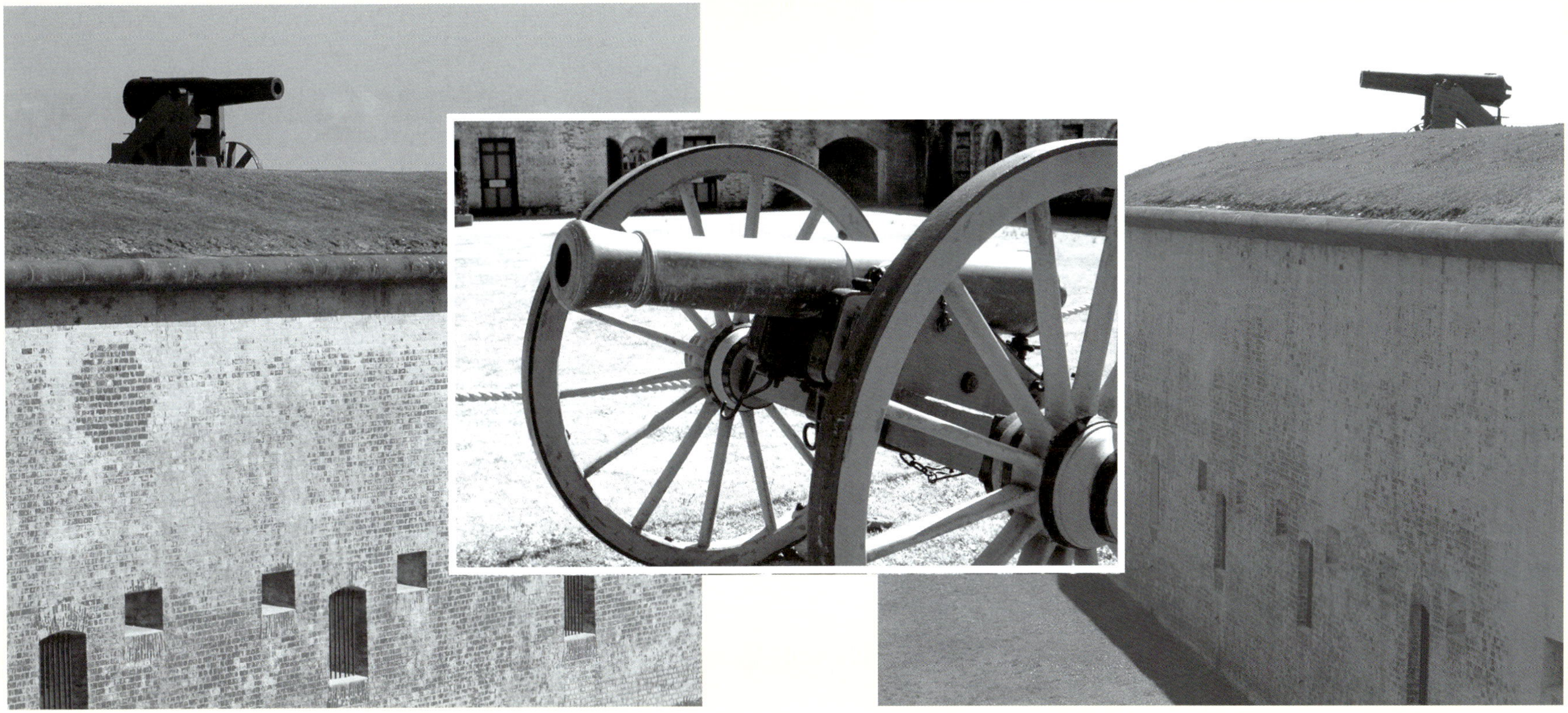

Louisa Bliss Departs for the California Gold Rush

18" x 20"

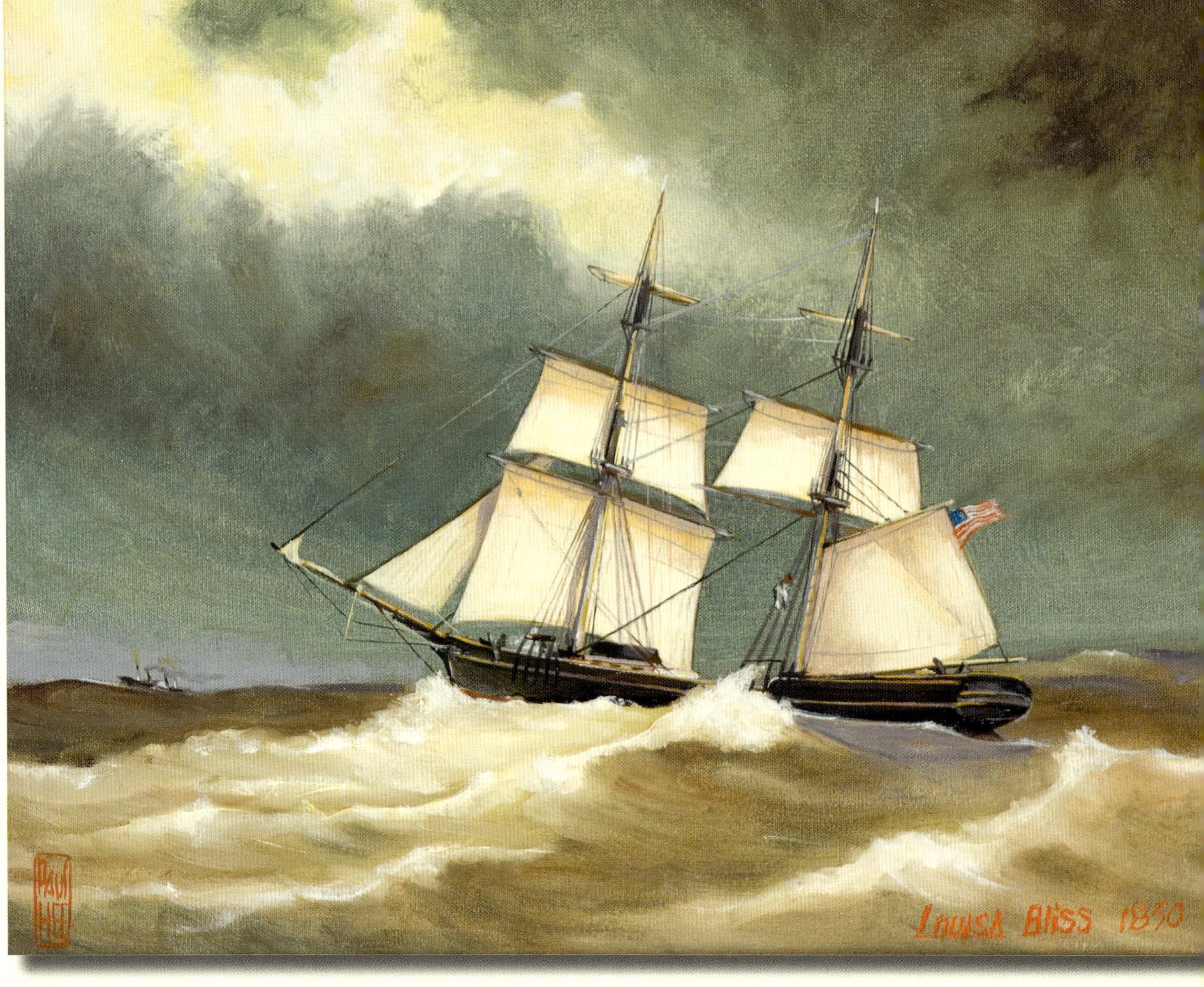

With a 10-man crew from Beaufort, North Carolina, Captain A.M. Fales sailed the 88-foot barque *Louisa Bliss* to San Francisco around Cape Horn with a cargo of lumber. The Beaufort crew included: Brian Rumley, S.S. Duffy, William Penn Hellen, LeRoy M. Piver, James Gillikin, David William Noe, William F. Hatsel, J. L. Manney, Charles Whitehurst, and James Busk. The *Louisa Bliss* was built in 1845 in Warren, Maine, as an immigrant ship. Owned by J.W. Elwell & Co., she sailed often to Bremen, Germany, and to Italy. After her 1850 voyage to San Francisco she returned to the North Atlantic and sank off Nova Scotia.

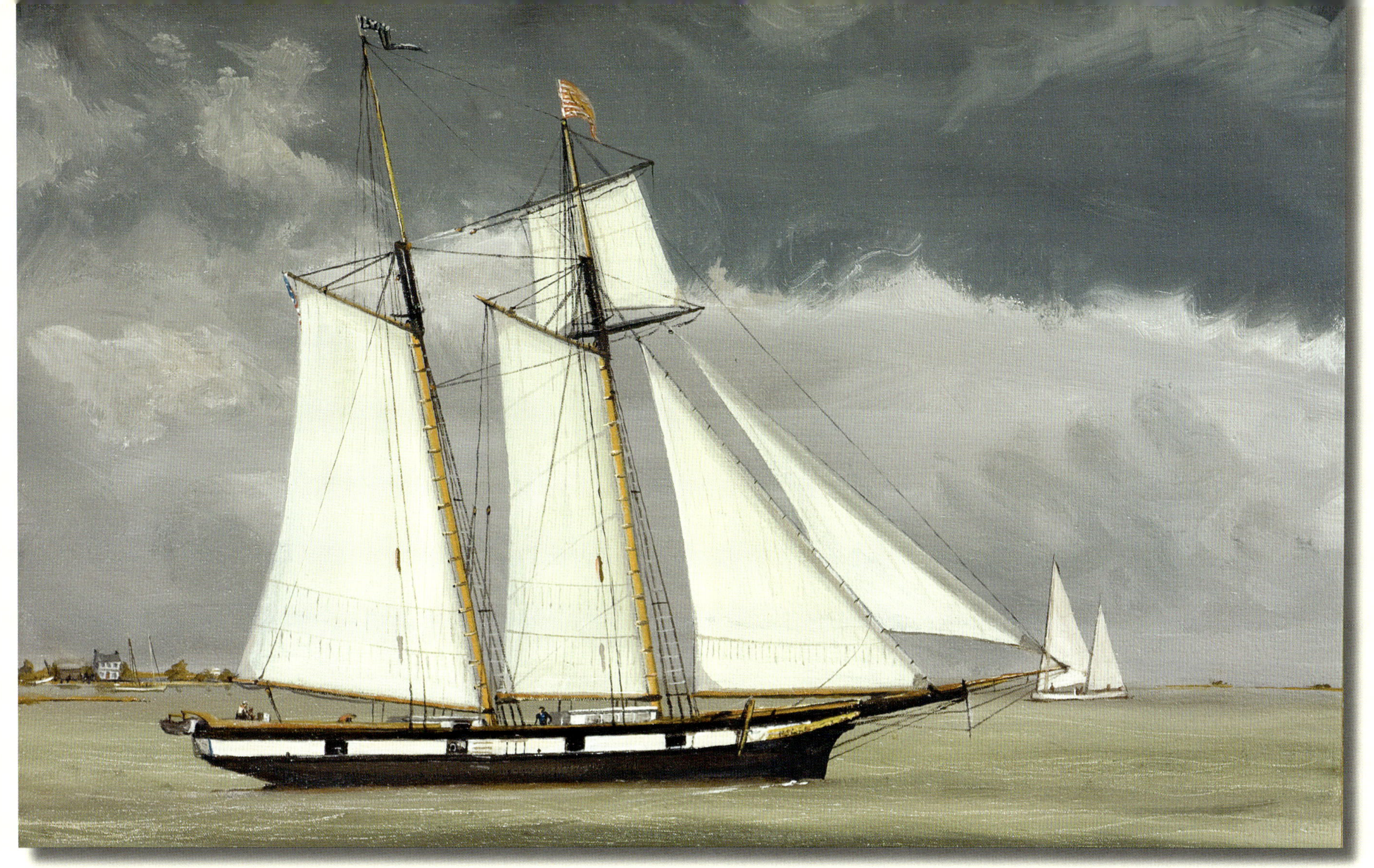

Privateer Schooner Lynx in Beaufort Harbor
18" x 28"

Lynx, a 122-foot square topsail schooner designed by Melbourne Smith and built at Rockport, Maine, is a modern recreation of a known successful Baltimore privateer from the War of 1812. She has operated since 2001 as a sail training ship out of Newport Beach, California. This view is in the style of early 19th Century ship's portraits.

George Taulane

18" x 28"

The schooner *George Taulane* of Beaufort, North Carolina, comes home after surviving the killer hurricane of 1899 that claimed lives, homes (it devastated Diamond City, the whaling village near Cape Lookout lighthouse on the island of Shackleford Banks), and more than 50 ships at sea. At Core Banks the day after the storm, *George Taulane*, bound to New Bern with fish scrap, ran ashore. Five men aboard were rescued.

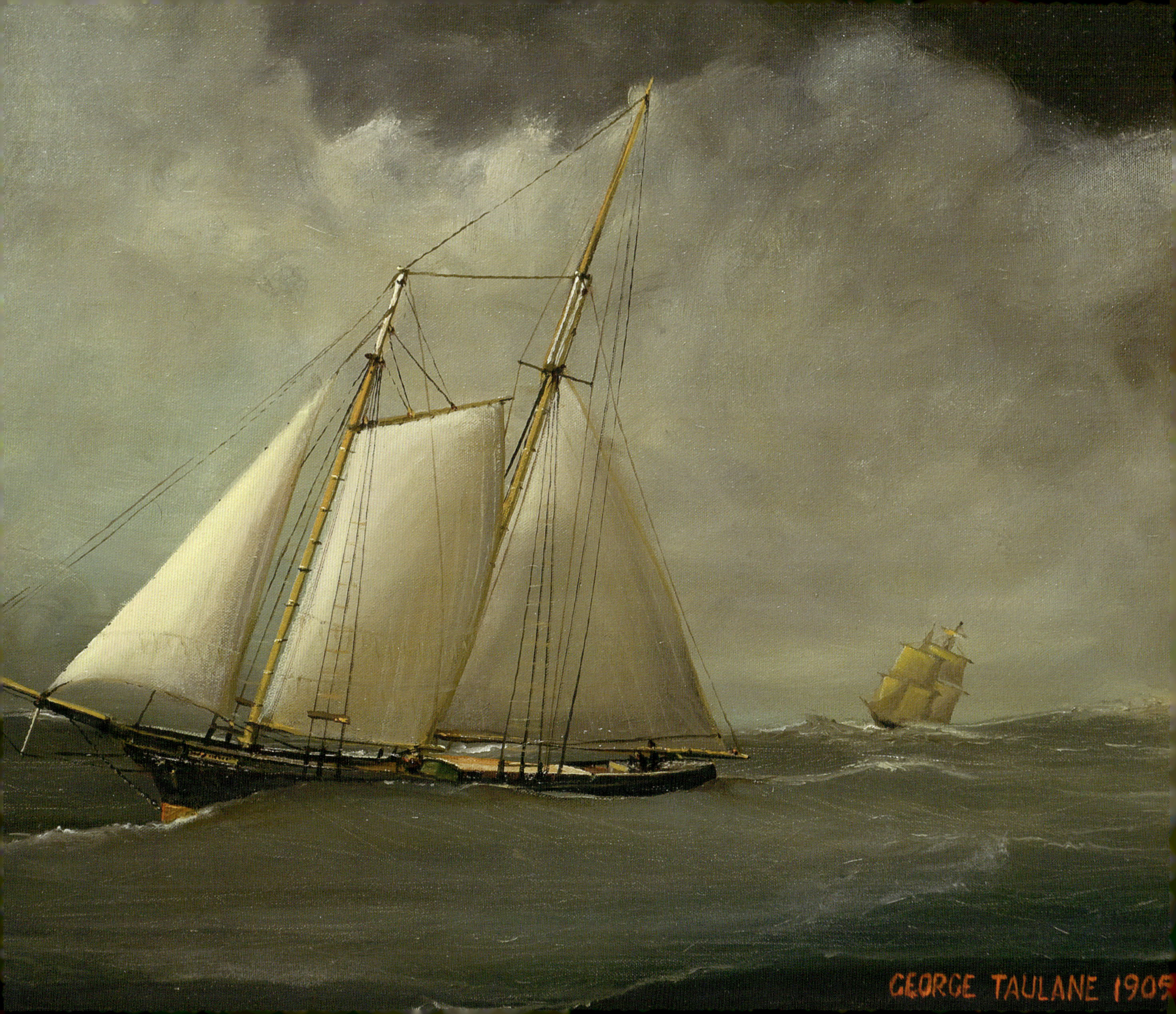
GEORGE TAULANE 1905

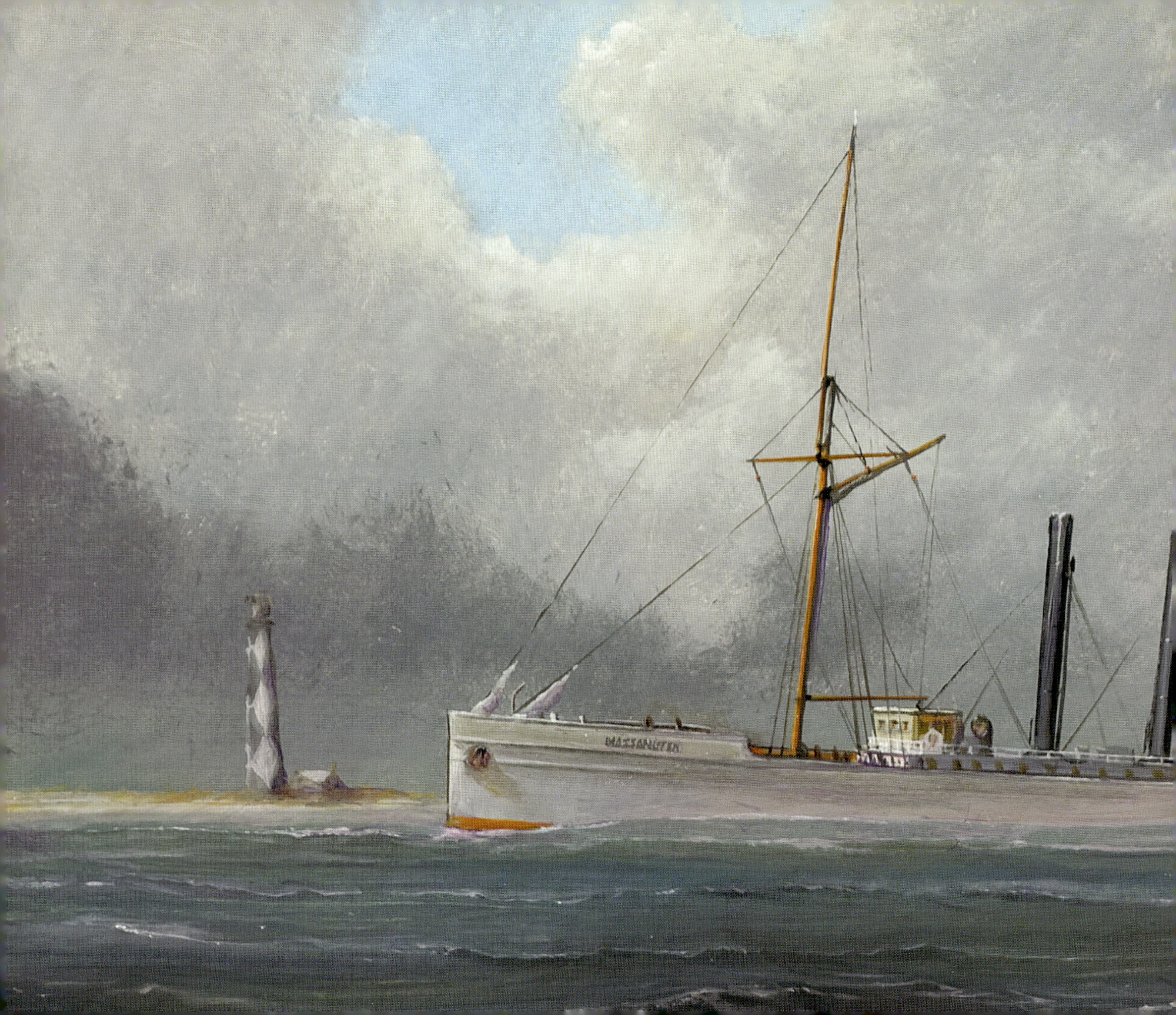

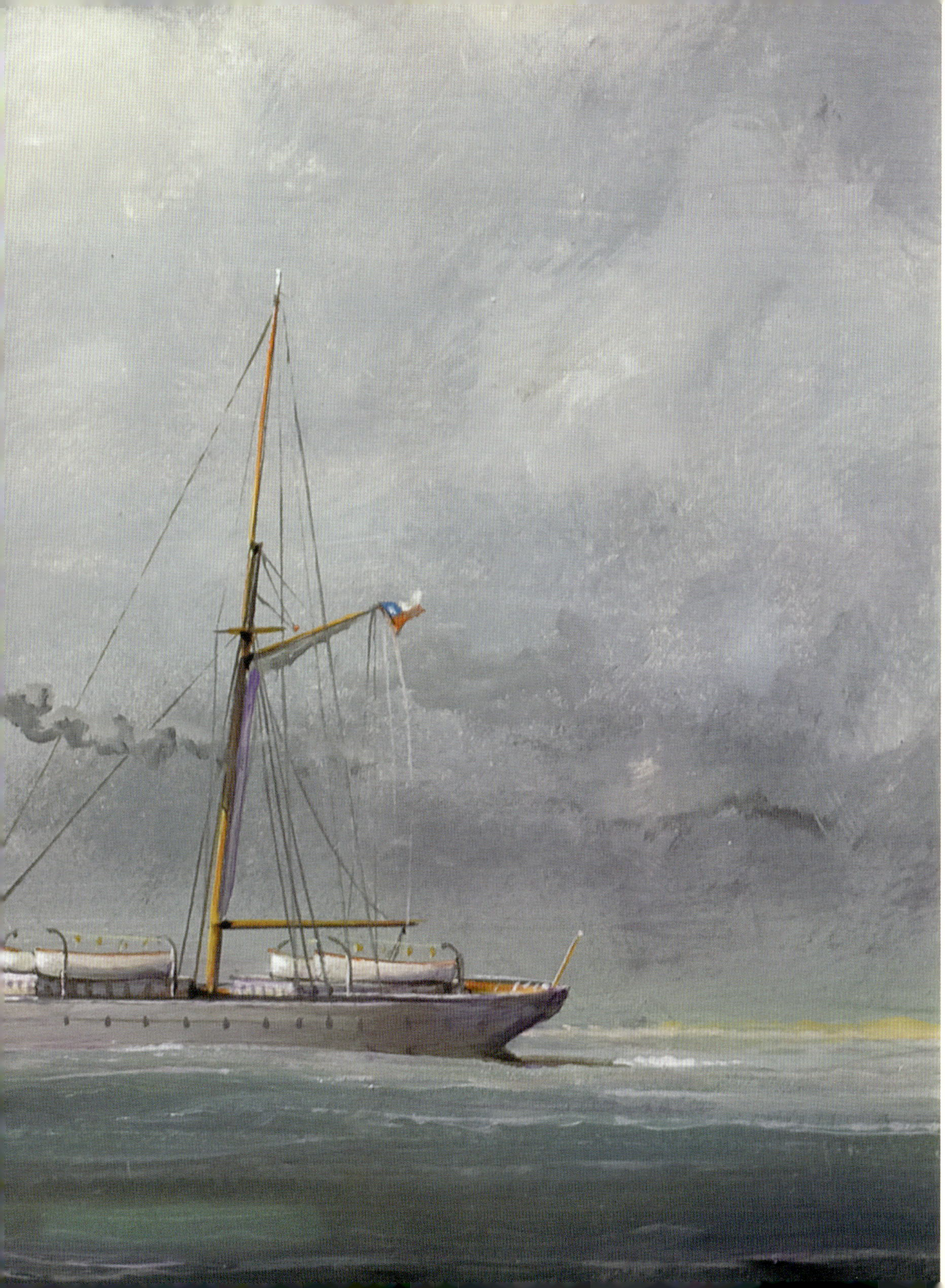

CSS Massanuten

18" x 28"

Confederate troopship steams by Cape Lookout enroute to Wilmington, North Carolina.

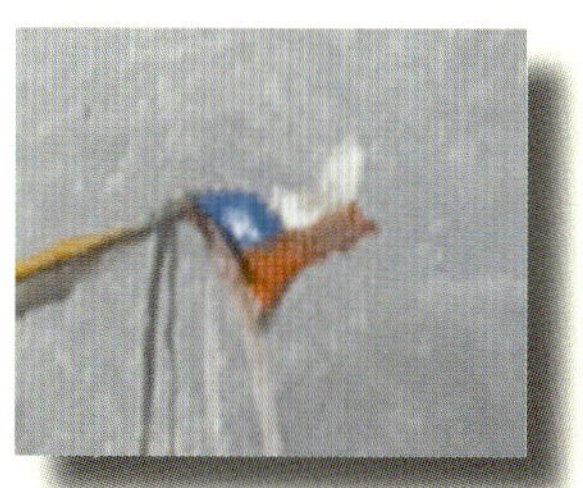

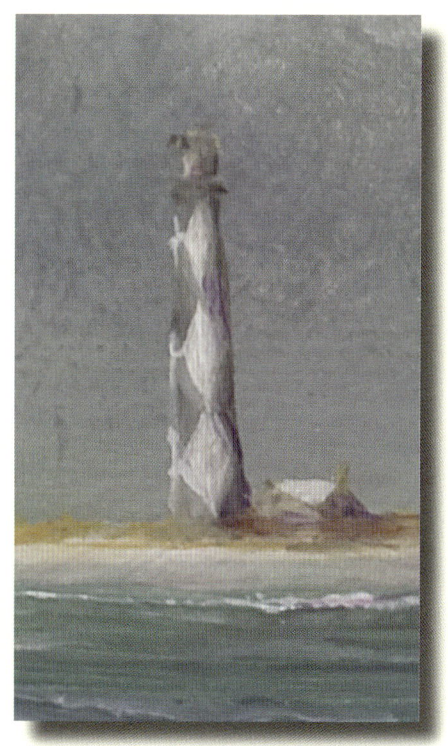

Snap Dragon

18" x 24"

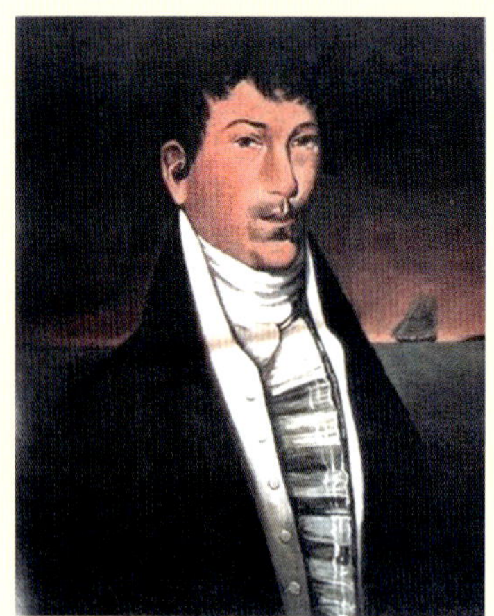

Otway Burns

In 1812, Otway Burns bought *Zephyr*, a Baltimore clipper, for $8,000, renamed it *Snap Dragon* and became the scourge of British ships on the Eastern coast. One of the most famous privateers in the history of the United States, Burns (1775-1850) is legendary for his seamanship aboard the swift 85.5-foot privateer during the War of 1812. In three cruises, from Nova Scotia to the Caribbean, *Snap Dragon* captured 300 sailors and 42 vessels valued at $4 million. When he died in 1850, he was laid to rest in Beaufort's Old Burying Ground with a *Snap Dragon* cannon atop his tomb.

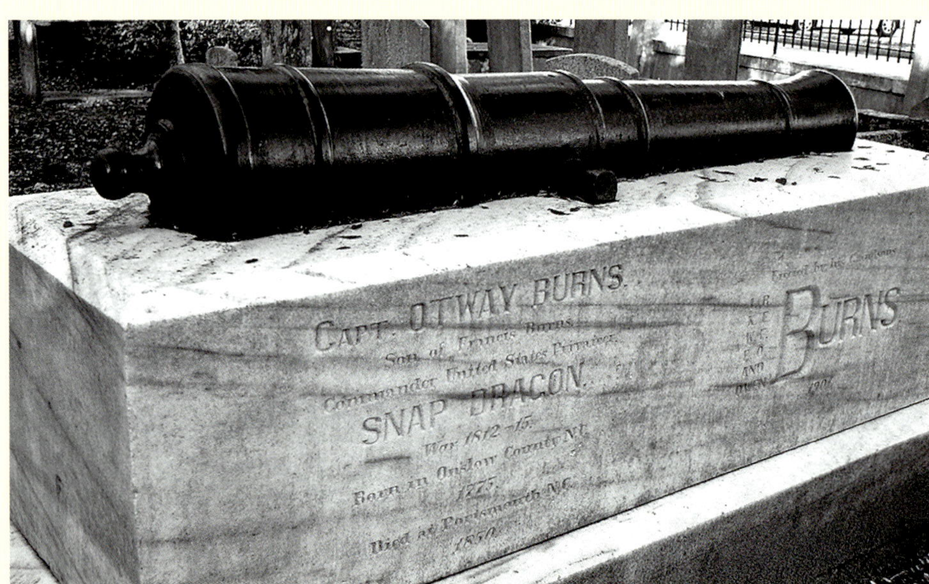

Silent Cannon on His Tomb

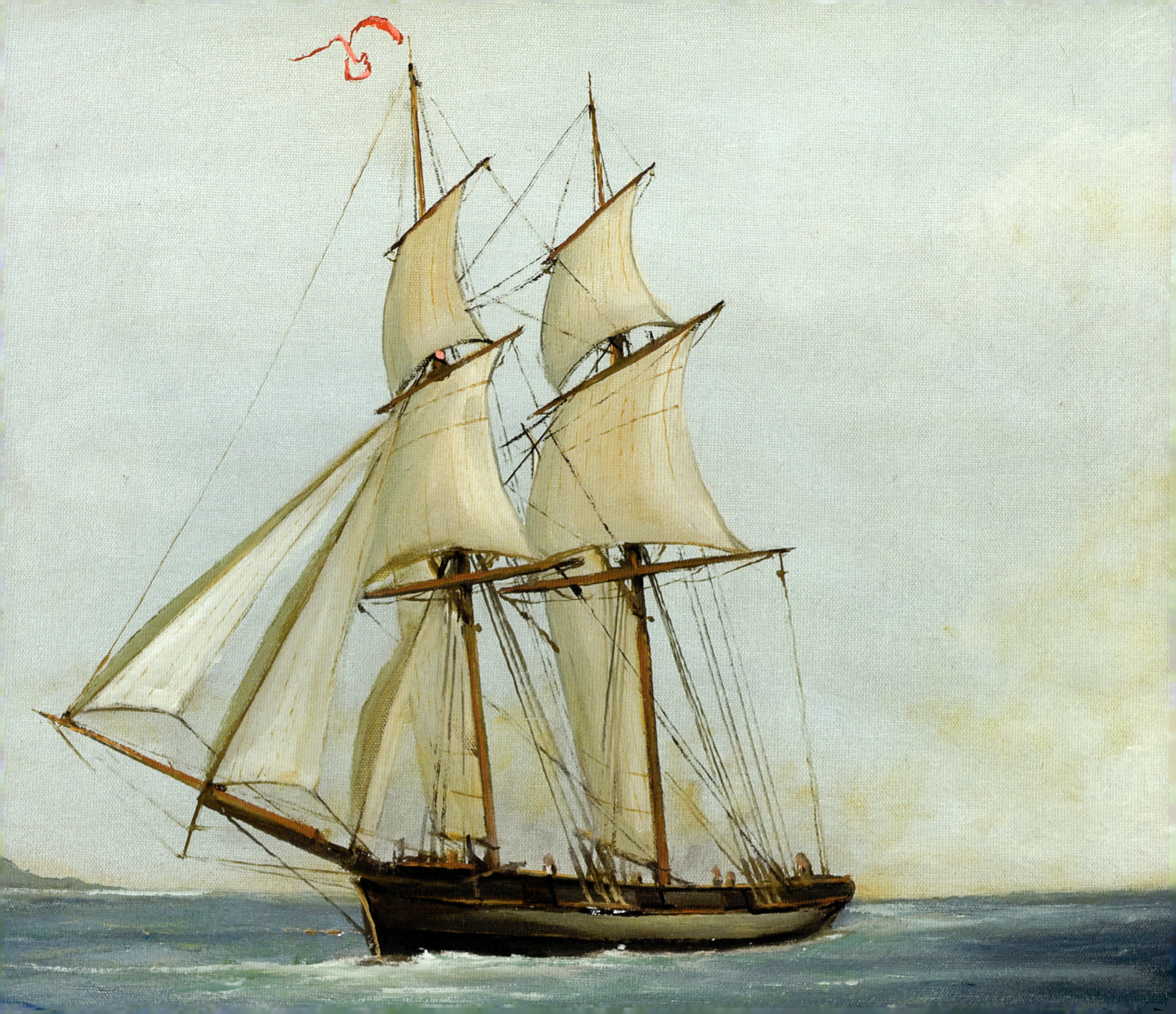

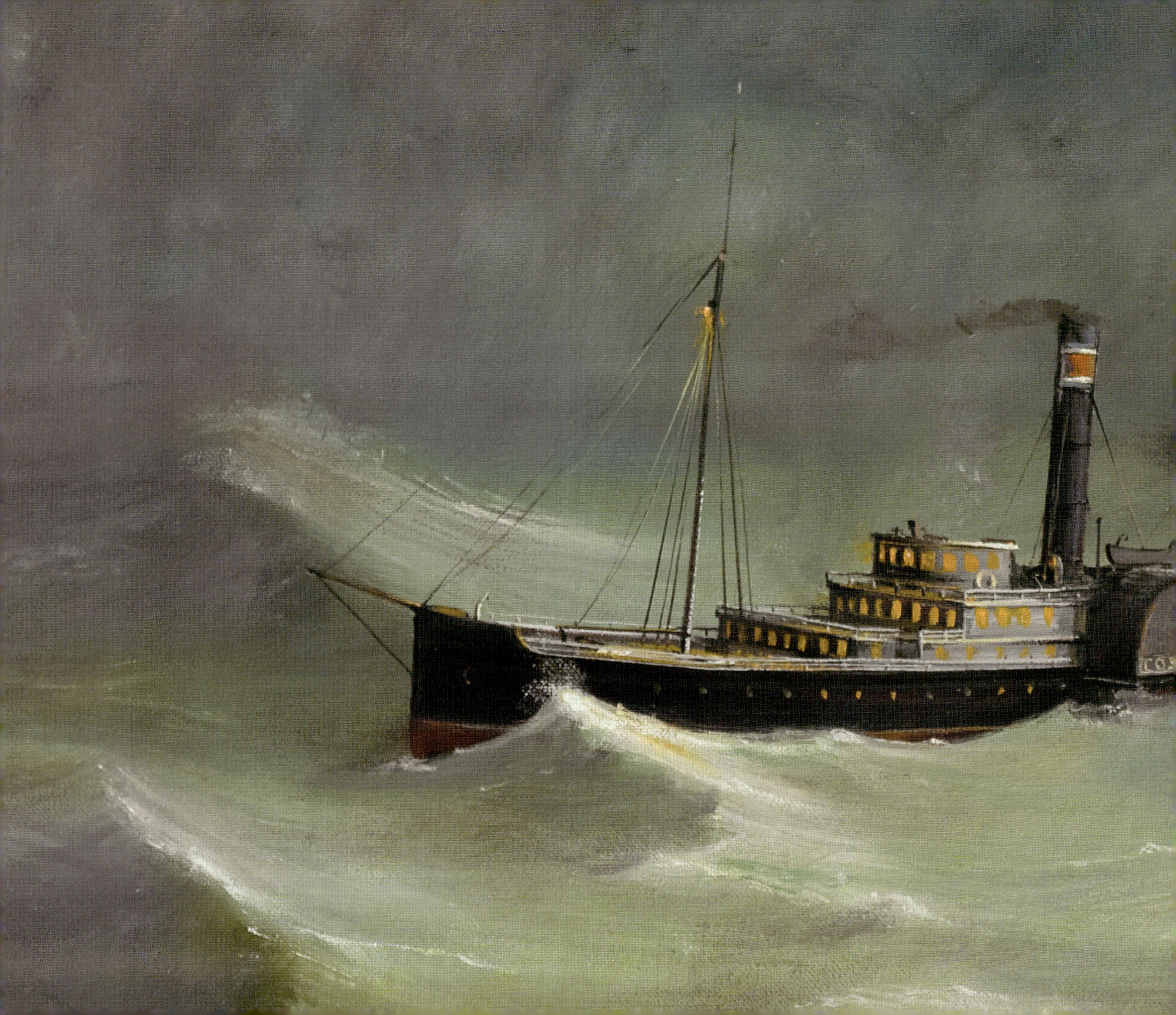

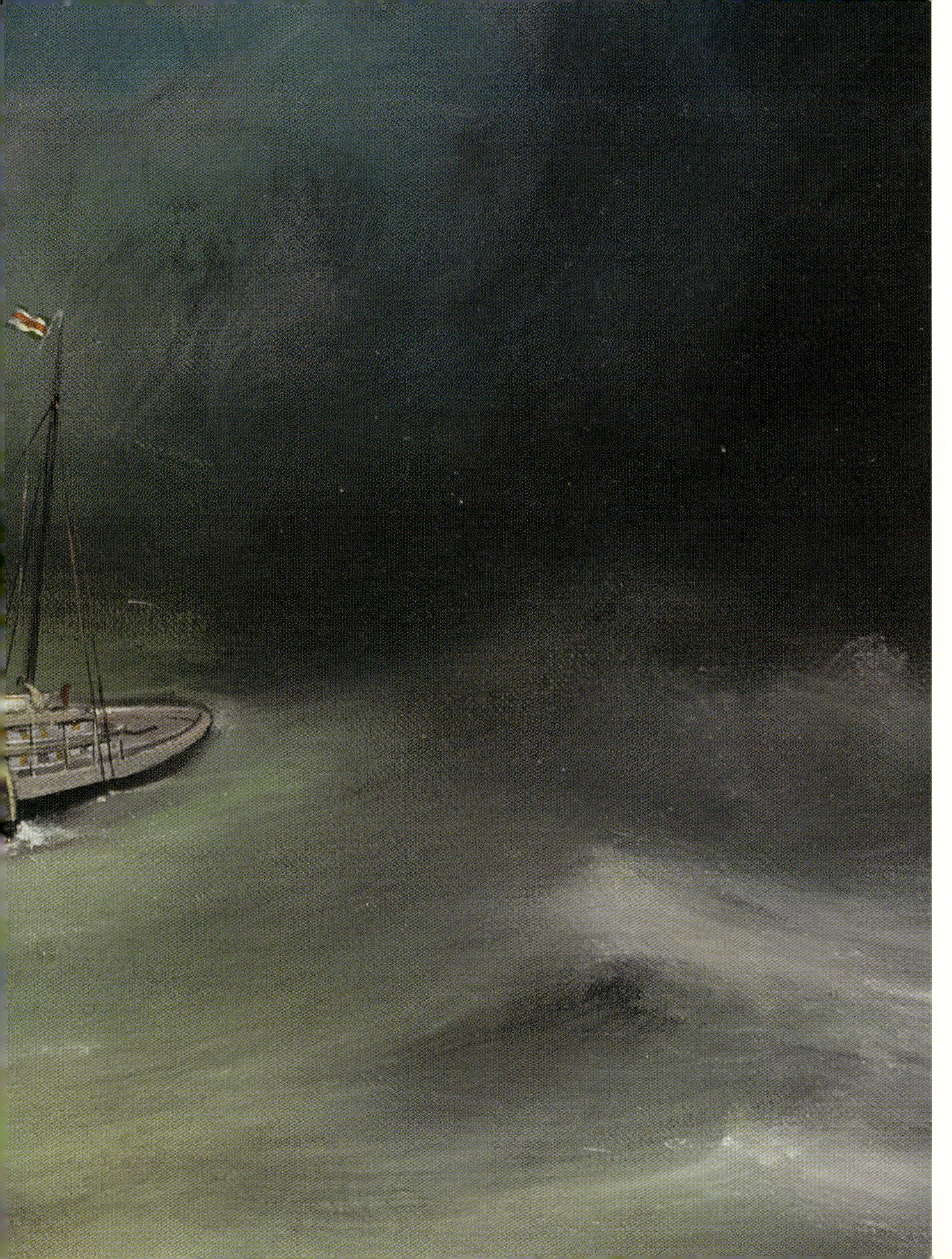

Lost Off Hatteras 1854

18" x 28"

Paddle-wheel steamer *Costa Rica* fights heavy seas off Cape Hatteras, North Carolina.

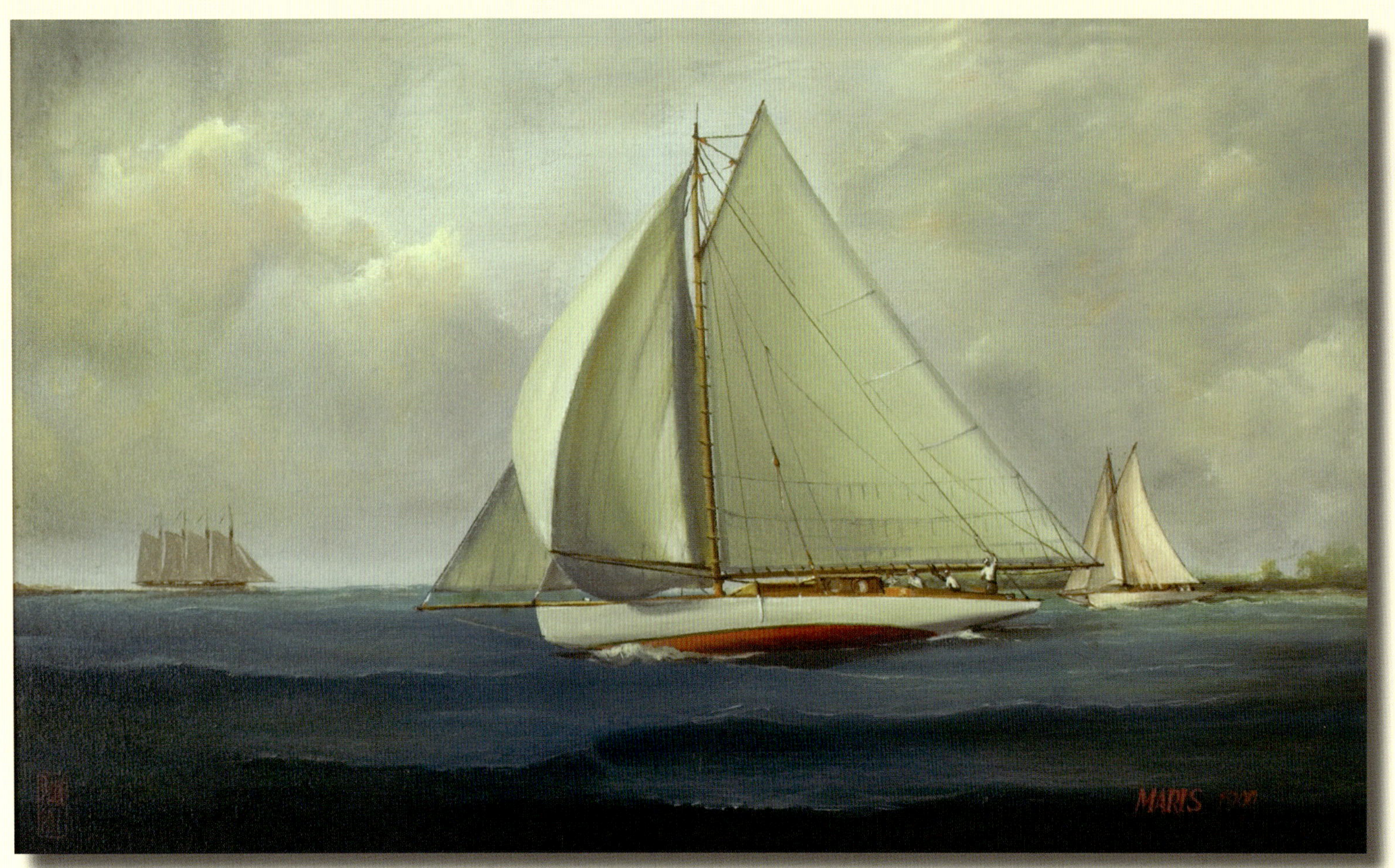

Maris

18" x 30"

Built for speed, the 51-foot racing sloop *Maris* lacked aesthetics and comfort but under full sail proved victorious for the Carolina Yacht Club of Charleston in 1900. On a test sail in Charleston Harbor on April 28, a day with "hardly a capful of wind," according to a reporter, *Maris* "flies with less wind than is required to raise a kite." With Captain Wilmot D. Porcher at the tiller *Maris* beat *Dragoon* in two consecutive races, each by 12 minutes actual sail time, to win the Inter-state Challenge Competition in Savannah, Georgia, in June 1900. The classic sloop was designed by Charles H. Crane and built in the South Boston yard of George Lawley & Son. This painting is on exhibit at Carolina Yacht Club, Charleston, South Carolina.

A Sharpie on Taylor's Creek

16" x 20"

Two-masted sharpie sails on Taylor's Creek past the Front Street houses of Beaufort, North Carolina. The flat-bottom sharpie is a local adaptation of a New Haven, Connecticut oyster boat introduced to Beaufort in 1876 by George Ives, an oysterman. The basic rig was the "leg-o-mutton" spritsails, shown here.

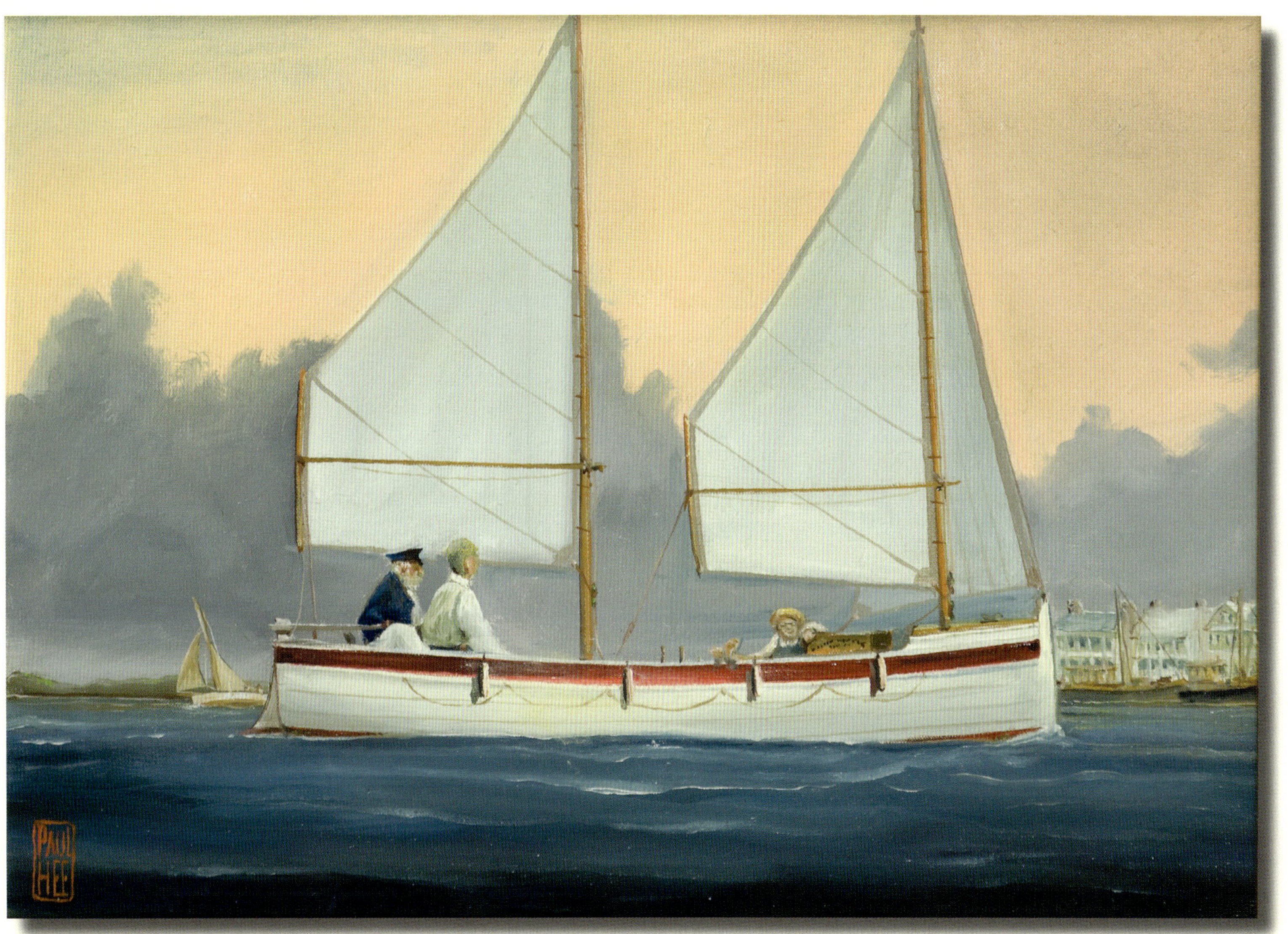

Queen Anne's Revenge Sinks 1718

18" x 28"

In 1709, the infamous Blackbeard seized the French slaver *La Concorde* as his flagship, renamed her *Queen Anne's Revenge* and set off marauding in the Caribbean Sea with 300 pirates. After a year of plundering, Blackbeard sailed into Topsail Inlet (the early name for Beaufort, North Carolina) and, either accidentally or on purpose, ran aground. In 1996, divers salvaged anchors, ballast, cannons, gold dust and remains of a ship of that era; they also raised a bronze bell dated 1709. All evidence now surfacing leads archaeologists to believe the wreckage is that of *Queen Anne's Revenge.* This fanciful image recalls the moment the ship went down. Many relics on exhibit at North Carolina Maritime Museum.

1709 Cast Bronze Ship's Bell Found at Beaufort Shipwreck Site

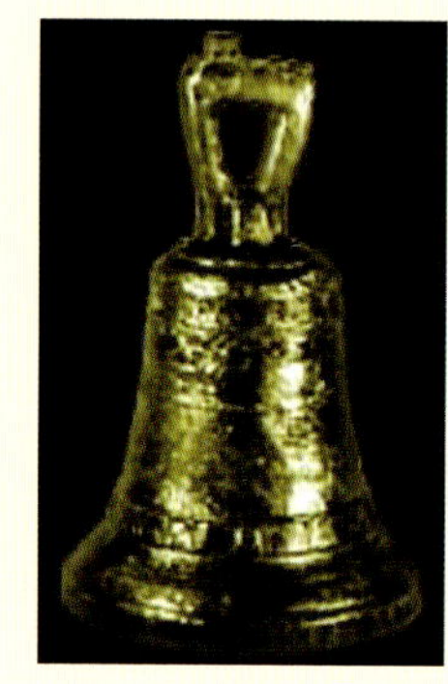

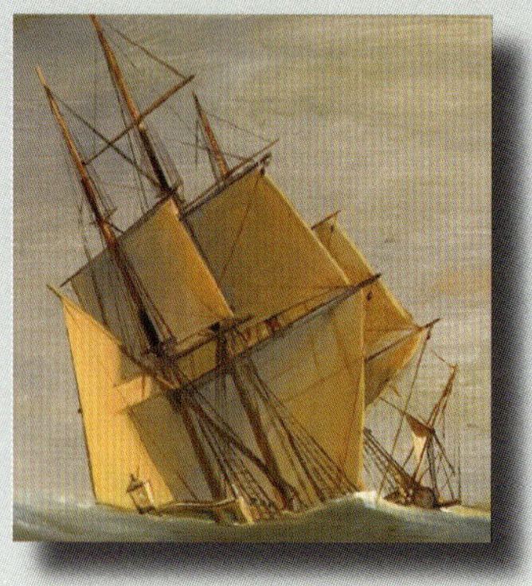

"On the 10th of June or thereabouts a large pyrate Ship of forty Guns with three Sloops in her company came upon the coast of North carolina ware they endeavour'd To goe in to a harbour, call'd Topsail Inlett, the Ship Stuck upon the barr att the entrance of the harbour and is lost; as is one of the sloops".

—July 12 1718 letter to the Lords of Admiralty written by Capt Ellis Brand of *HMS Lyme.*

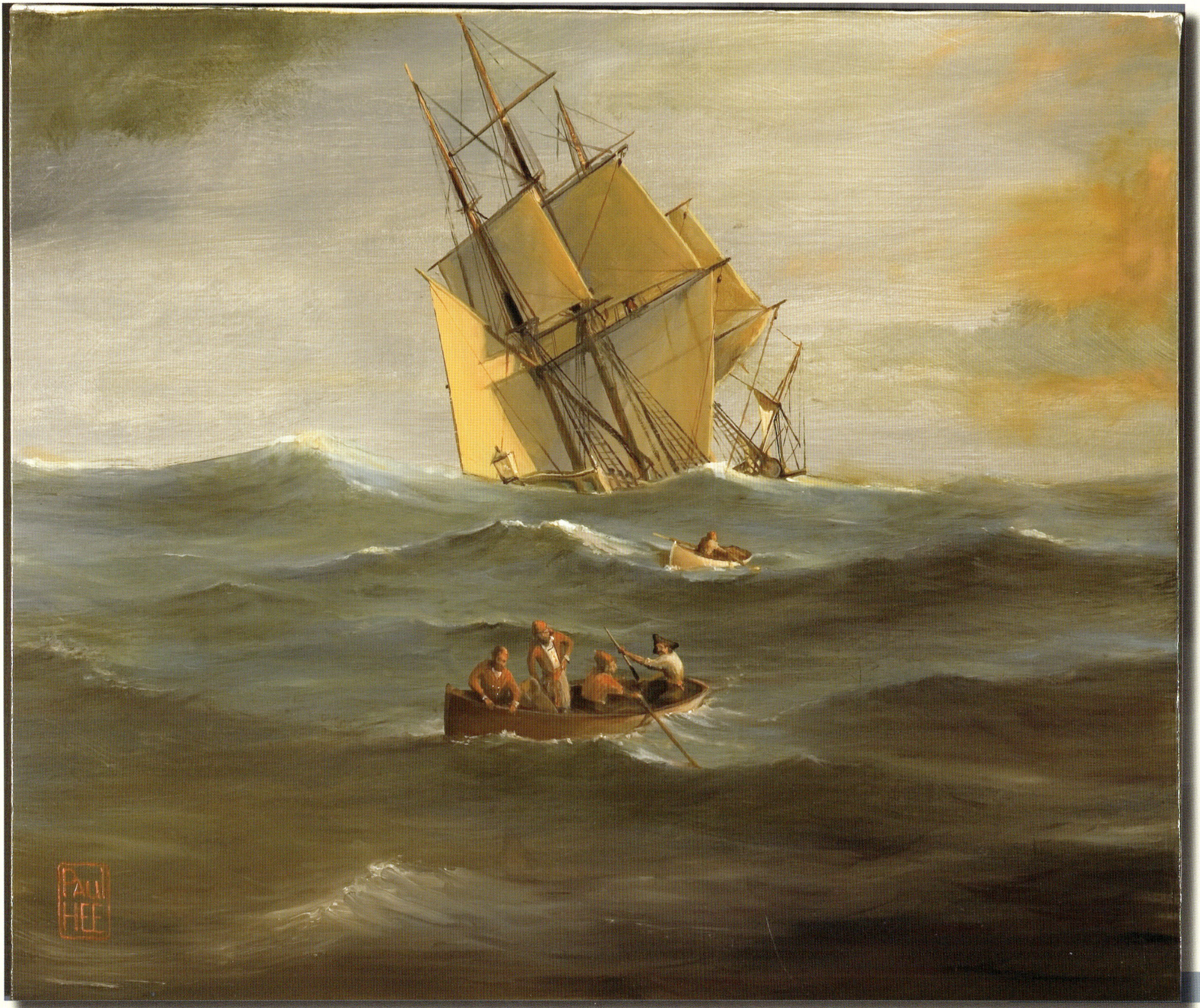
PAUL
HEE

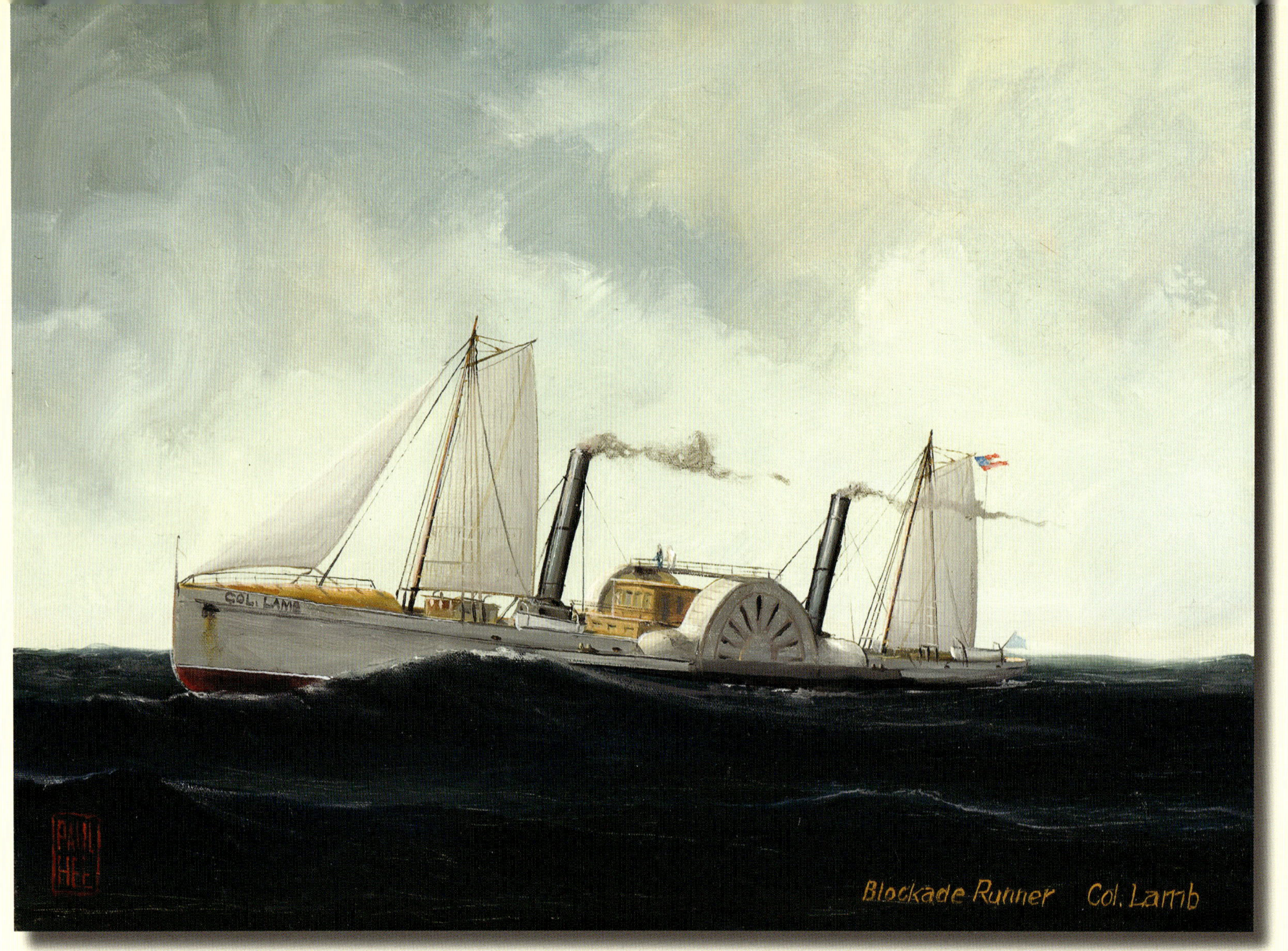

Colonel Lamb
18" x 28"

One of the fastest Confederate blockade runners, *Colonel Lamb*, (named for William Lamb, commander of Fort Fisher, North Carolina) this 281-foot steel hull side-wheel steamer was built in Liverpool by William Quiggin and transferred to the Confederate Navy. She survived the war but blew up at anchor in Mersey, Liverpool, in 1867 with explosives bound for Brazil.

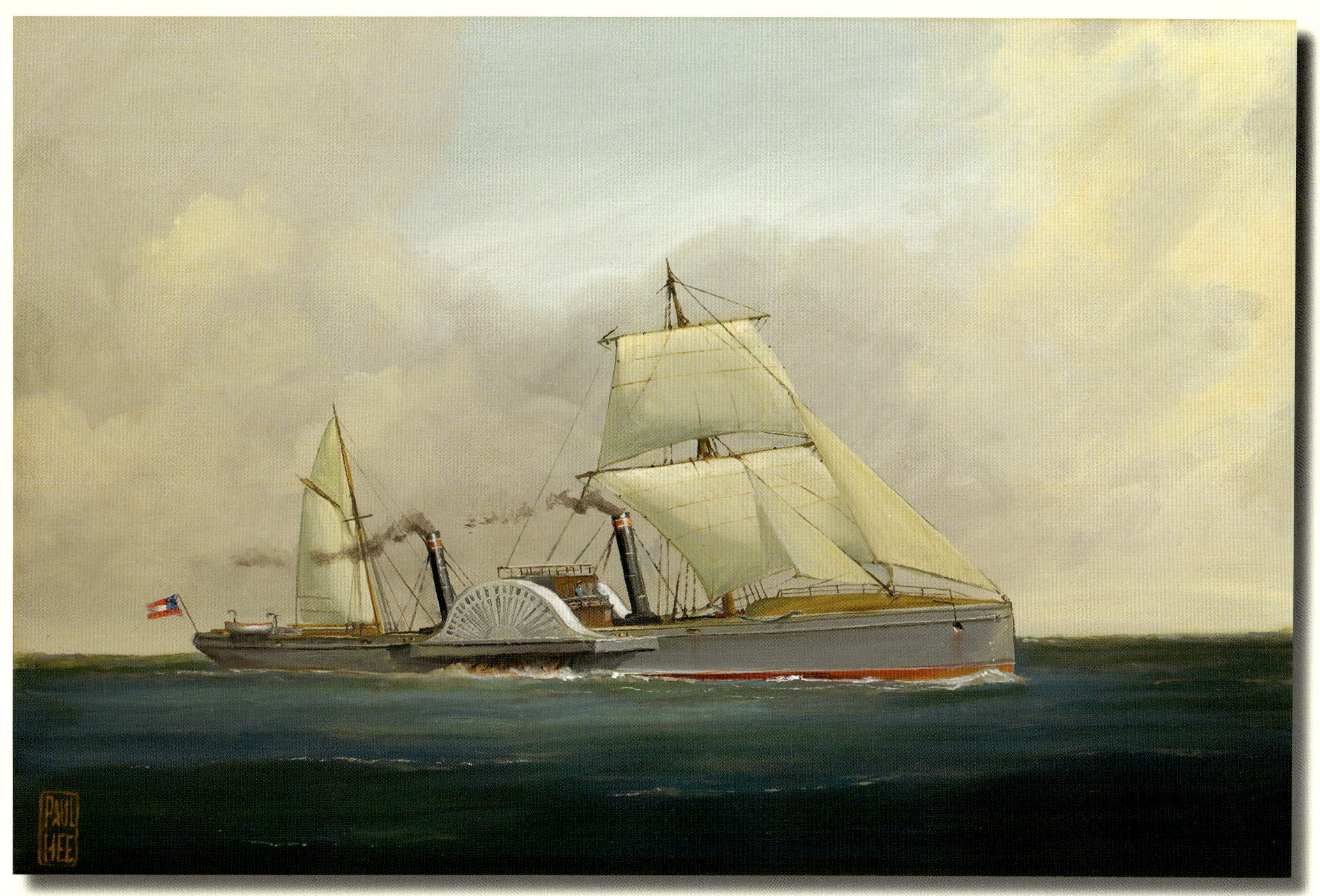

CSS Hope 1864

18" x 28"

Once the "finest and fastest steamer in the trade" the iron and steel paddle-wheeler *CSS Hope* was built in the Liverpool yard of Jones & Quiggin & Co., and procured there by the Confederate Navy. With two fore and aft engines and a top speed of 16 knots, the 281-foot steamer could outrun most vessels. Yet, on October 22, 1864, the US steamer *Æolus* captured the blockade-runner at the mouth of the Cape Fear River, after a 65-mile chase.

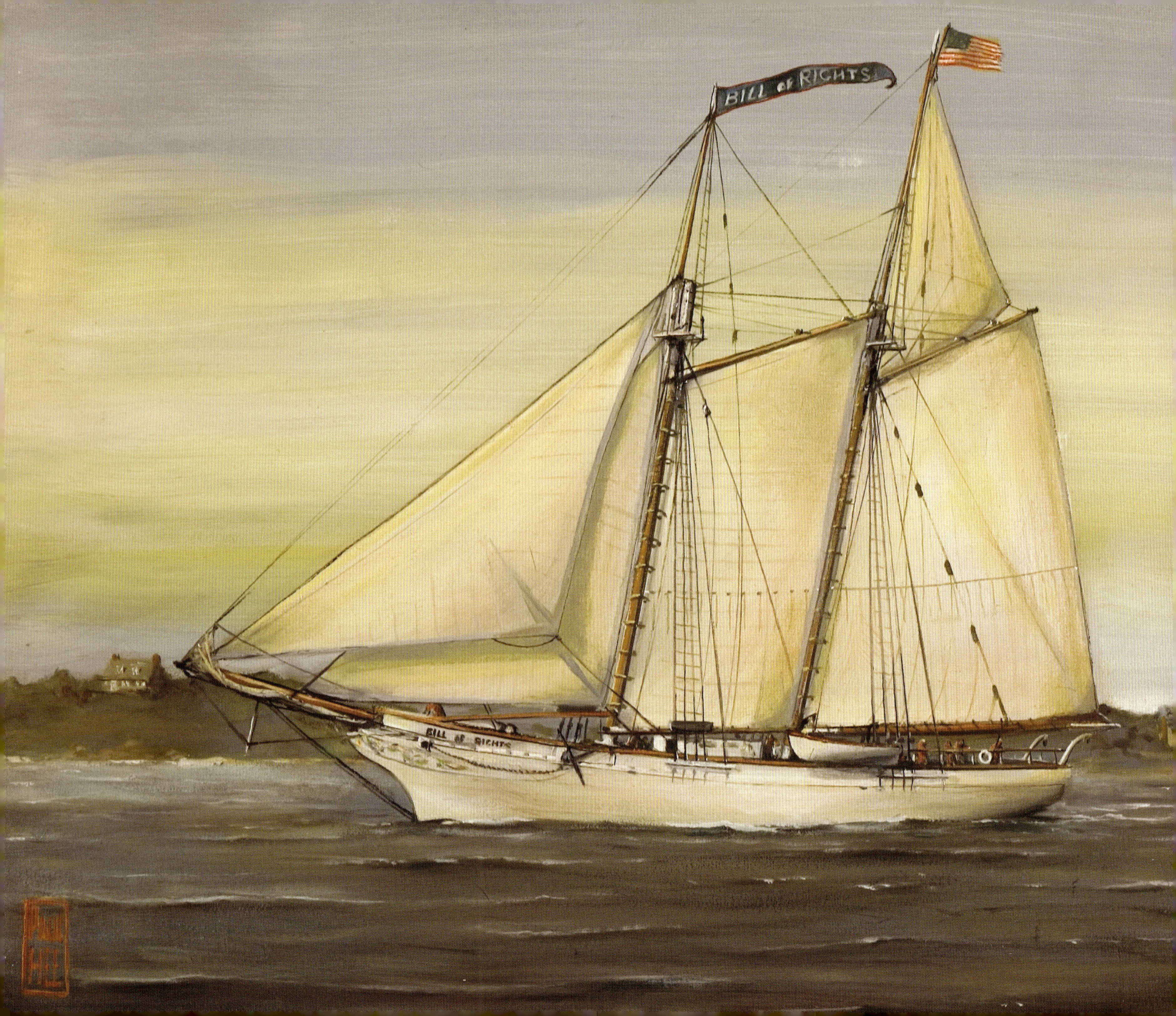
BILL of RIGHTS
BILL of RIGHTS

Bill of Rights

18" x 28"

Built in 1971 by Harvey Gamage of South Bristol, Maine, this 129-foot, two-masted, gaff-topsail schooner carried 6,300 feet of sail. The schooner operated as an Atlantic Ocean sail-training vessel out of Norfolk, Virginia for almost three decades. On March 7, 1998, Captain Chris Welton and *Bill of Rights* departed Norfolk for the Pacific, stopping at Beaufort, North Carolina, en route to Los Angeles. She joined *Swift of Ipswich* as a Topsail Youth Program training vessel for the Los Angeles Maritime Institute in San Pedro, California.

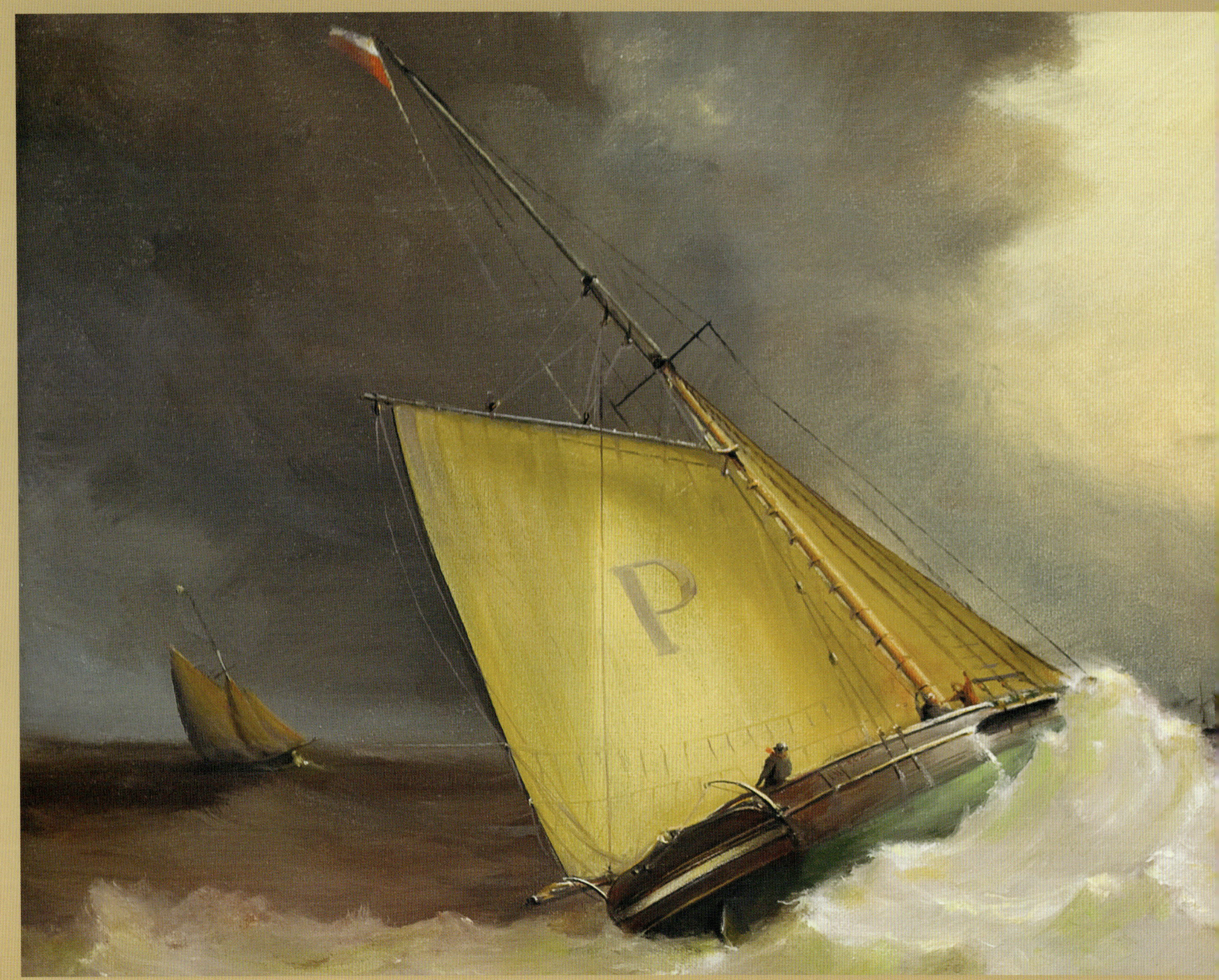

P

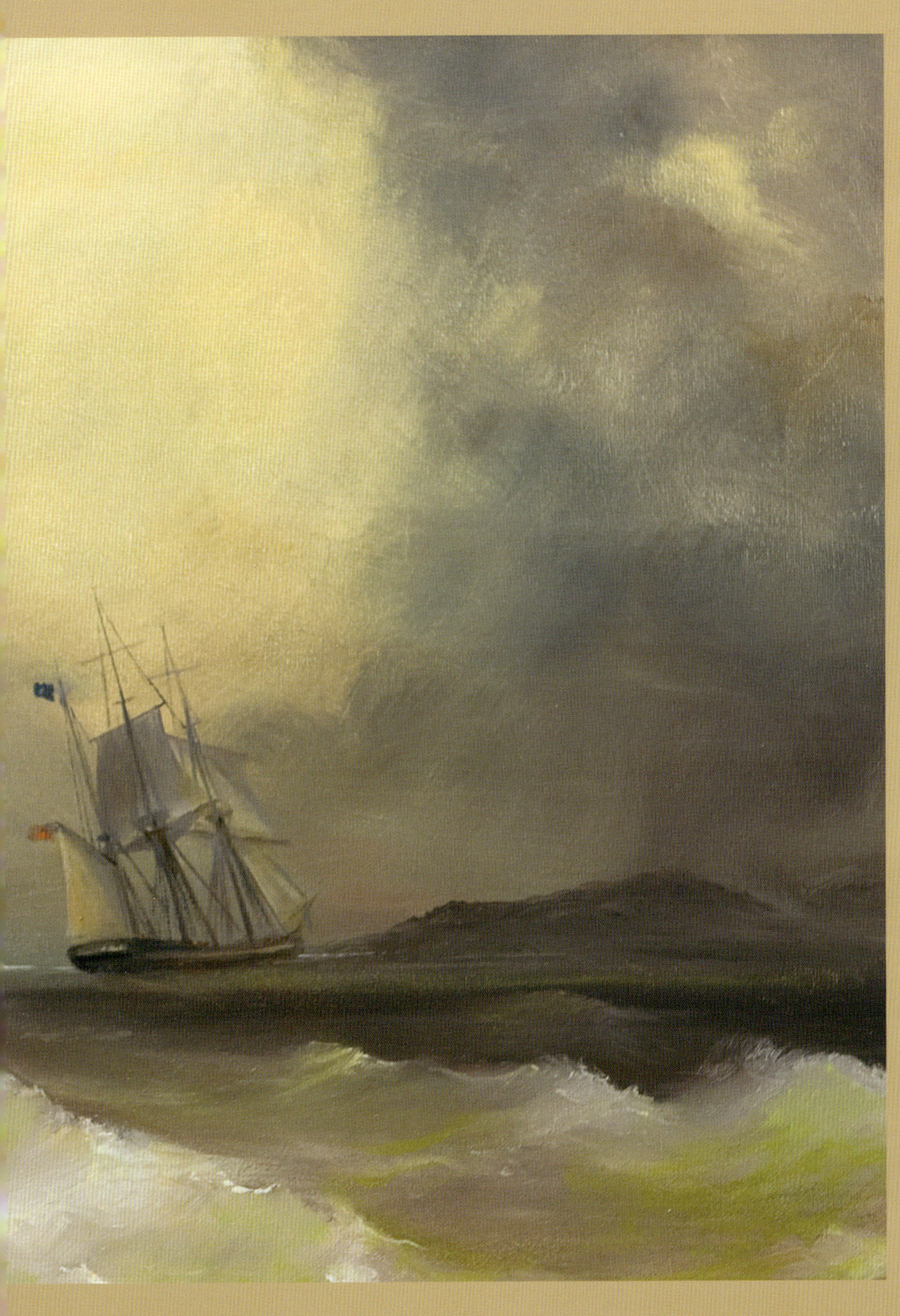

CHAPTER IV

GOLDEN AGE OF SAIL & STEAM

Pilot Cutter 1872

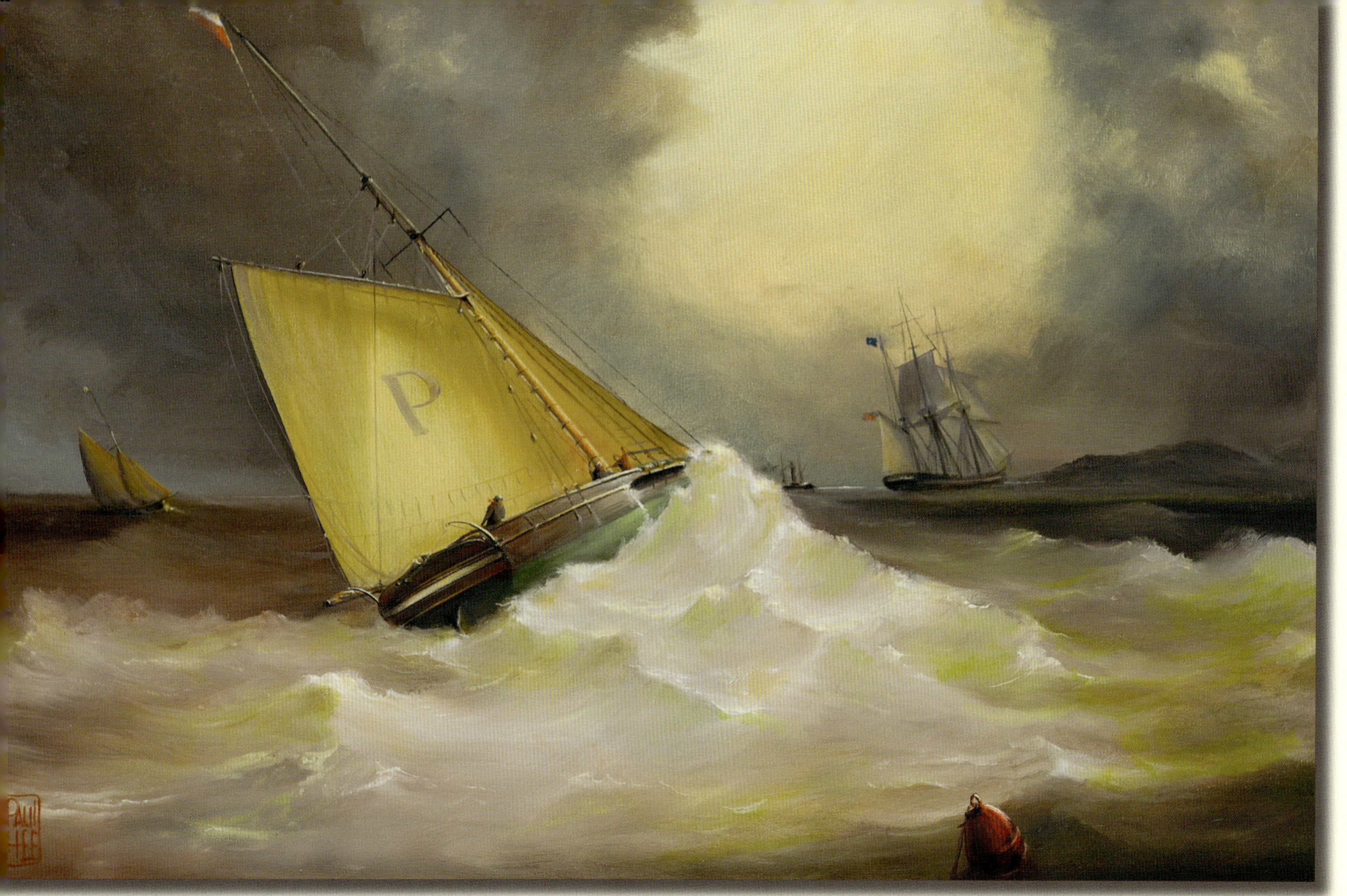

Pilot Cutter 1872
20" x 30"

Pilot Cutter was inspired by Admiral Richard Brydges Beechey's work of 1872. Pilot cutters were designed both for speed and seaworthiness. The ship at right is waiting for the pilot to arrive and board to guide it safely into port. The "P" on the mainsail identifies the Pilot Cutter.

Ontario

18" x 28"

Built in Newcastle, Maine, in 1854, the packet ship *Ontario* served the Swallow Tail Line between New York and Liverpool until 1863. It is shown off Point Lynas, Wales, after dropping its pilot who is transferring to the pilot schooner in the distance.

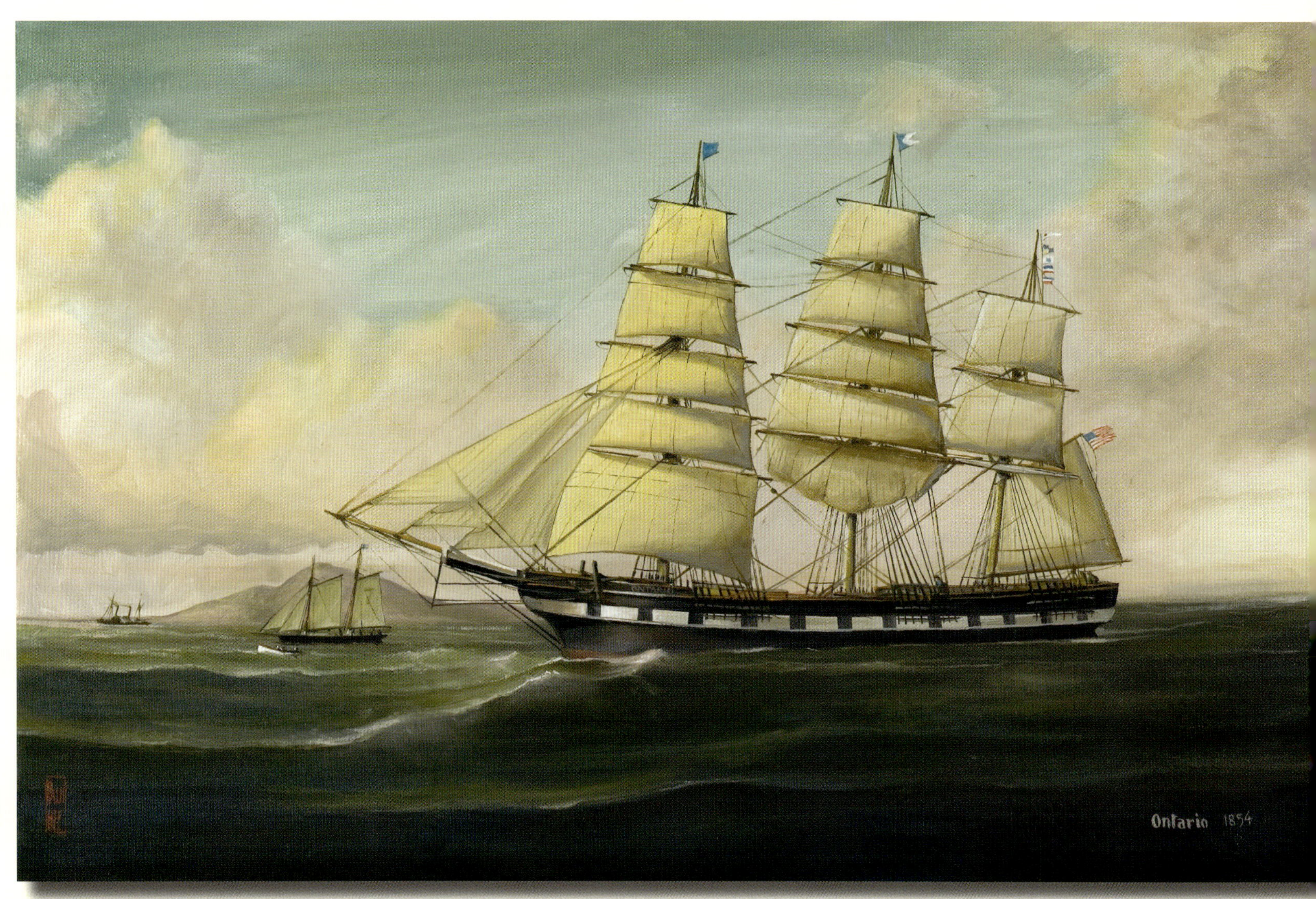

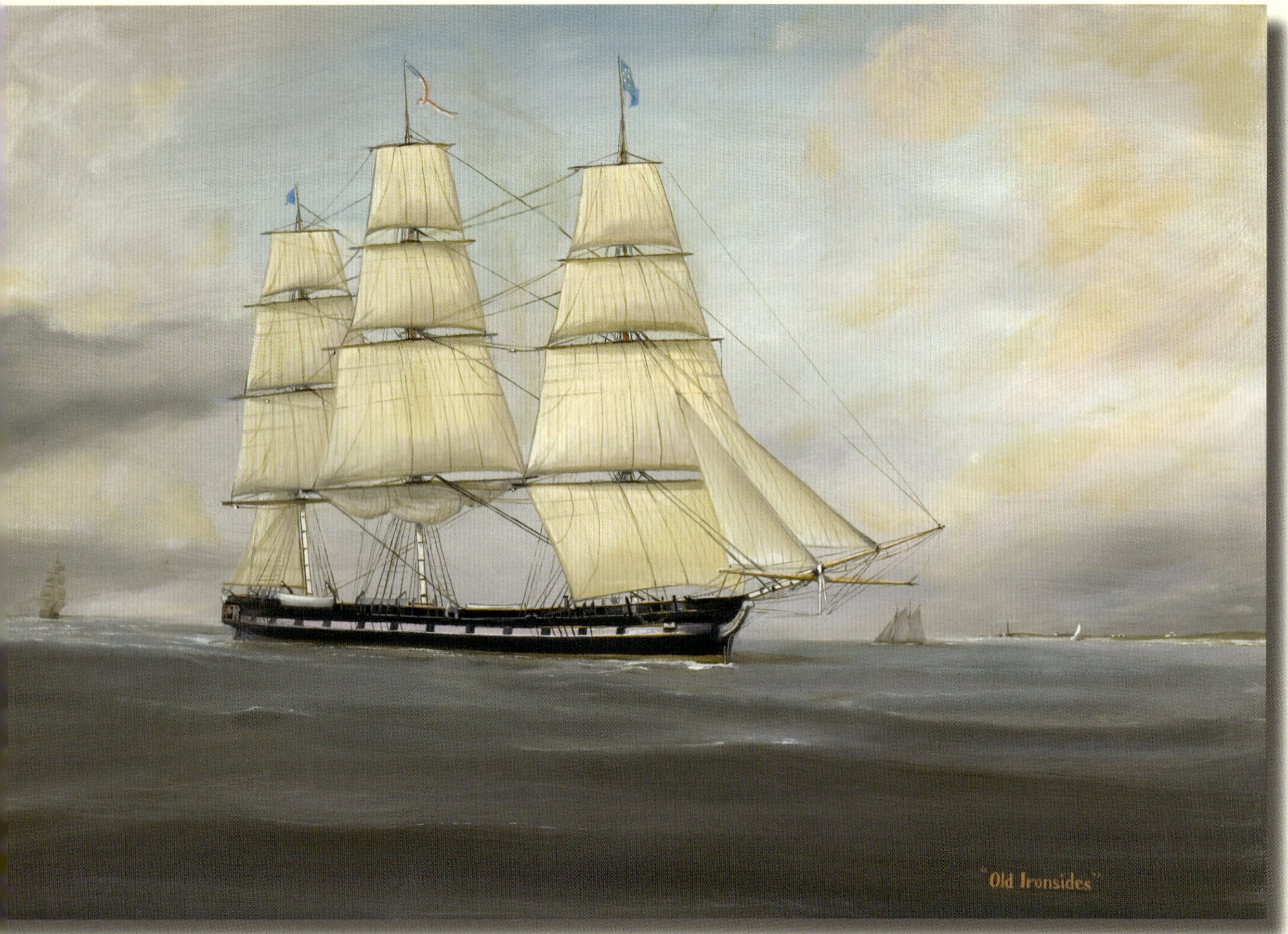

Old Ironsides

Ay, tear her tattered ensign down!
Long has it waved on high,
And many an eye has danced to see
That banner in the sky;
Beneath it rung the battle shout,
And burst the cannon's roar;
The meteor of the ocean air
Shall sweep the clouds no more!

Her deck, once red with heroes' blood,
Where knelt the vanquished foe,
When winds were hurrying o'er the flood
And waves were white below,
No more shall feel the victor's tread,
Or know the conquered knee;
The harpies of the shore shall pluck
The eagle of the sea!

Oh, better that her shattered hulk
Should sink beneath the wave;
Her thunders shook the mighty deep,
And there should be her grave;
Nail to the mast her holy flag,
Set every threadbare sail,
And give her to the God of storms,
The lightning and the gale!

—Oliver Wendell Holmes

USS CONSTITUTION

18" x 20"

The oldest warship afloat, *USS Constitution* was one of six frigates ordered and named by President George Washington in 1794 to defend America against the Barbary pirates. Built in Edmond Hartt's Boston shipyard, and launched October 21, 1797, she put to sea in 1798. Made of 2,000 trees from Maine to Georgia, armed with cannons cast in Rhode Island, fastened with copper spikes forged by Paul Revere, the 54-gun, 204-foot ship is a true national landmark. She became known as "Old Ironsides" in the War of 1812, when cannonballs from the British frigate *Guierriere* bounced off her hull. "Huzzah! Her sides are made of iron!" a sailor exclaimed, according to legend. The sturdy ship, with its two-foot-thick planks, survived 42 battles in three major wars. "Old Ironsides" is docked at Charlestown Navy Yard, off Chelsea Street in Boston.

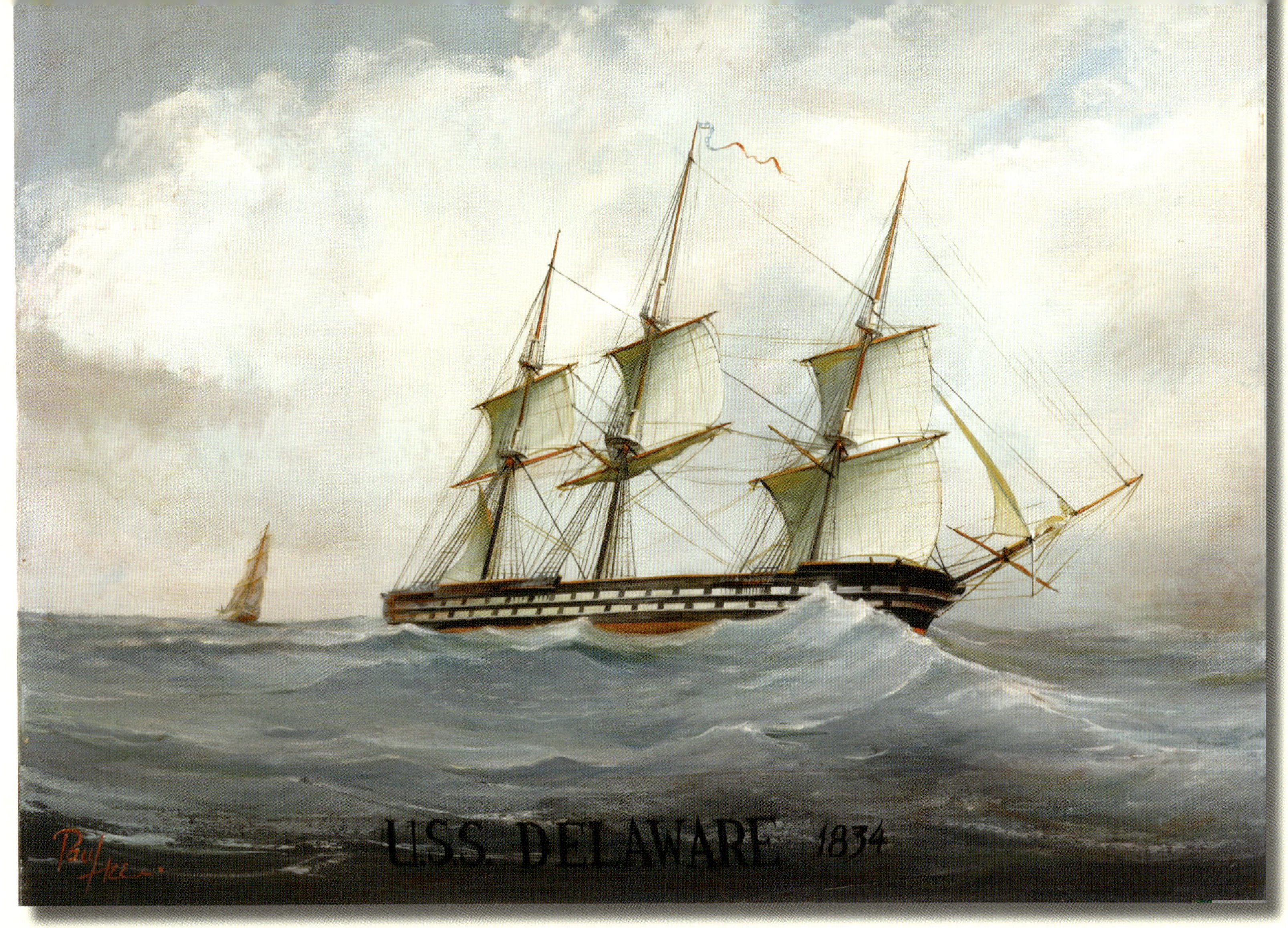

USS Delaware 1834

18" x 22"

Delaware and her sister ship *North Carolina* were designed by William Doughty as the definitive model for the United States Navy's 74-gun ships. Built in Norfolk Navy Yard, she was launched October 21, 1820. *Delaware* served in the Mediterranean and in Brazilian waters. The ship-of-the-line is shown here en route to France in 1834. She was burned to the waterline in Norfolk in 1861 to prevent capture by the Confederates.

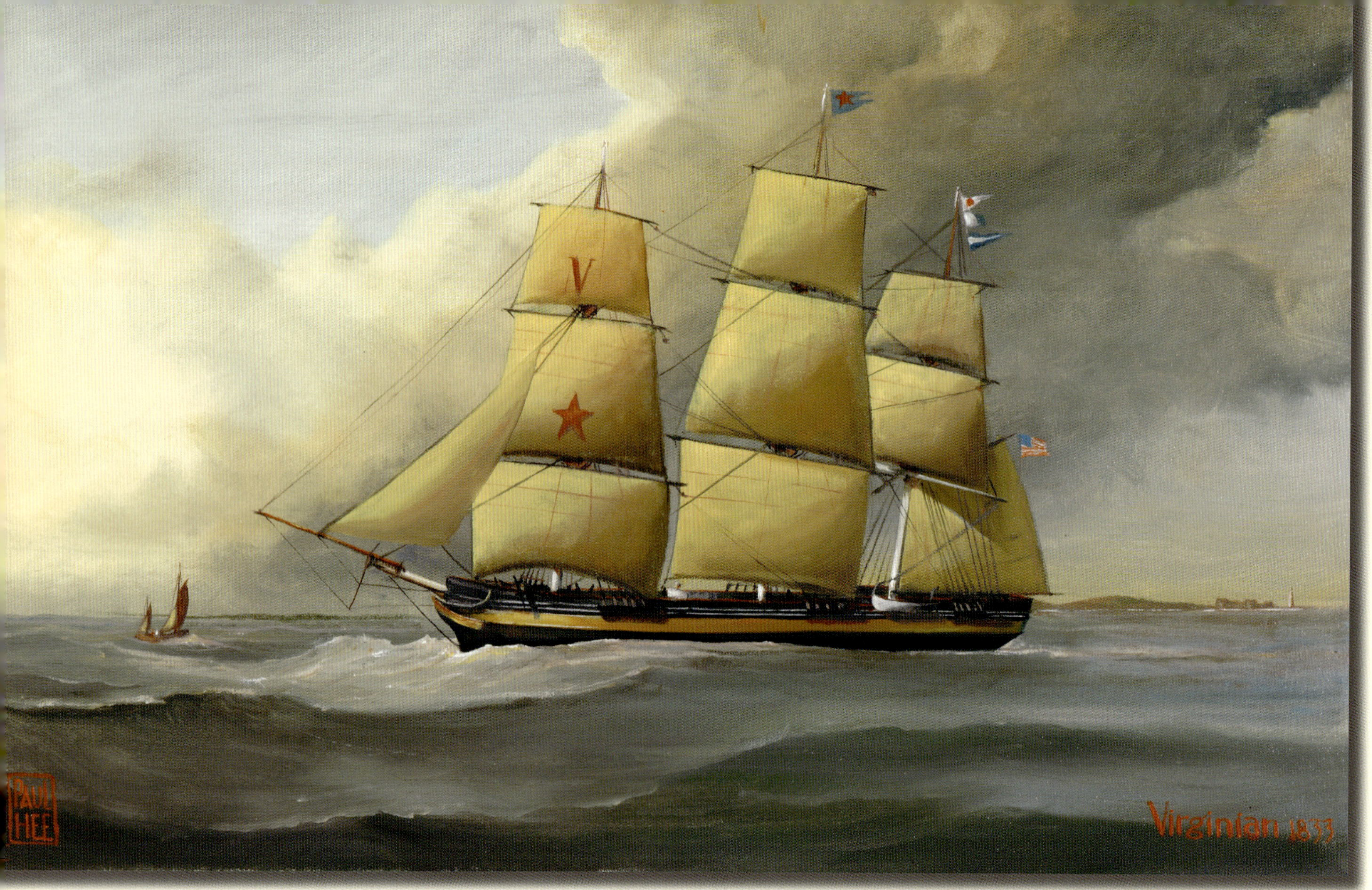

Virginian
18" x 28"

In 1842, *Virginian* sailed from New York to Liverpool in 15 days, a record crossing. Her speed made *Virginian* ideal for the New York-San Francisco route, carrying fortune seekers to the California Gold Rush. The *Virginian* operated on Robert Kermit's Liverpool line from 1832 to 1847, one of the longest sea services of any trans-Atlantic sailing packet.

Cimbria 1867

19" x 28"

In the spring of 1878, the steamship *Cimbria* anchored for six months in Southwest Harbor, Maine, with 700 officers and men of the Russian Imperial Navy. The ship, under charter to the Emperor of Russia, stood armed and ready to prey upon British commerce on America's shore. When the threat of war between England and Russia eased, the man-of-war sailed on. Built for the Hamburg American Line, the brig-rigged 330-foot steamship made her maiden voyage to New York on April 13, 1867. She served this route more than a decade. On January 19, 1883 in dense fog near Borkum Island Germany, *Cimbria* collided with the British vessel *Sultan* and sank, carrying 402 passengers. Only 54 survived in seven lifeboats.

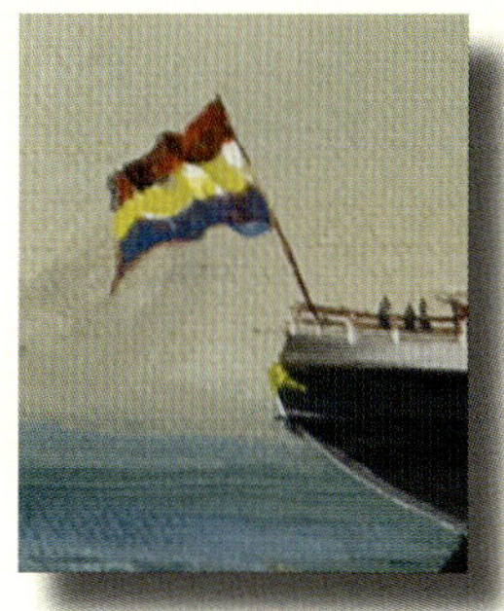

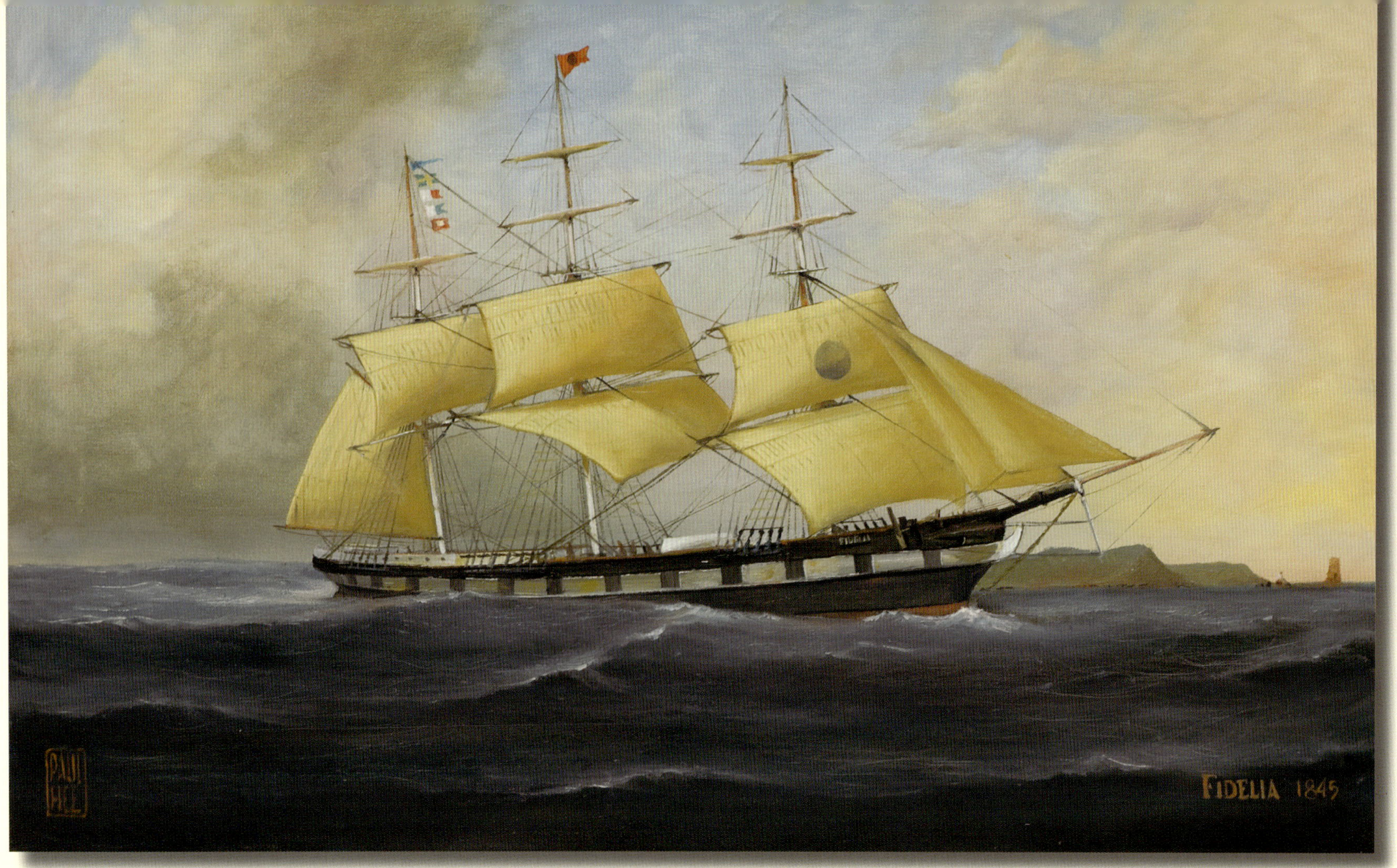

Fidelia

18" x 28"

Bound for New York from Liverpool, *Fidelia,* the clipper of the Black Ball fleet, leaves Mersey River on an easterly wind to pass South Stack Light en route to Scar Light and the open sea. On the return leg, *Fidelia* ran from Boston to North-West Light Ship at the mouth of the Mersey River in 13 days, 7 hours. A typical packet, she was built by William Henry Webb (1816-1869) of New York, considered America's first naval architect. Webb built many of America's finest and fastest clippers, like *Guy Mannering, Ocean Monarch* and *Young America*, popular on the California Gold Rush run.

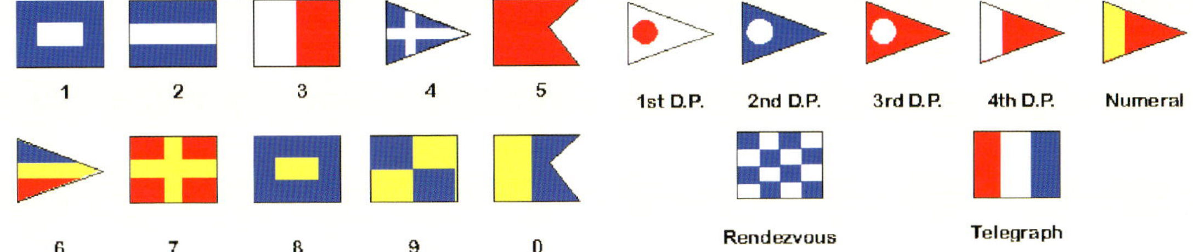

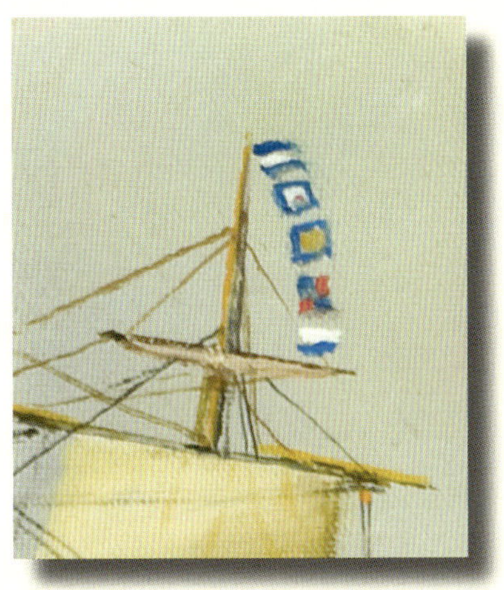

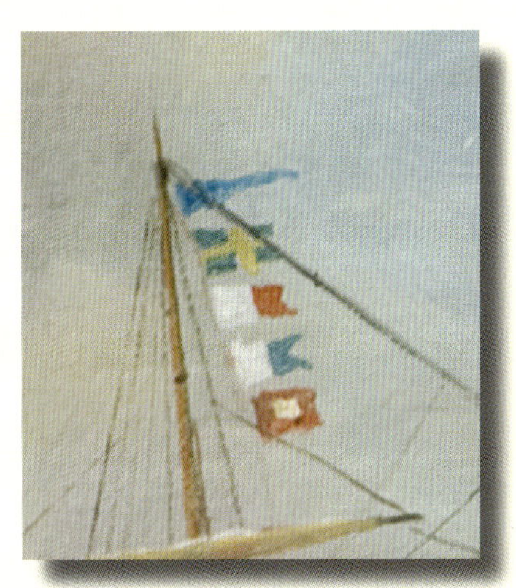

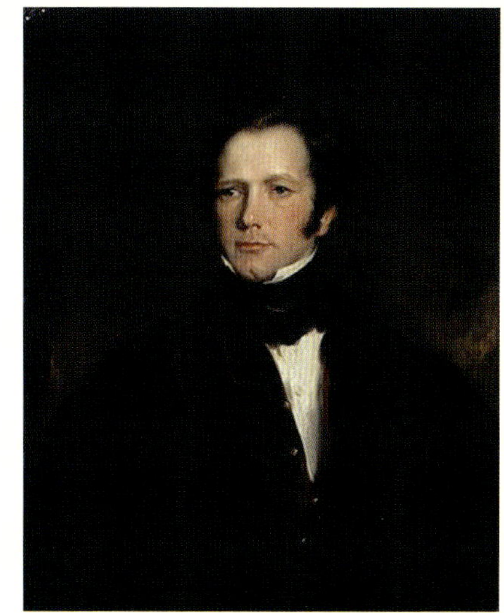

Captain Frederick Marryat

Captain Frederick Marryat of Westminster, London, impressed by Lord Nelson's state funeral in 1806, went to sea as a midshipman in the Royal Navy. He served in the War of 1812, and distinguished himself by capturing nine enemy ships and saving the lives of five seamen. In 1817, he created a system of flags to identify ships that became today's International Code of Signals. The following year he invented a lifeboat, and won the Gold Medal of the Royal Humane Society. After a ridiculous search for a "non-existent, but reported island in the mid-Atlantic" which he never found, Marryat retired from the Navy in 1828 to write the first of 26 well-received books, *The Naval Officer Scenes & Adventures in The Life of Frank Mildmay.*

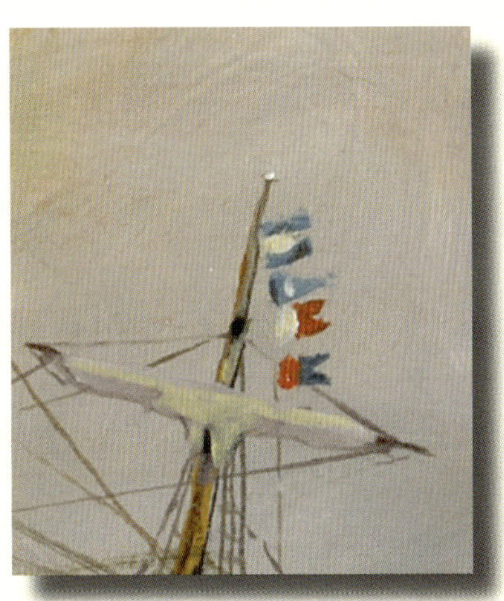

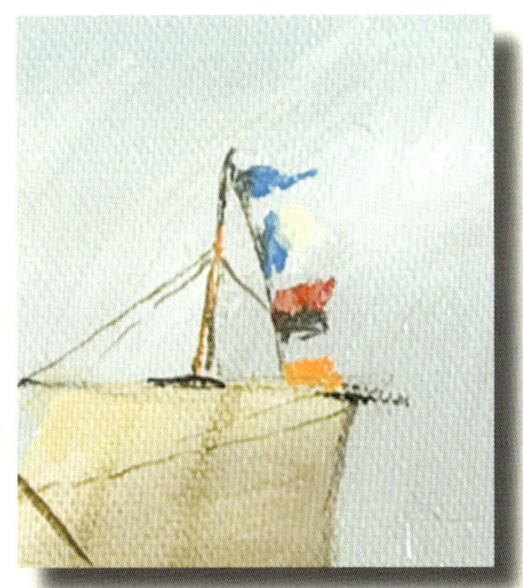

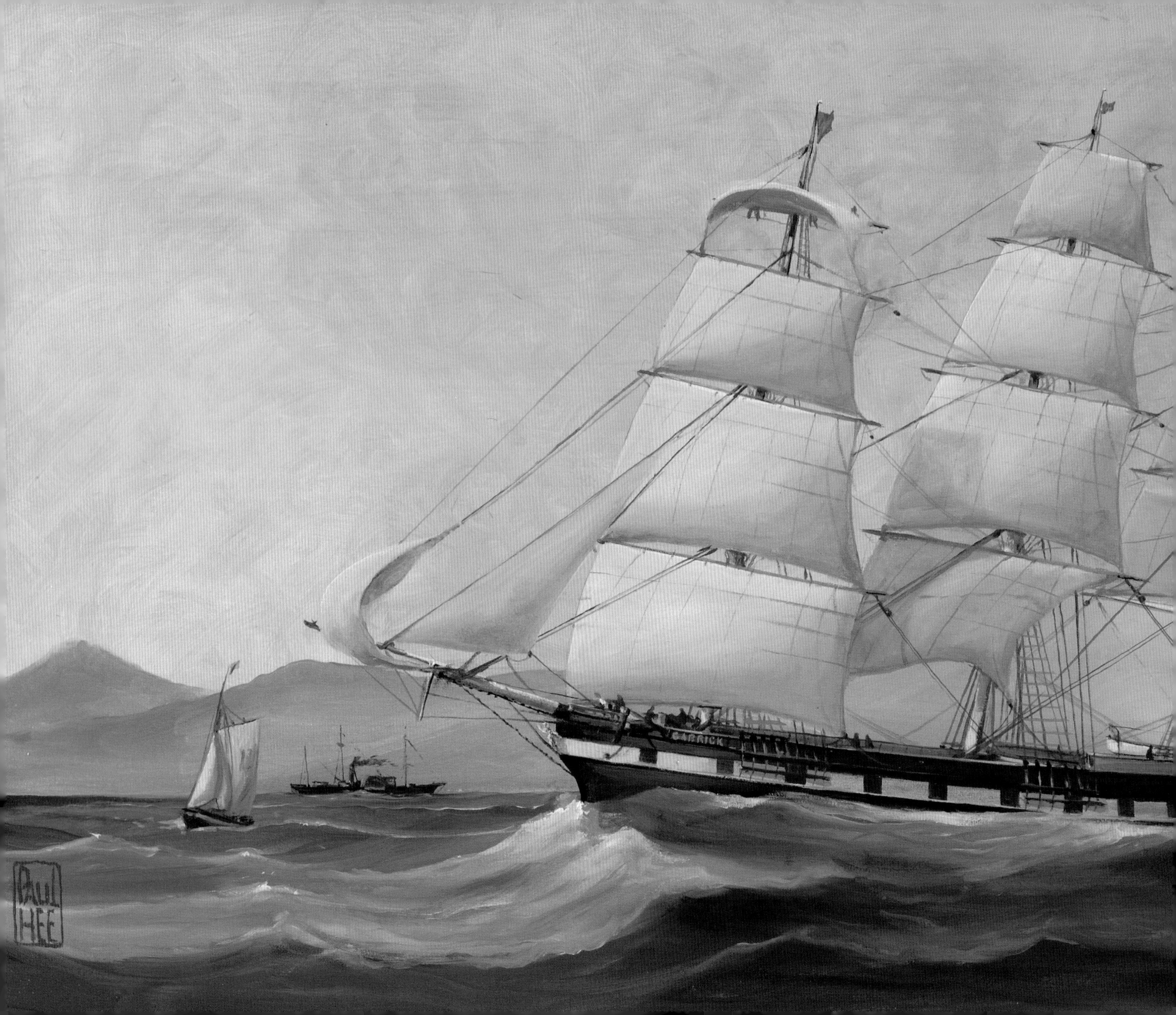
GARRICK
Paul
HEE

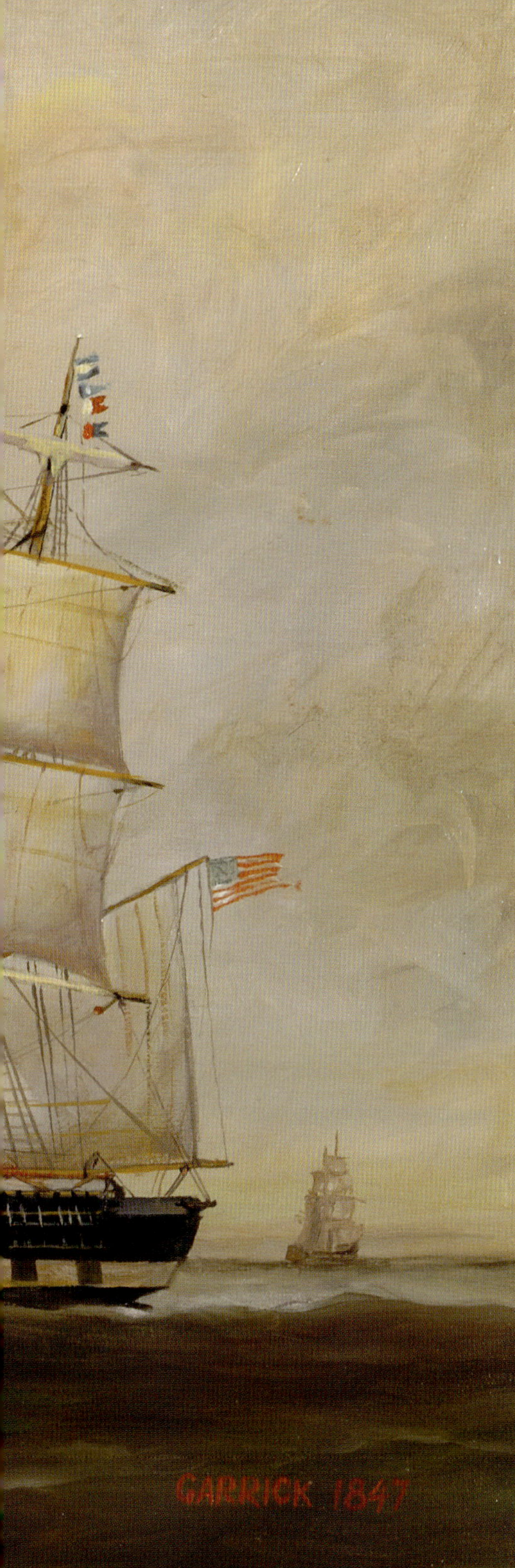

Garrick

18" x 28"

Garrick, one of several packet ships designed by Captain Nathaniel B. Palmer (1799-1877), was the fastest on the sea. The three-masted, square-rigged ship, built in New York in 1836, ferried many an immigrant fleeing the Irish potato famine to a new life in America. Lead designer of American clipper ships, Palmer was the first American to set foot on the Antarctic Continent in 1820 while on a sealing expedition.

TAPSCOTT'S

LINE OF AMERICAN PACKETS

FOR NEW YORK.

TO SAIL POSITIVELY ON THE 6th AUGUST,

THE MAGNIFICENT NEW AMERICAN LINE PACKET-SHIP

CONSTITUTION

CAPTAIN BRITTON, 2500 Tons Burthen.

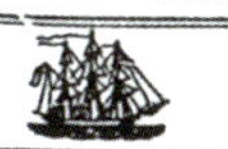 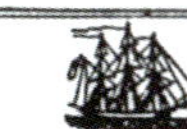  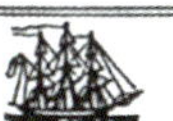

This splendid new Packet-ship is one of the largest and most magnificent ships afloat, has three decks, and fitted with every modern improvement for the comfort of Passengers, which with Captain Britton's uniform kindness and attention, should obtain for this noble ship a decided preference; and parties about to cross the Atlantic, should examine the accommodations of the CONSTITUTION, before making other engagements.

For terms of Passage, which will be moderate, early application should be made to

W. TAPSCOTT & CO.,

St. George's Buildings, Regent Road, Clarence Dock, Liverpool.

N.B.—The "Constitution" made her last Passage to New York in the short space of TWENTY Days, and returned here in NINETEEN Days!

Persons wishing to go by this fast-sailing favourite Ship, should send Deposits of £1 each, to secure good berths.

**** The splendid Packet-ship "GARRICK," so long and favourably-known, to the Emigrating public, is the succeeding Packet, and Sails on the 11th of August.*

ALSO, FOR NEW YORK.

SHIP.	CAPTAIN.	TONS.	TO SAIL.	Steerage. Adults. £	s.	Children £	s.
RICHARD COBDEN	Barrell,	1500	19th July				
J. Z.,	Zerega,	1500	23rd ,,				
A. Z.,	Chandler,	1500	8 Aug	3	5	2	5
CAMBRIDGE,	Peabody,	1800	1st Aug.	3	5	2	5
CONSTITUTION	Britton,	2500	6th ,,	3	"	2	10
GARRICK	Howe	2000	11th ,,	3	"	2	10
J. H. SHEPPARD	Ainsworth	1500					
FIDELIA,	Yeaton,	2000	16th ,,				
ARLINGTON,	Ryan,	1500					
WEST POINT	Allen,	2000	26th ,,				
E. Z.,	Hartshorne,	1500					
ISAAC WRIGHT	Marshall	2000	1st Sept.				
HOTTINGUER,	Bursley,	2000	6th ,,				
ROSCIUS,	Eldridge,	2000	11th ,,				
YORKSHIRE,	Hackstaff,	2000	16th ,,				
FOR NEW ORLEANS.							
ELIZABETH,	Hasty,	1800	1st Aug.				
And to be succeeded every Ten Days after.							
FOR PHILADELPHIA.							
WILLIAM PATTEN,	Decker,	1500	25th July.				
FOR BOSTON.							
HENRY WEAR,	——	1000	27th July.				
NEW SHIP	——	1000	10th Aug.				

☞ For the information of those whose friends sailed per **Constellation**, we are pleased to inform them that the Ship arrived safe at New York, after **Twenty-six Days** passage.

Second Cabin, 10s., and Rooms, £1 a-head extra.

PASSENGERS' CHECK TICKET.

Ship *Garrick* for *New York*

Ticket, No. *252* Berth

Souls. *5*

Adults. *3*

To receive from the Ship daily during the Voyage,

3 lbs. Bread. *or*

3 lbs. Meal, or Flour.

9 quarts Fresh Water.

Passage paid at the Office of **W. TAPSCOTT & CO.**

LIVERPOOL, *6 Dec* 184*7*

Signed,

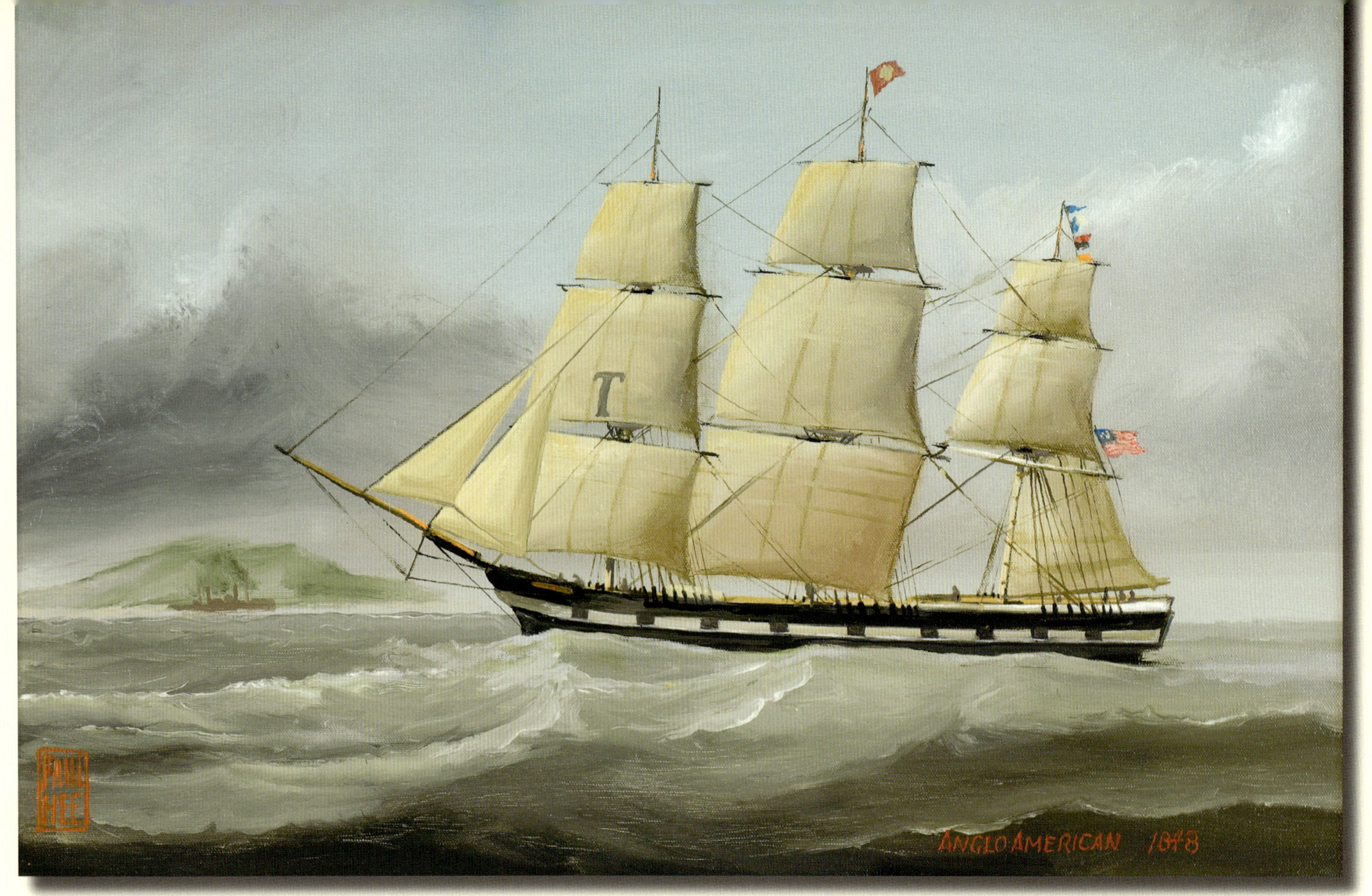

Anglo American 1848

18" x 28"

The 704-ton packet ship *Anglo American,* built by Donald McKay at East Boston in 1848, is shown arriving in Liverpool under the command of Captain A.H. Brown for her first voyage to carry Irish immigrants to Boston. The ship's passenger list includes Kellys, Campbells, Kilpatricks, Reillys and Ryans. Their various occupations included tailors, dressmakers, weavers, and one chocolate maker.

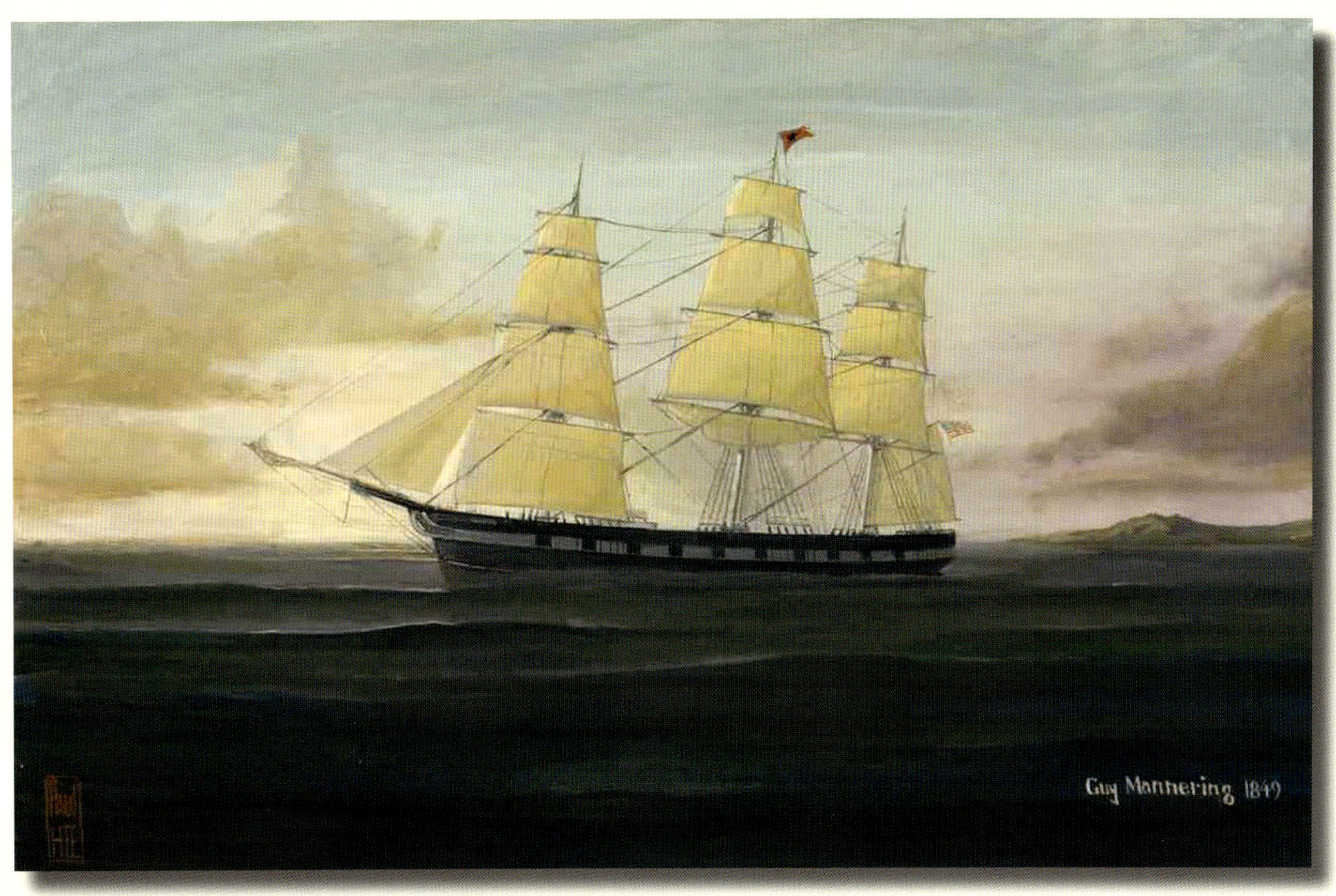

Guy Mannering 1849

18" x 24"

Named after the hero of Sir Walter Scott's 1815 popular novel, *Guy Mannering* was the first three-deck merchant ship built in the United States, launched in March 1849. *Guy Mannering* sailed with the Black Star line between New York and Liverpool until New Year's Eve 1866, when a hurricane shredded sails and masts, and the ship capsized. The 190-foot long, 1,419-ton ship was found wrecked on the west coast of the Island of Iona with loss of 17 souls.

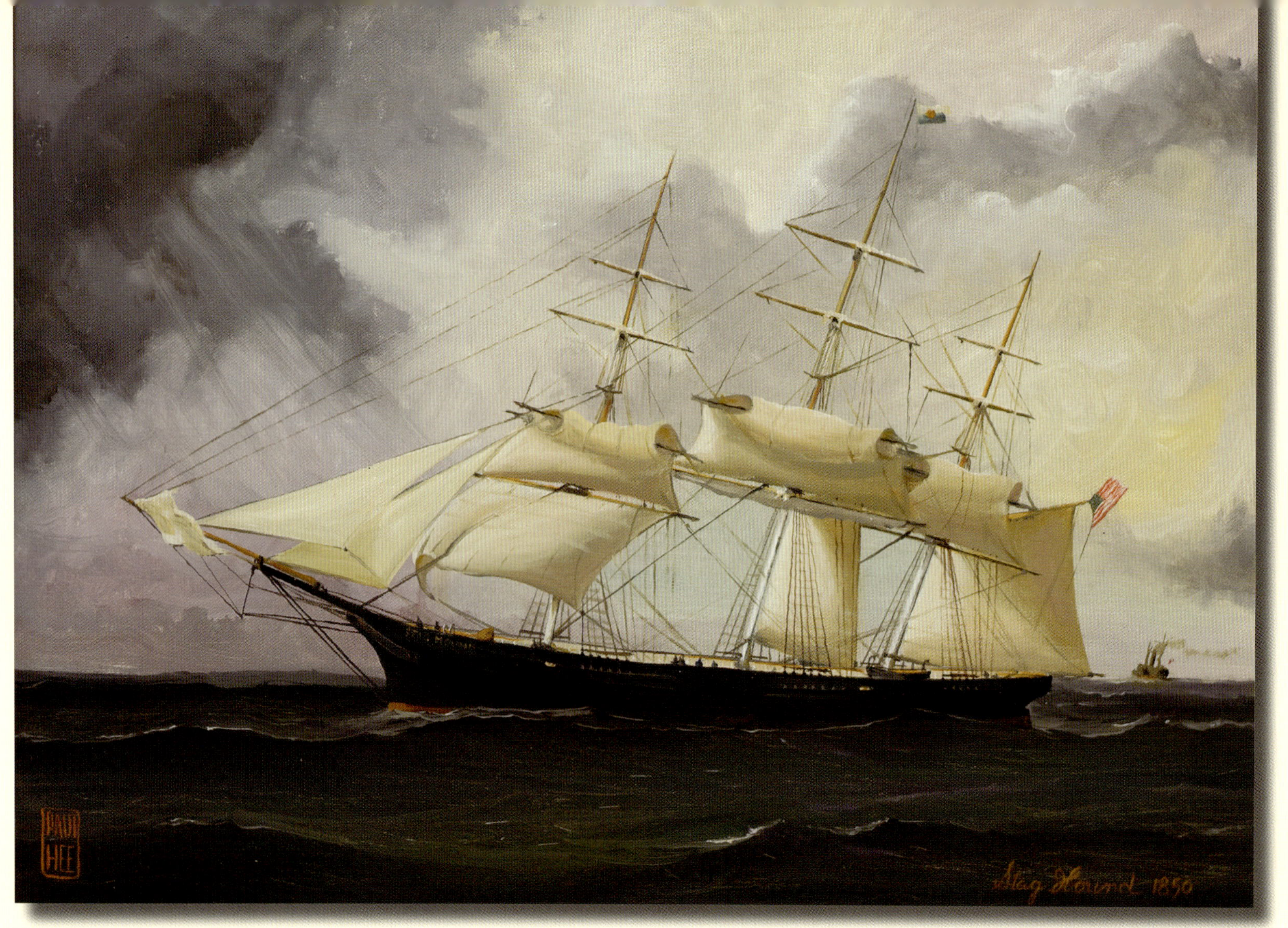

Staghound 1850

18" x 28"

Largest merchant ship built in 1850, the 215-foot extreme clipper ship *Staghound* unfurled 9,500 square yards of sail with an 88-foot main mast. A carved golden staghound was its figurehead. Built by Donald McKay for the California trade, the ship in 1851 reached San Francisco from New York, a voyage of 16,408 miles in 107 sailing days, a record it never equaled. A decade later, on October 12, 1861, laden with coal, the ship caught fire off Brazil's coast and was abandoned with all hands saved.

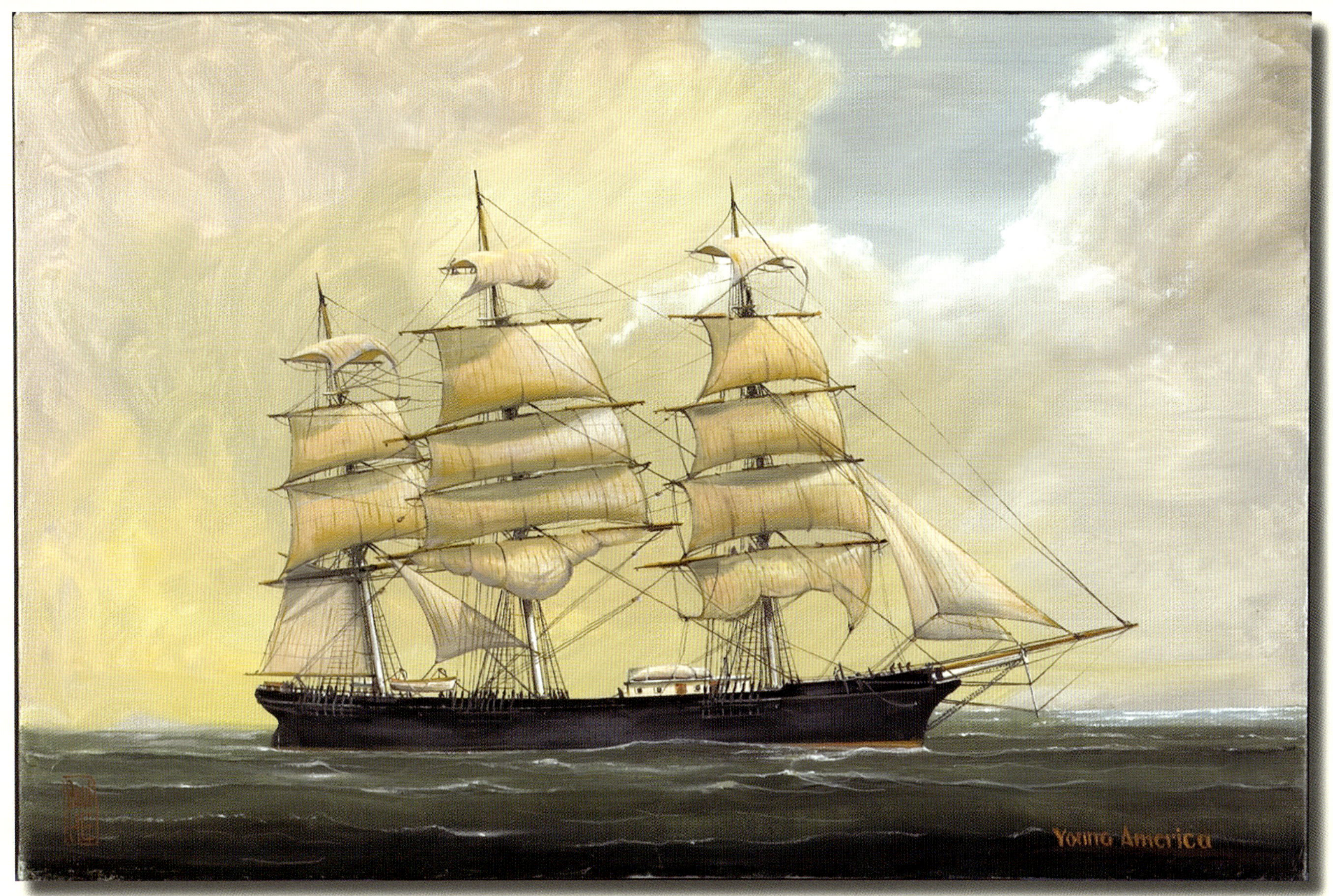

Young America

18" x 28"

The extreme clipper ship *Young America*, built by William Webb, launched in 1853 from his New York boatyard. Designed for speed the 243-foot, 1,961-ton clipper sailed with 100-man crew from New York to San Francisco 20 times, averaging 118 days a trip. *Young America* sailed to Hawaii, China, the Philippines, Australia, and New Zealand in a 30-year career. In 1886, she departed Delaware on a trading voyage and vanished, never to be seen again.

John Elliott Thayer 1857

20" x 30"

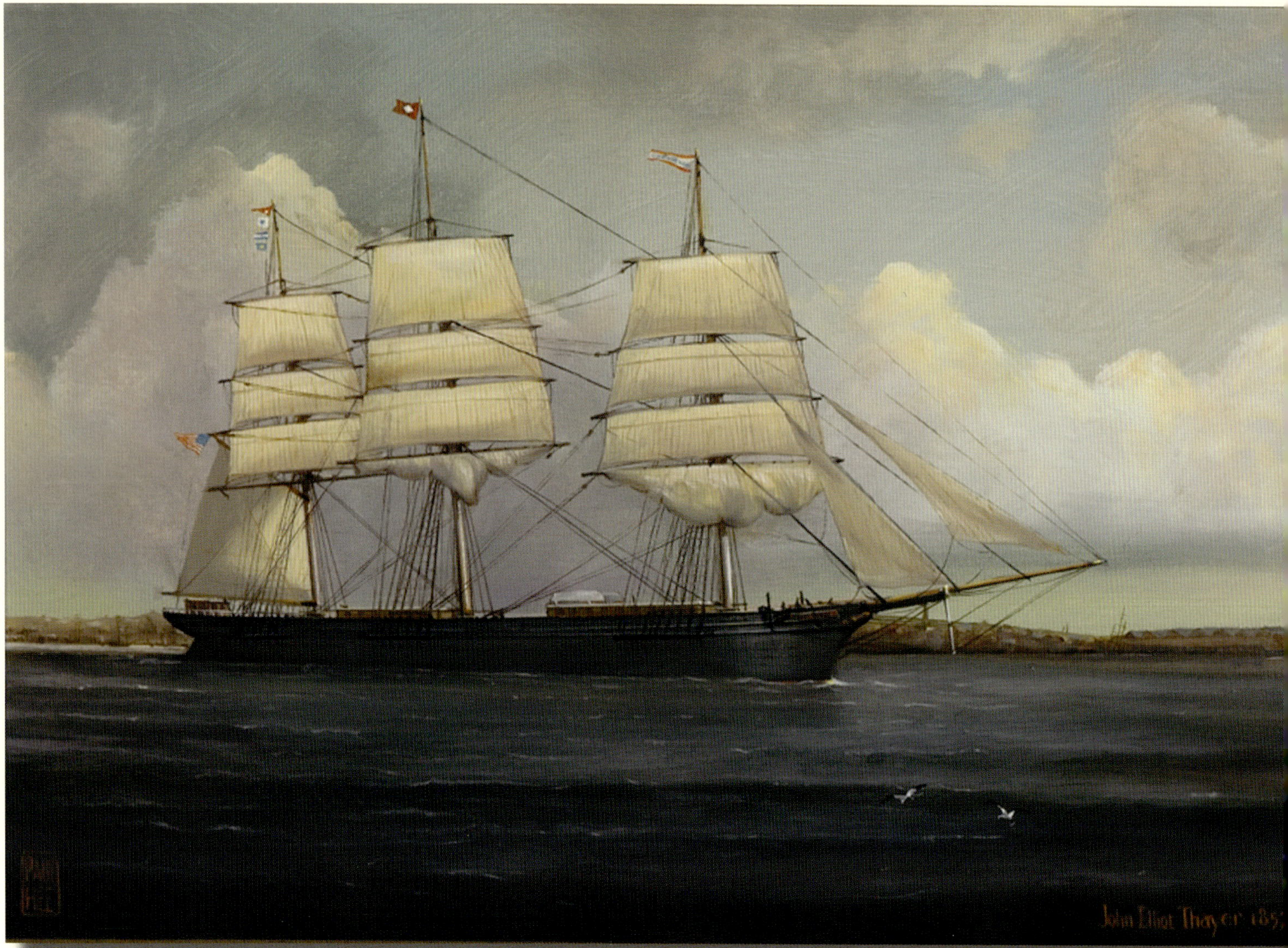

Built in the East Boston yard of Donald McKay, the clipper *John Elliot Thayer* was one of 12 superb vessels "all famous for beauty of design, attractiveness of equipment and, above all, speed." McKay gained fame as the builder of the fastest clippers of the day. His *Flying Cloud* ran from Boston to San Francisco in a record 92 days. His fame inspired Henry Wadsworth Longfellow's poem, "The Building of the Ship."

"Build me straight, O worthy Master!
Stanch and strong, a goodly vessel,
That shall laugh at all disaster,
And with wave and whirlwind wrestle!"

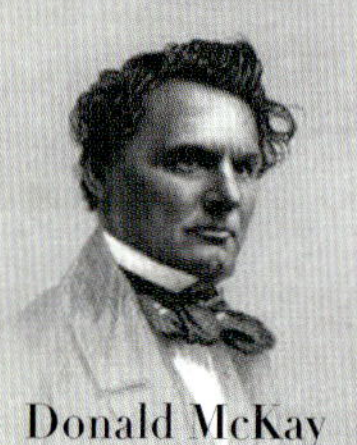
Donald McKay

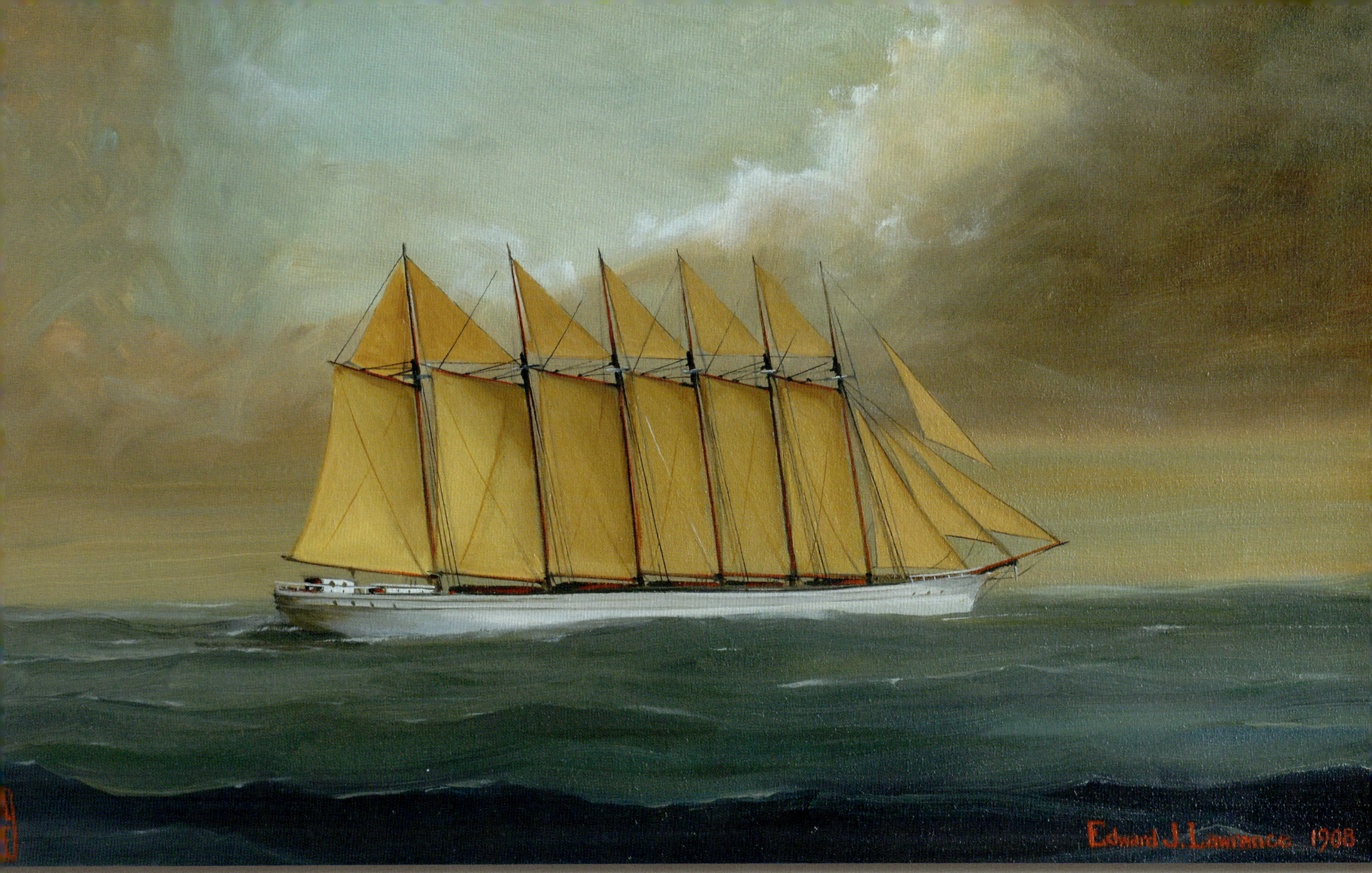

Edward J. Lawrence 1908

18" x 28"

The last big schooner afloat when it burned at Portland, Maine, on December 17, 1925, the *Edward J. Lawrence* was built in Bath, Maine, at Percy & Small shipyard in 1908. The 320-foot ship was one of five six-masted schooners J.S. Winslow & Co. used to haul coal from Southern fields to New England cotton mills.

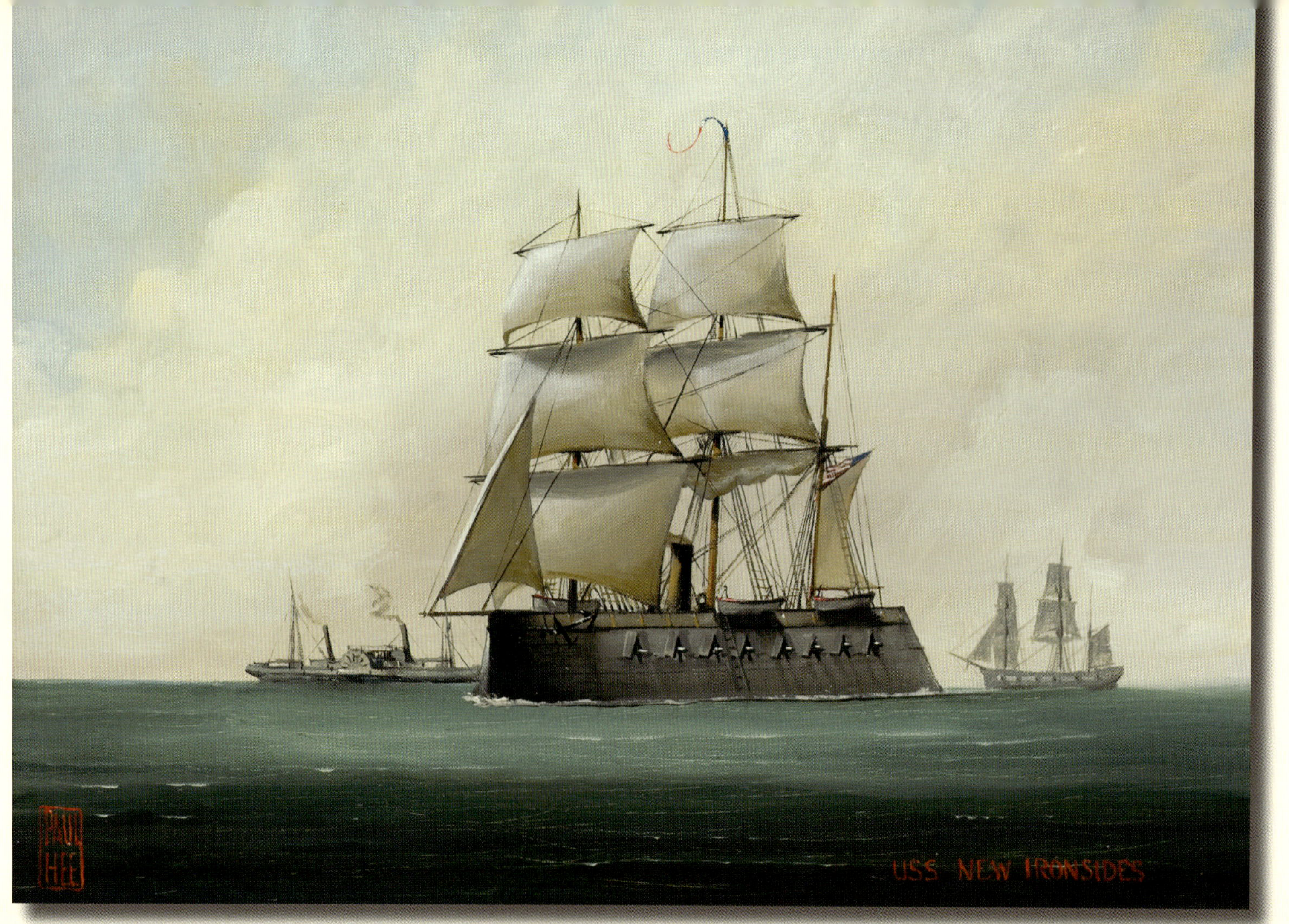

USS New Ironsides
18" x 28"

With eight heavy guns on each side, *USS New Ironsides*, a 230-foot armor-plated steamship, was America's first true battleship. Launched at Philadelphia in 1862, the Union's flagship deployed for the Siege of Charleston to blockade the harbor and bombard Fort Sumter. The 3,486-ton ironclad helped take Fort Wagner, bombarded Fort Sumter and Fort Fisher, North Carolina, to stop blockade running into Wilmington. A $100,000 ransom offered to anyone who could sink *New Ironsides* was never claimed. The Confederate submarine *H. L. Hunley*, secret hope of the South, was created in Mobile for that mission, but failed. After the war, at homeport in Philadelphia, an unattended stove fire took the ironclad down.

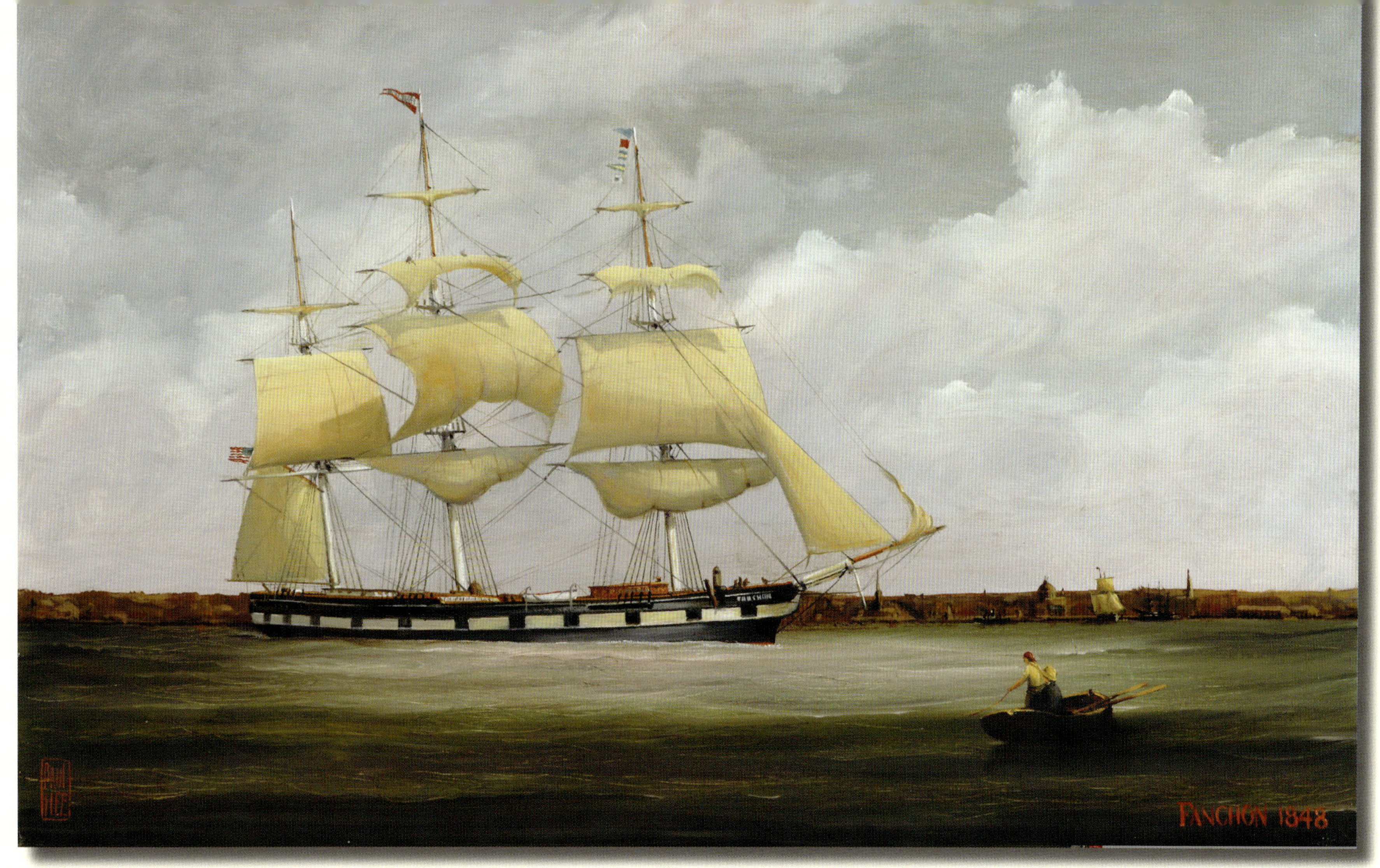

Fanchon 1848

18" x 28"

The packet ship *Fanchon* arrives at Liverpool in 1848 with Marryat Code identification flags flying. Just forward of the bowsprit is St. Paul's Church. To the far right is the spire of St. Mary's Church. Neither landmark exists today. A Mersey sailing flat is seen "bow on" in middle ground.

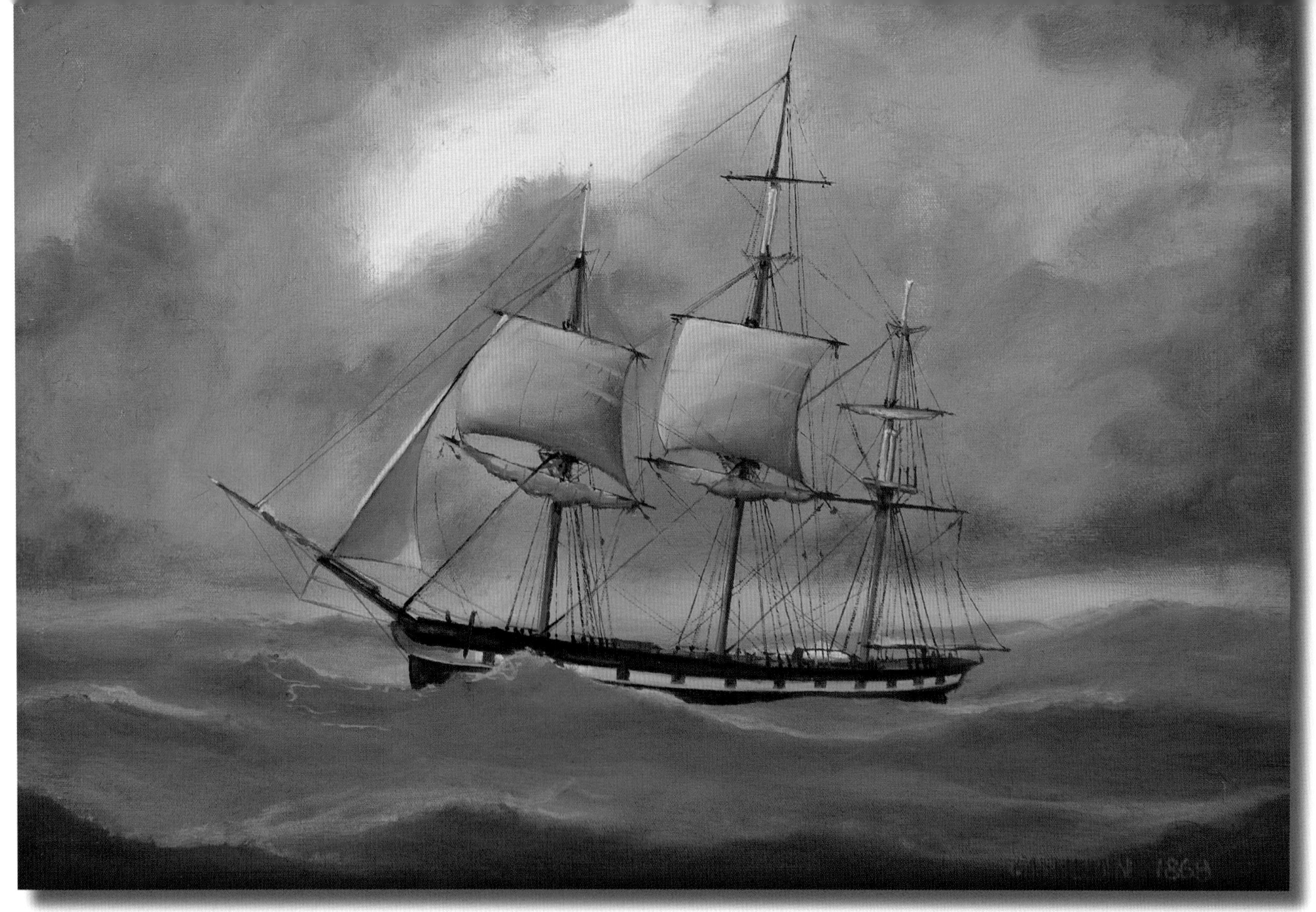

Castillian 1868

18" x 28"

The steamship *Castillian* encounters a "white squall," a sudden, violent windstorm at sea which can catch mariners unaware because it lacks the usual ominous dark clouds that warn of heavy seas. The name refers to the white-capped waves and broken waters that challenge ships during such an event. *Castillian* operated on the Allan Line out of Liverpool as an immigrant ship until 1899.

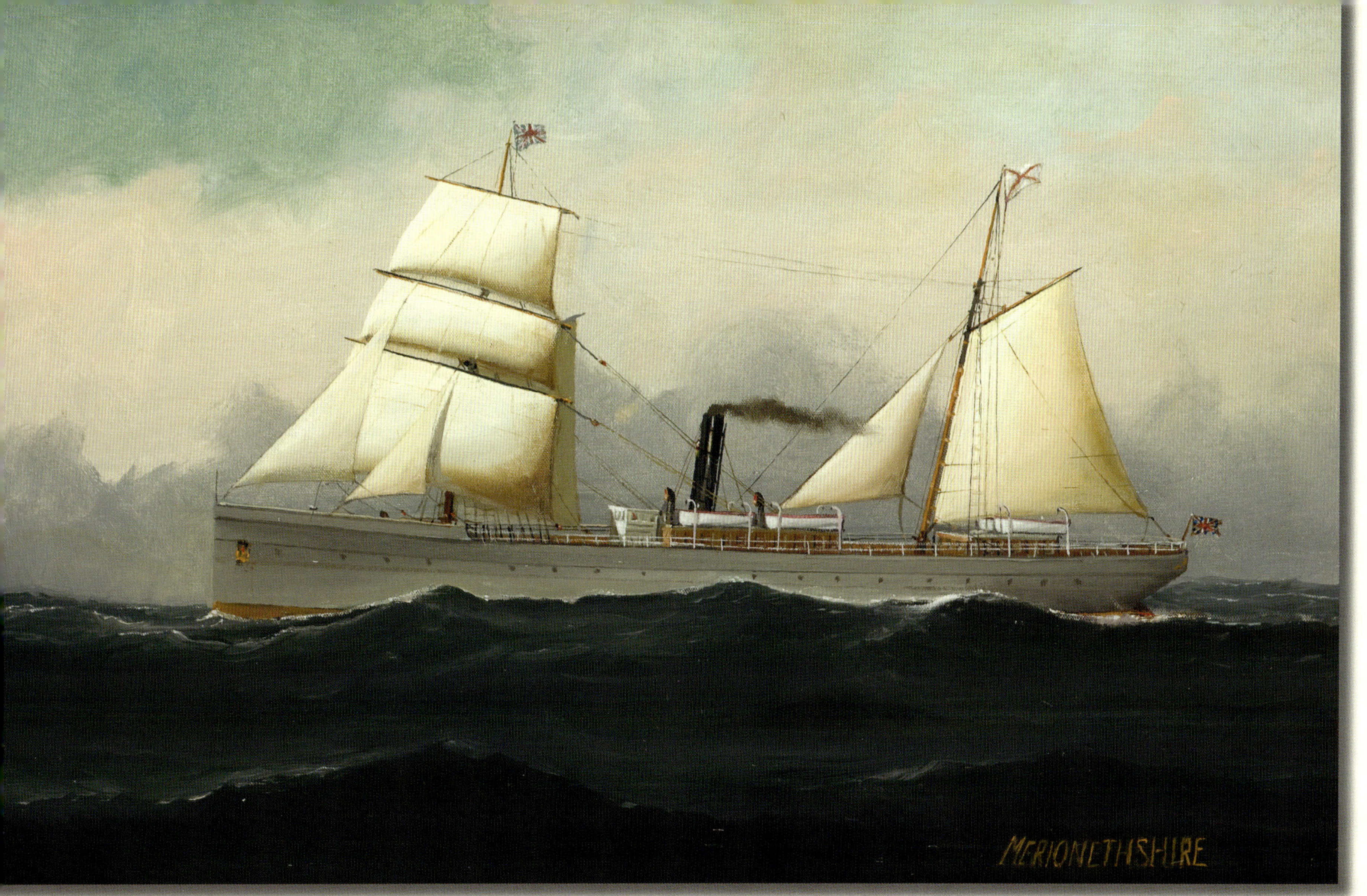

Merionethshire
18" x 28"

David Jenkins ordered the screw steamship *Merionethshire* in 1878 from London & Glasgow Shipbuilding Co. The ship operated for Jenkins' Shire Line between London and Japan until 1890. Renamed *Caribee*, it sailed between the United Kingdom and St. Lawrence until it foundered in a storm off the east coast of the United States on June 8, 1908.

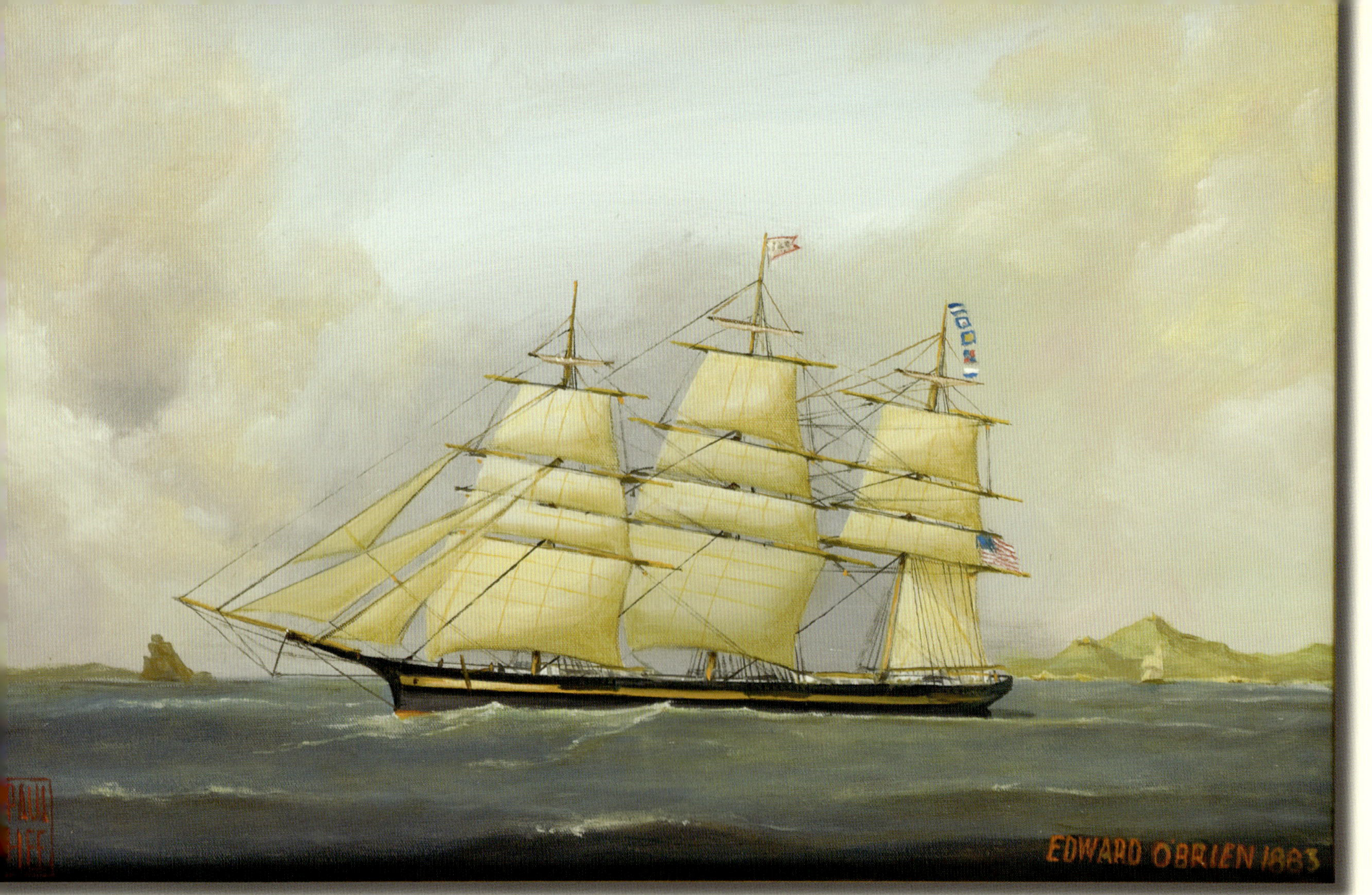

Edward O'Brien 1883

18" x 26"

This large "Down Easter" was launched at Thomaston, Maine, in 1863. It was the largest ship built there, displacing 2,157 tons and measuring 259 feet overall. It is shown at the approach to Liverpool just off the South Stack Light. The flags on the mizzen mast are the ship's Marryat Code identification numbers.

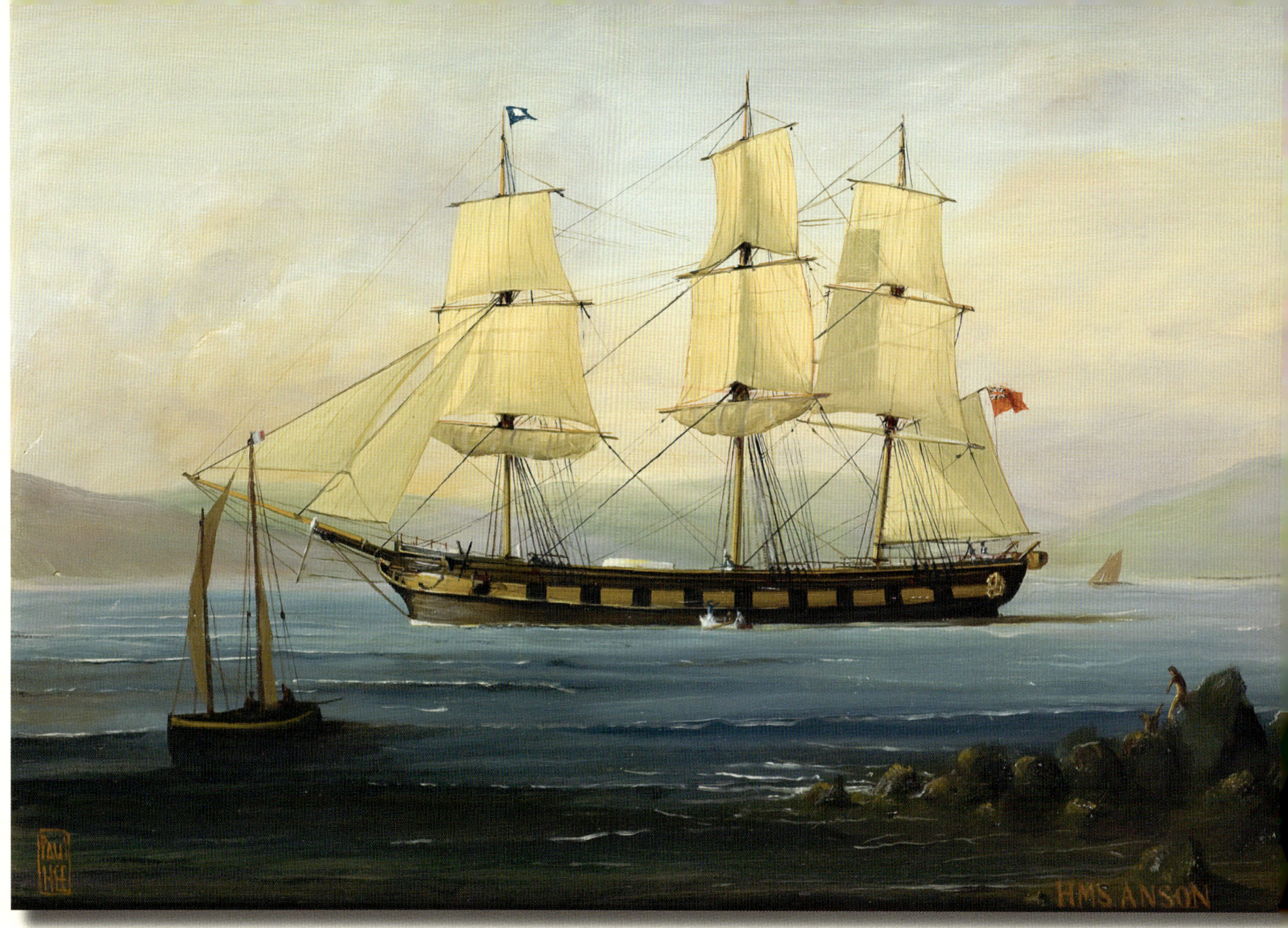

HMS Anson
18" x 28"

Named for Admiral George Anson, the 44-gun razee frigate was launched January. 4, 1781, at Plymouth Dockyard in England as a two-deck 54-gun ship and cut down one deck in 1794. (A razee is a nautical term for an armed ship having her upper deck cut away, thus reduced to the next inferior rate.) Then-commodore Anson circumnavigated the globe (1740-1744) on his flagship *Centurion*, seized a Manila galleon laden with a million pieces of eight, and capped his career by becoming First Lord of the Admiralty from 1751-1758. The frigate wrecked on Loe Bar, near Porthleven, Cornwall, on December 29, 1807. Seven British war-ships were named *Anson*. Anson County in North Carolina is named in his honor. The novels, *The Golden Ocean* and *Unknown Shore,* by Patrick O'Brian are based on Anson's circumnavigation.

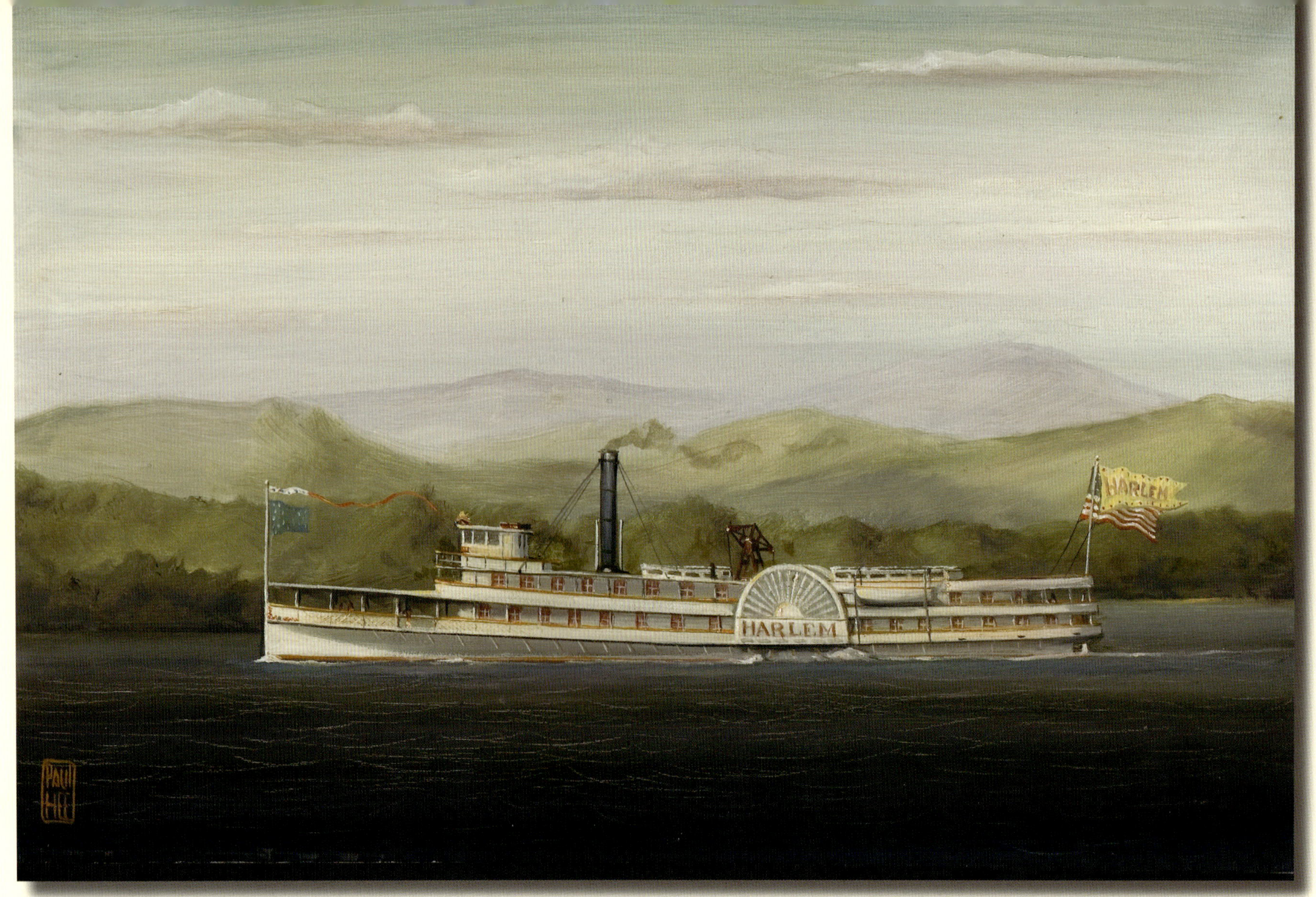

Harlem

18" x 20"

Harlem, a dandy Hudson River side-wheeler, and *Norwich*, (next page) are inspired by the folk art of twin brothers John and James Bard, self taught artists who at age 12 began to capture the romance of the steamboat age in paintings now prized by collectors and museums.

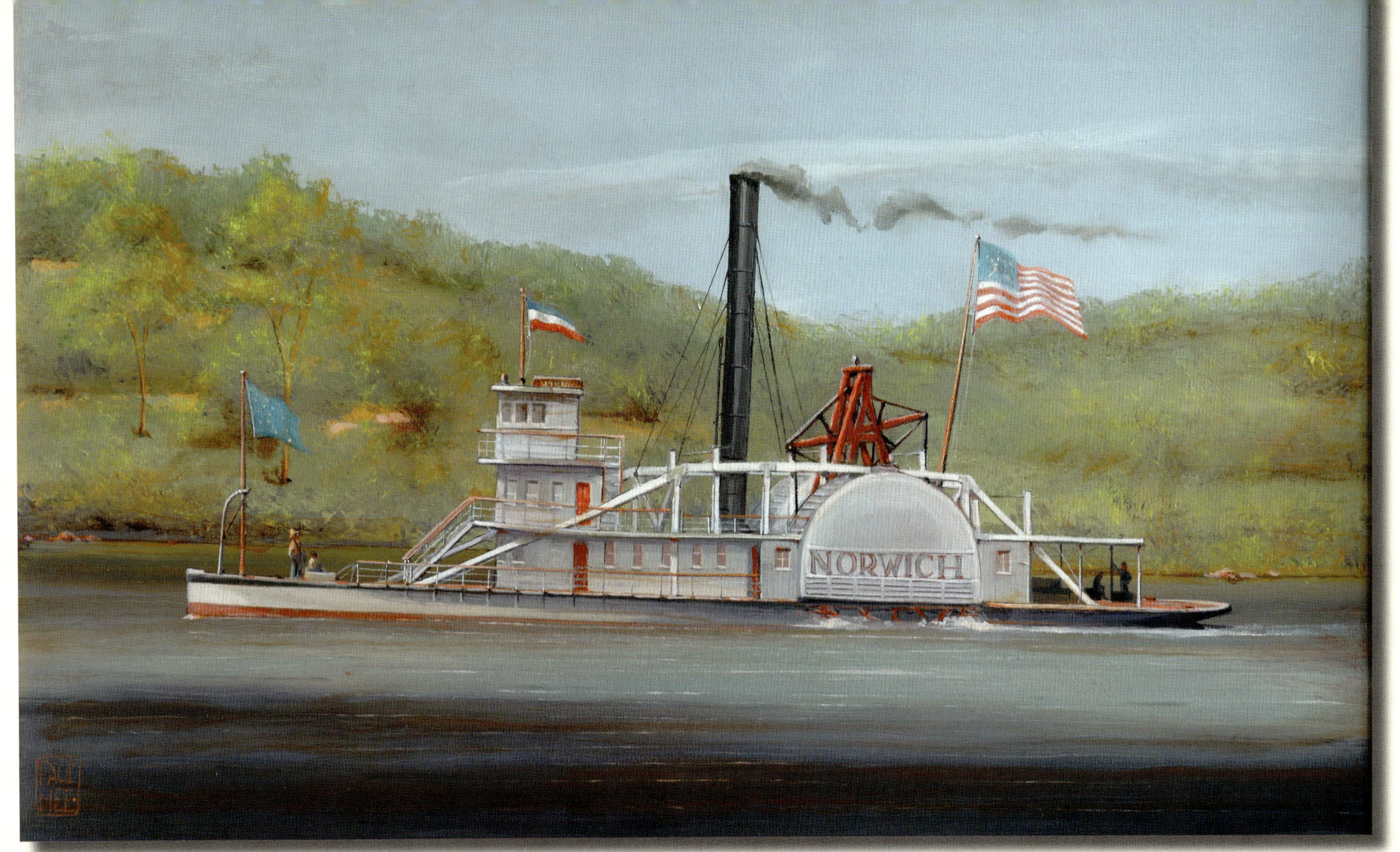

Norwich
18" x 20"

Oldest steamboat in the world, *Norwich*, built in 1836, was known on the Hudson River as the "Ice King." With stout hull and powerful engines, she was the first boat out in Spring to break the ice. She may be the last of the "up and down beam boats," so called because its steeple engine operates a horizontal cross beam up and down, as depicted here. *Norwich* remains in commission as a towboat on the upper river.

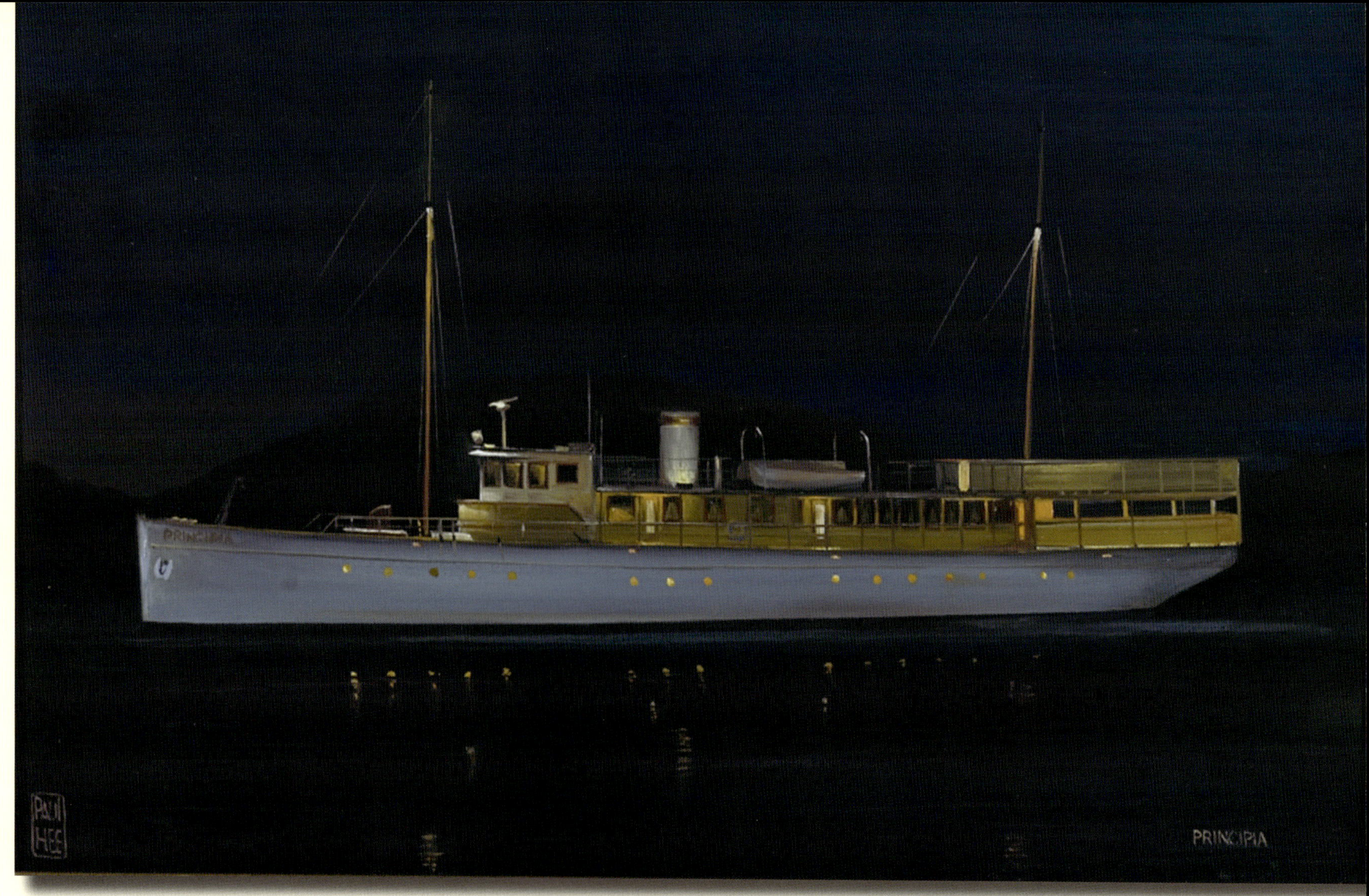

Principia

18" x 28"

Designed by Ted Geary (1885-1960) of Seattle, who built luxury motor yachts for West Coast millionaires and Hollywood movie stars in the '20s and '30s, *Principia* is one of four 96-foot sister ships, and the first and only single-screw 96-foot yacht built in 1928 at Lake Union Dry Dock. She was launched that year for San Francisco yachtsman L.A. Macomber. *Principia* epitomizes the era of elegant luxury yachts. Now restored, she sails from the Independence Seaport Museum of Philadelphia.

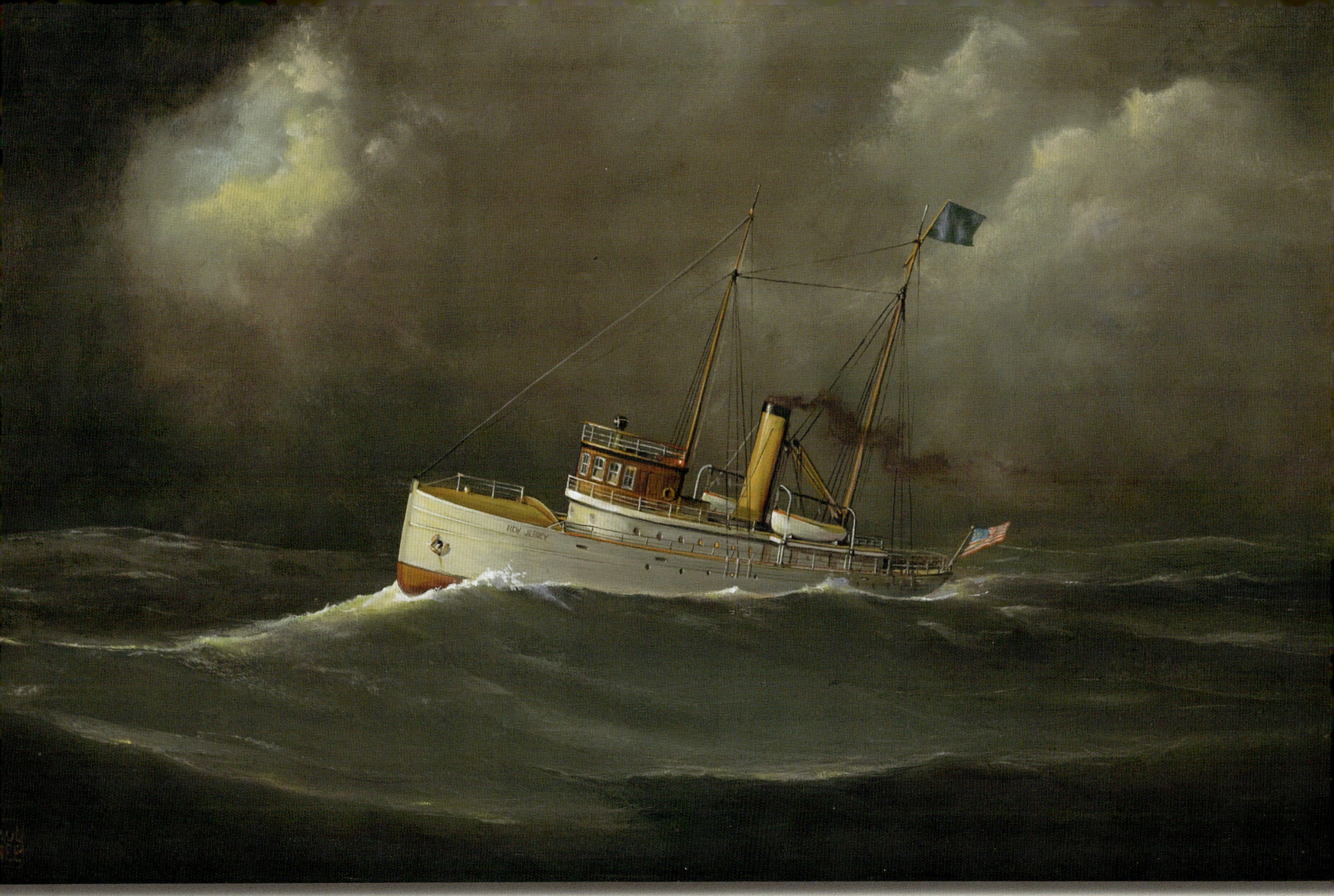

New Jersey
18" x 20"

Tug heading out.

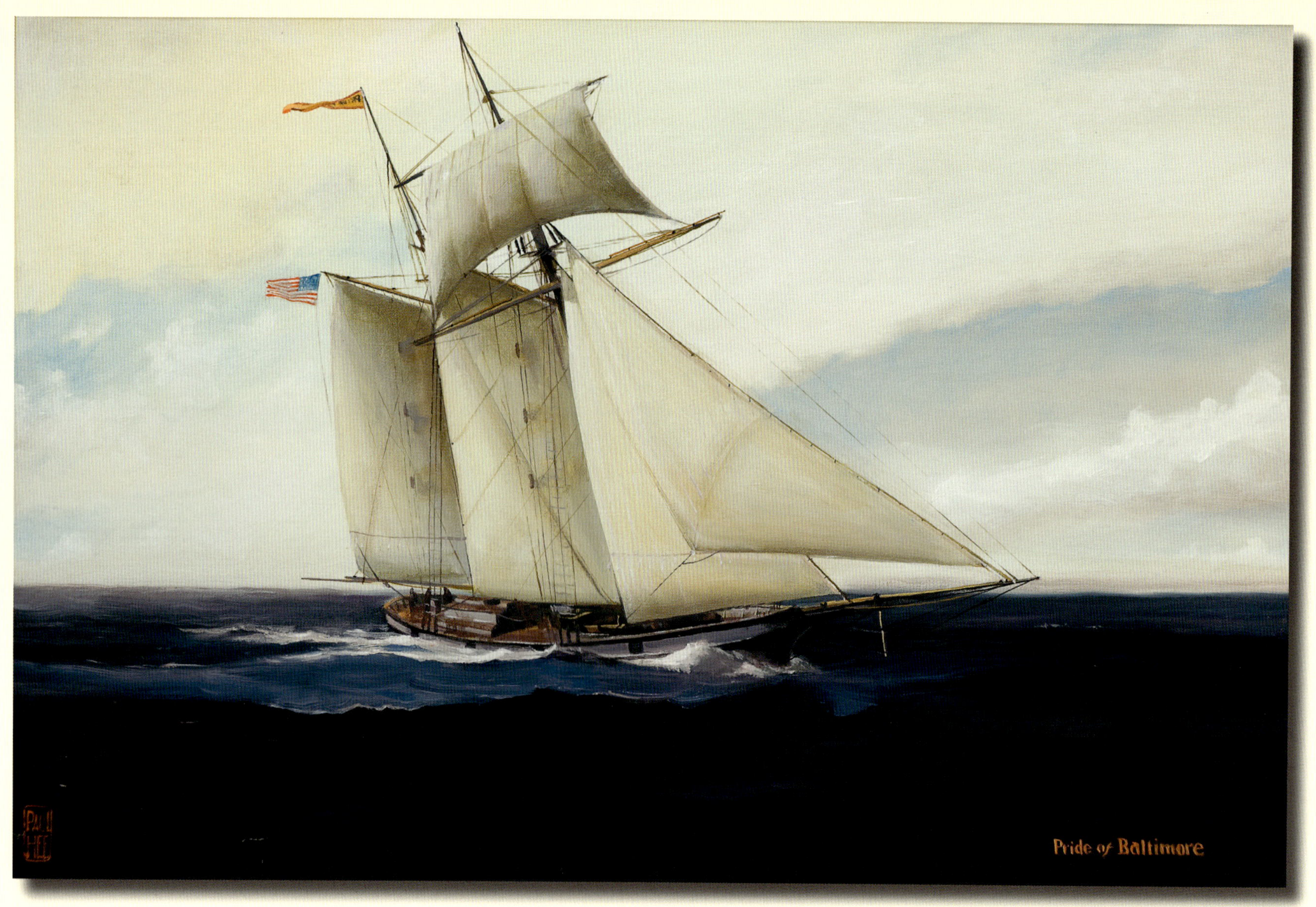

Pride Of Baltimore II

18" x 20"

Her sharply raked masts, abundant sail and sleek profile catch eyes wherever she goes. *Pride II*, as she is known, has sailed 200,000 miles and visited 200 ports in 40 countries as a goodwill ambassador. *Pride of Baltimore II*, designed by Thomas G. Gillmer and built by G. Peter Boudreau in the Baltimore Inner Harbor, was launched on April 30, 1988 to replace the

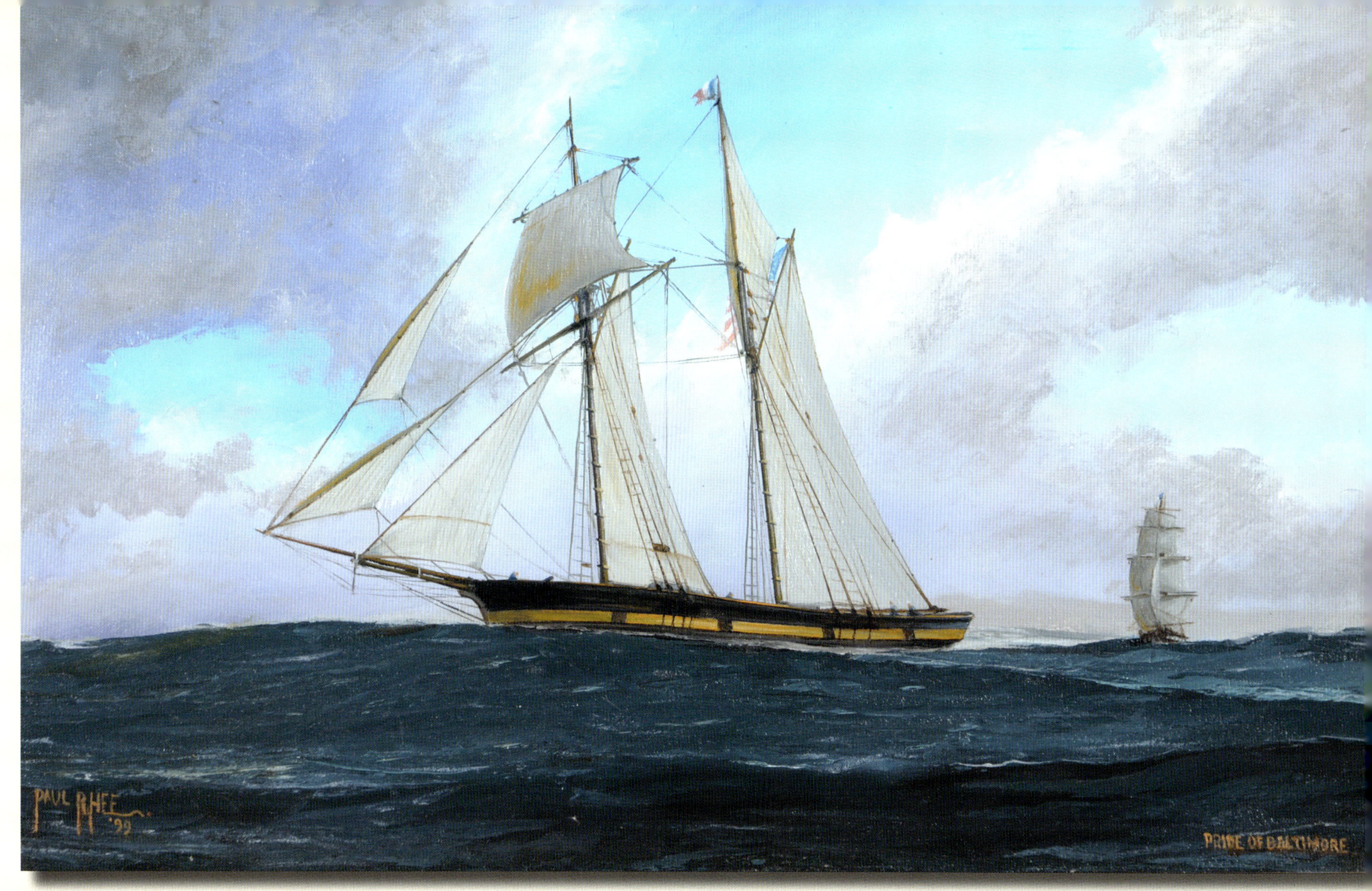

Pride Of Baltimore

18" x 28"

original vessel. The original topsail schooners of the Baltimore Clipper type served with distinction as privateers in the War of 1812. The first *Pride of Baltimore* was built in 1977 as a replica of type to celebrate its importance in American maritime history. The 157-foot ship, caught in a squall off Puerto Rico, sank with the loss of the captain and three crew members in 1986.

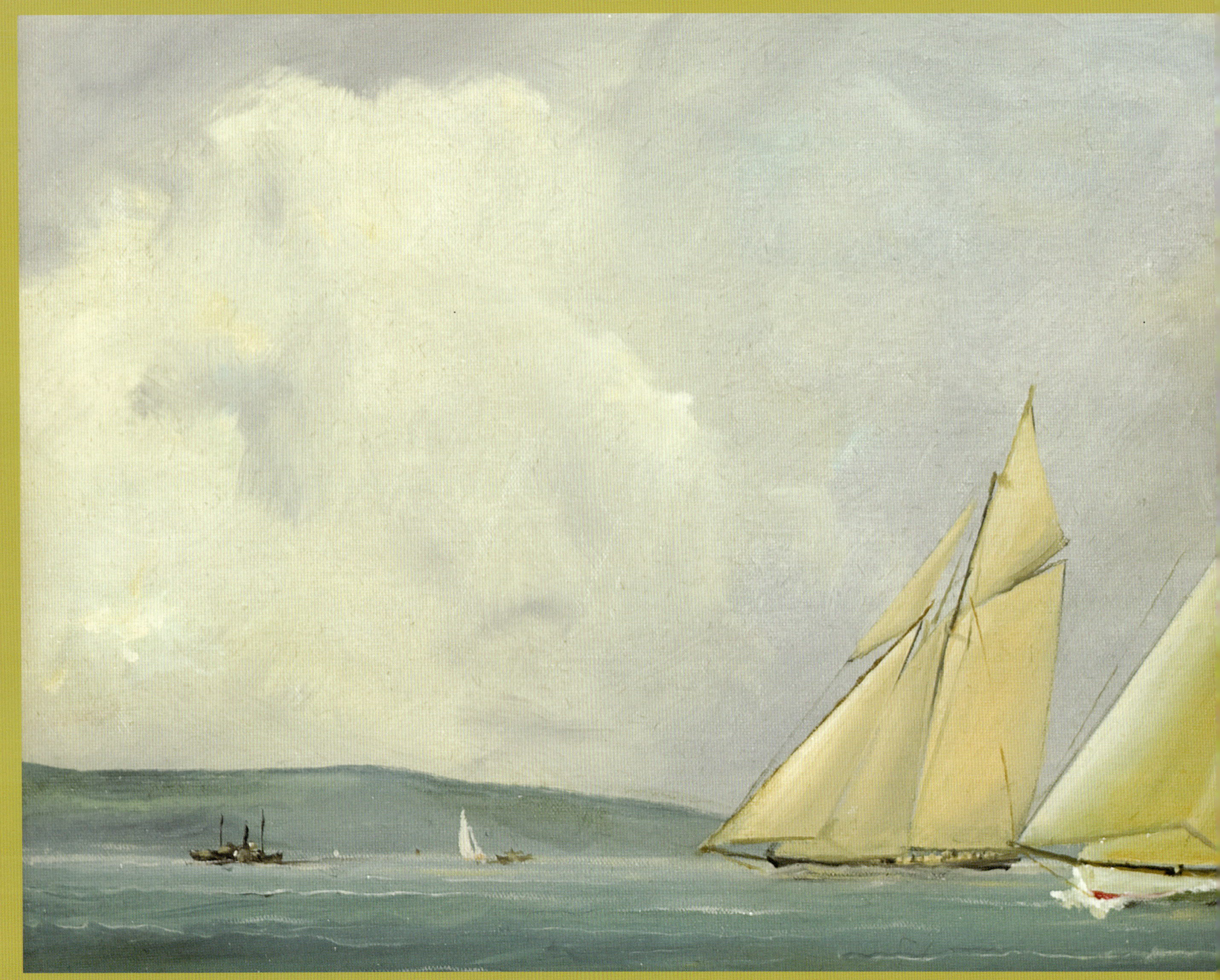

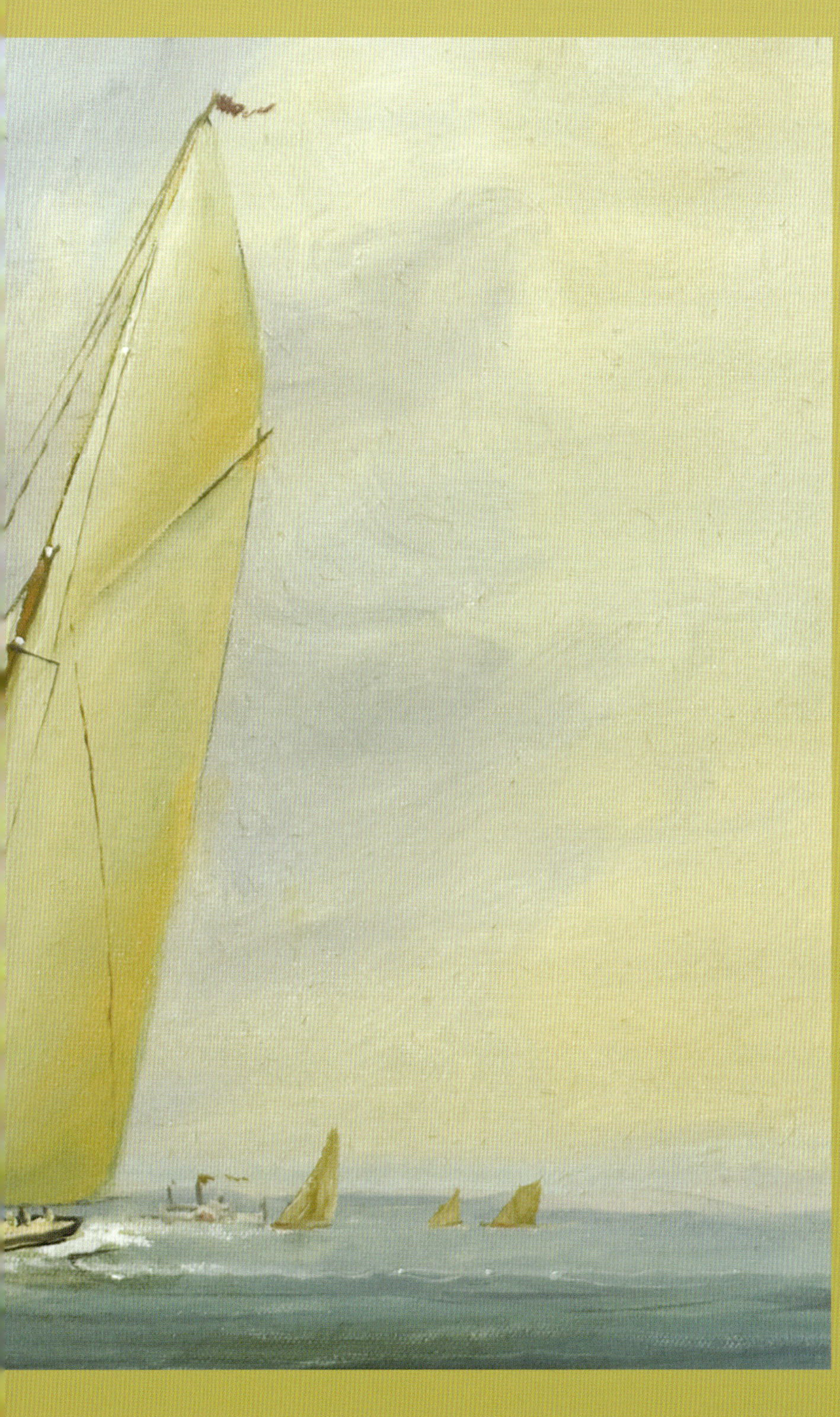

CHAPTER V

RACE DAYS

Vigilant vs. Valkyrie II 1893

Vigilant vs. *Valkyrie II* 1893

18" x 30"

Vigilant, a centerboard sloop designed and skippered by Nathanael Greene Herreshoff of Bristol, Rhode Island, won the eighth America's Cup against the British gaff-rigged cutter *Valkyrie*.

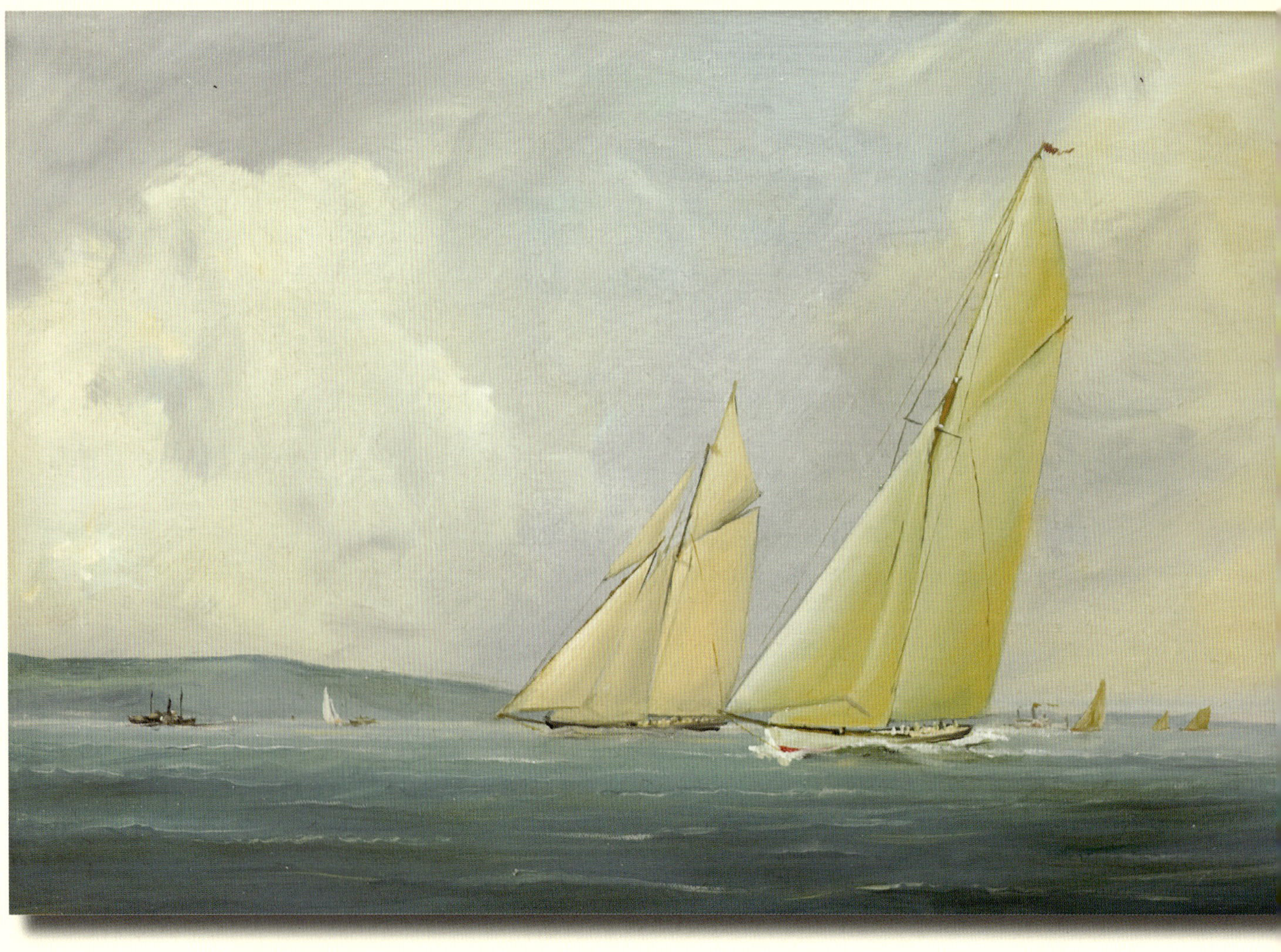

"For A Great Contest Both Valkyrie & Vigilant In Fine Racing Trim"

—New York Times 1893

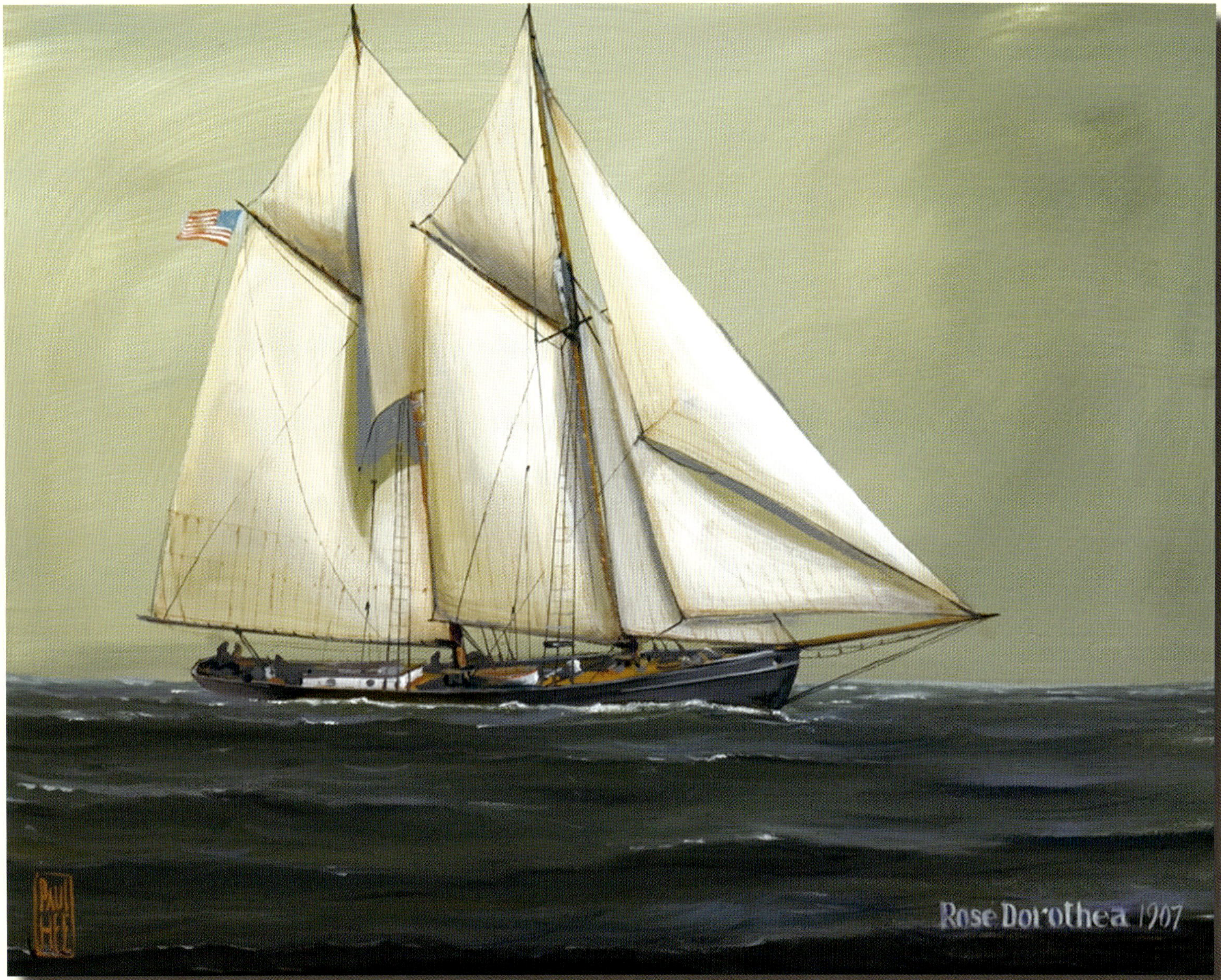

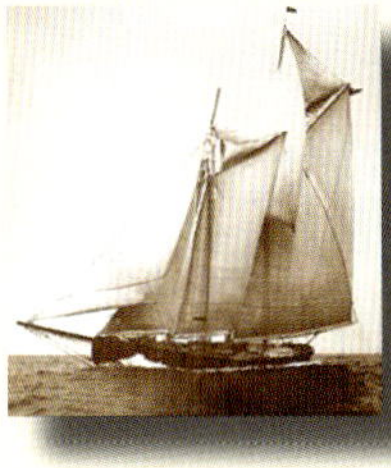

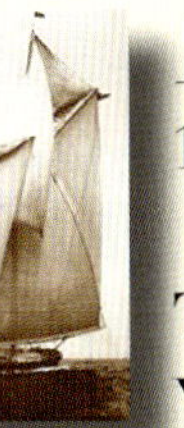

Rose Dorothea 1907

18" x 28"

The 108.7-foot, 108-ton fishing schooner designed by Tom McManus and built at the Tarr & James Yard in Essex, Massachusetts, sets out from Provincetown to compete in the first Fishermens Cup Race.

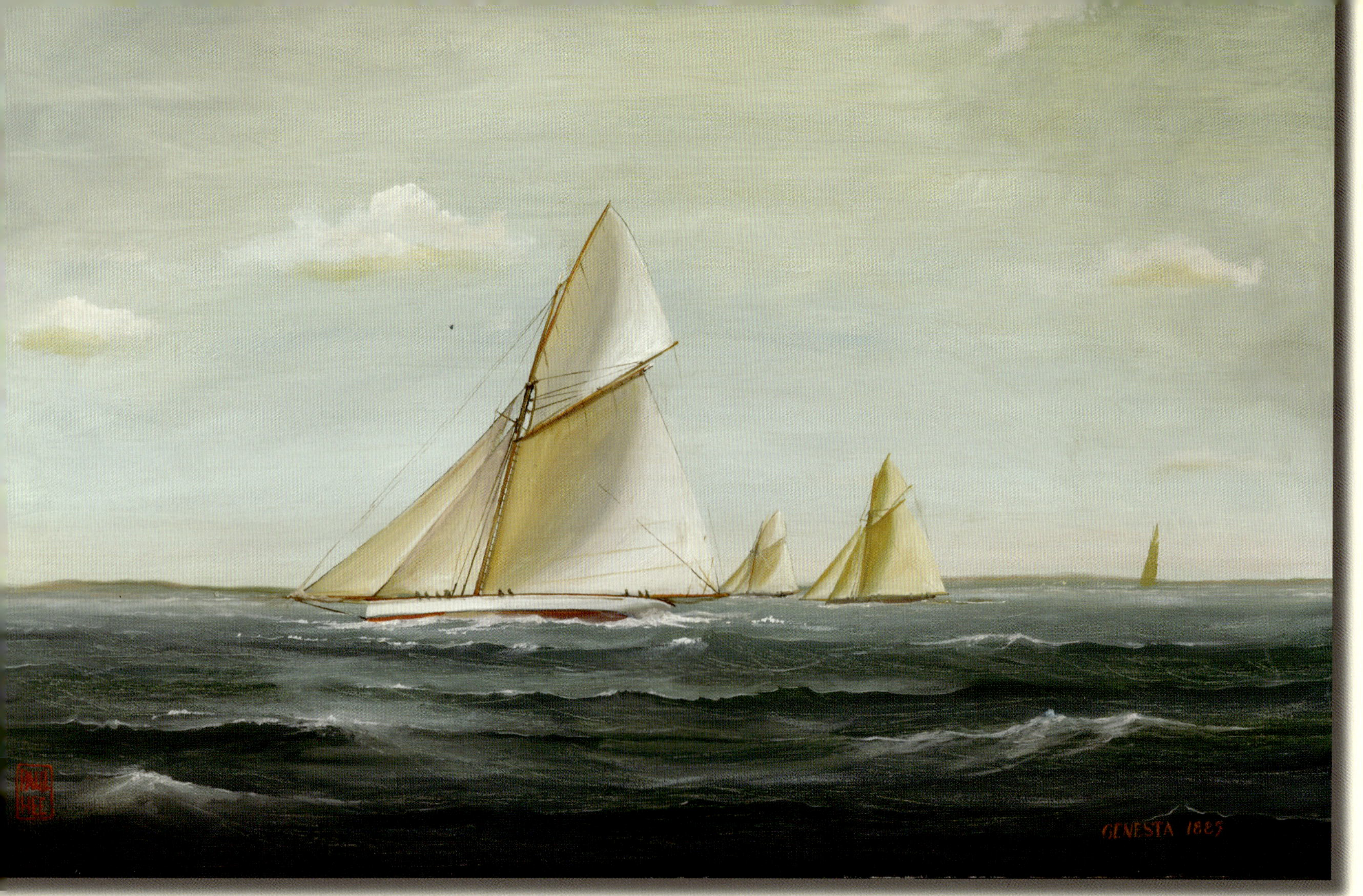

Genesta vs. Dauntless

18" x 28"

After the swift British cutter *Genesta* lost to American defender *Puritan* in the America's Cup in 1885, she posted an easy victory over *Dauntless* in the Cape May Challenge Cup. "Little more than a walkover for *Genesta*," the *New York Times* reported. "She held the lead from start to finish and came in many hours ahead." Built of oak planks on steel frame, the deep, narrow 81-foot cutter was considered "unbeatable" in her day. Designed by John Beavor-Webb, she was built by D. & H. Henderson & Co. of Glasgow for Sir Richard Sutton and survived until 1900.

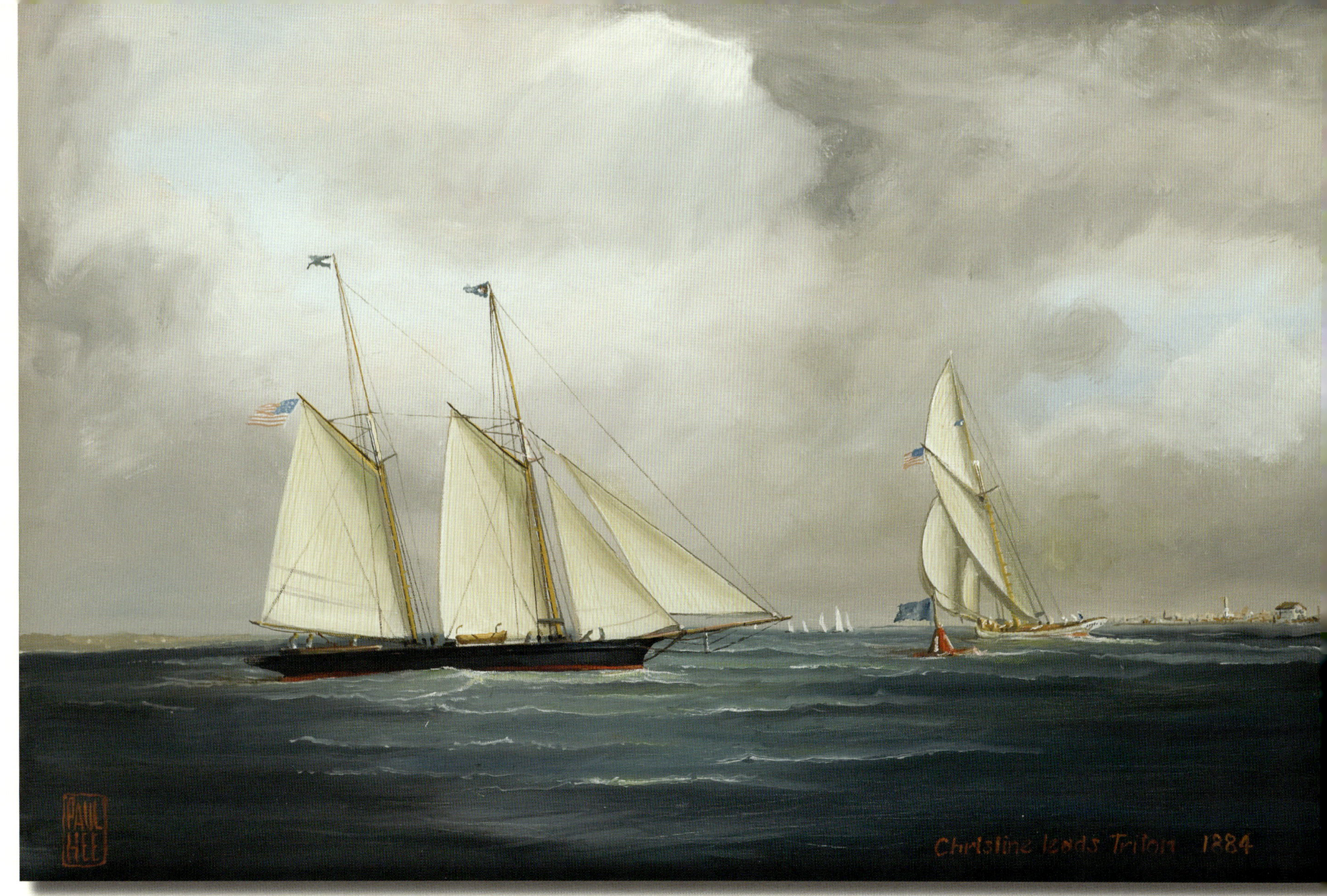

Christine Leads Triton 1884

18" x 30"

The schooner *Triton* and the sloop *Christine* are depicted racing in Newport Harbor in the style of the English maritime artist James Edward Butterworth (1817-1894).

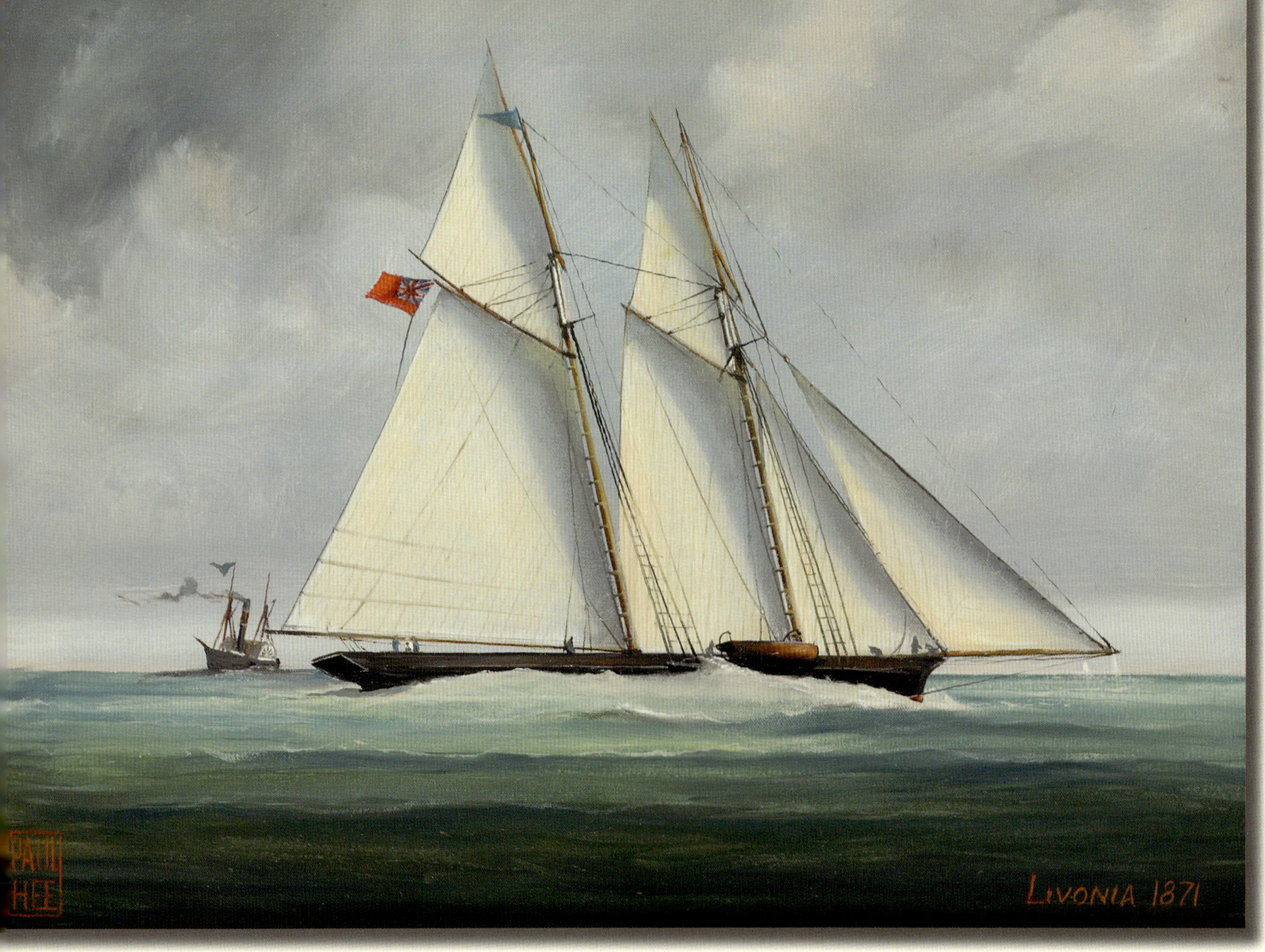

Livonia 1871
18" x 28"

James Ashbury, of the Royal Harwich Yacht Club in Ipswich, was the first challenger for the America's Cup, in 1870. After losing, he returned to challenge the New York Yacht Club in 1871 with his new yacht, *Livonia*. Skippered by R.W. Woods, the 127-foot yacht, with more than 18,000 square feet of sail, took on the New York Yacht Club's defender, *Columbia*. *Livonia* won one of the first three races, but *Columbia* was damaged in the third race. *Sappho* took *Columbia*'s place and went on to defeat *Livonia* twice, to retain the America's Cup for the New York Yacht Club.

Race Day 1907

18" x 20"

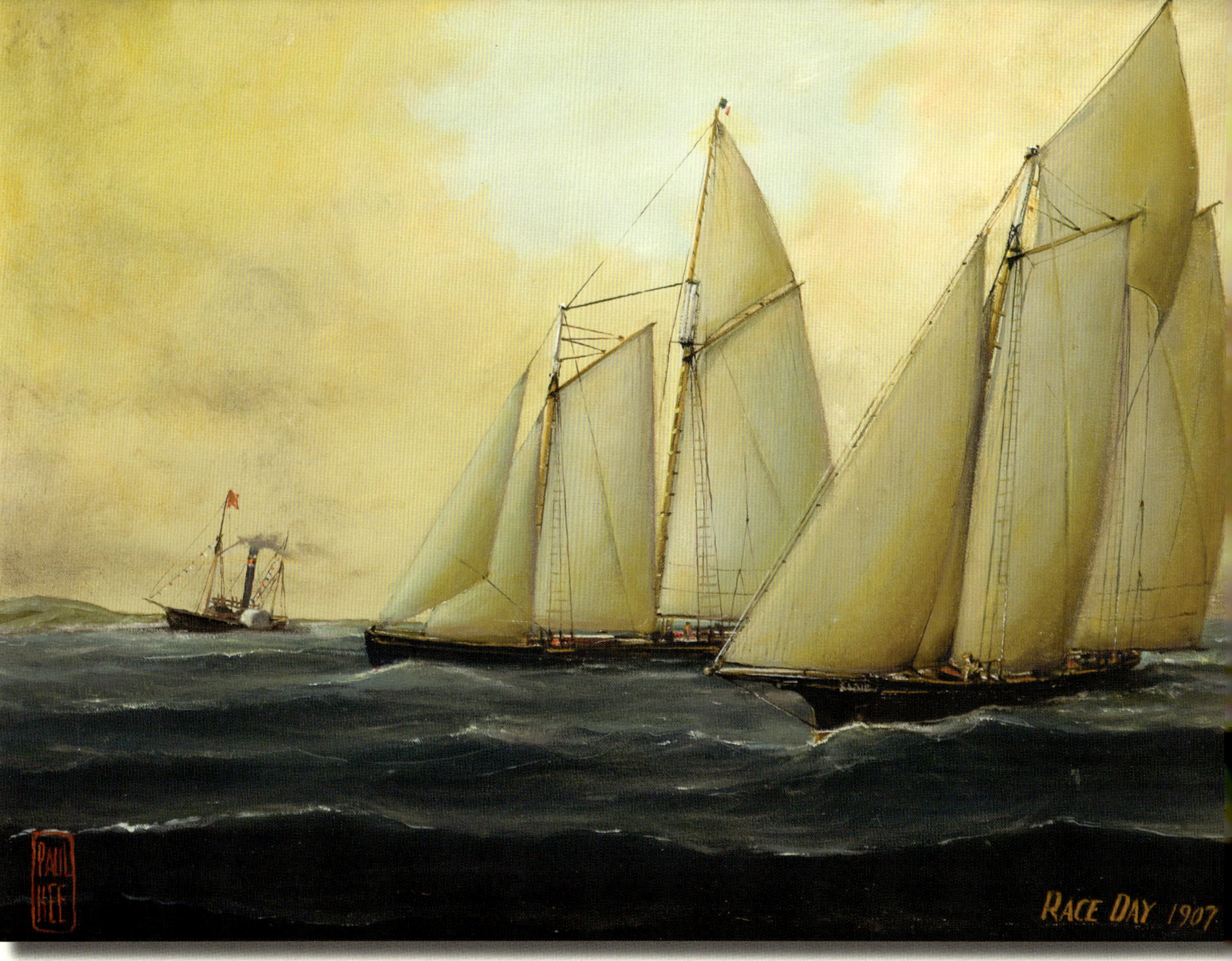

Two Gloucester fishing schooners race from Boston to Provincetown in the first Fishermens Cup race in 1907. The trophy, valued at the time at $5,000, was donated by Sir Thomas Lipton, a regular and famous contender in America's Cup races. The schooners *Rose Dorothea* and *Jessie Costa* are battling for the lead in the race, won by the former in 11 hours and 45 minutes (a lead of less than 2 minutes). The races became international in 1920 and continued until 1938. Modern schooner racers revived the contest in 2008.

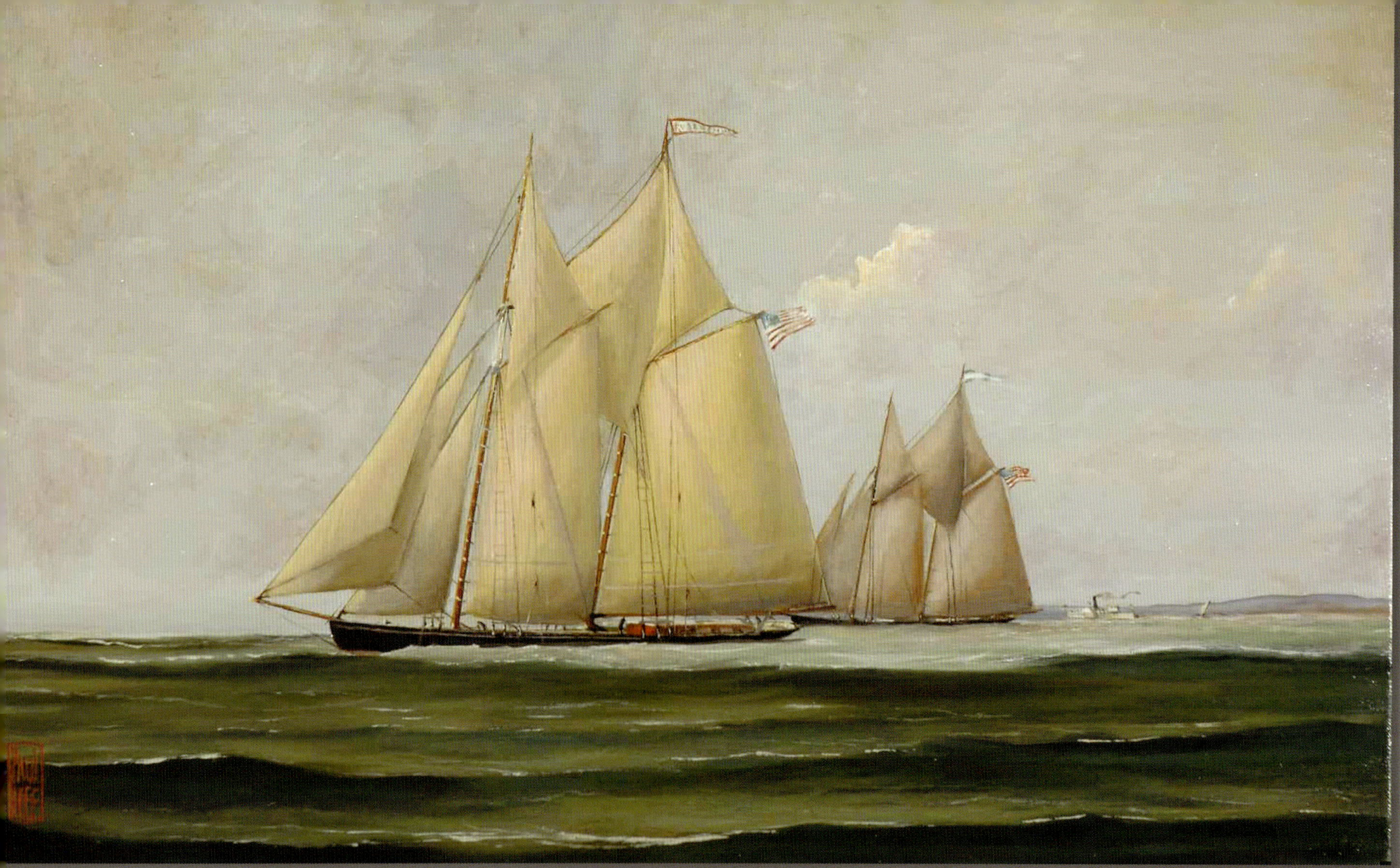

Rose Dorothea Wins Lipton Cup 1907

18" x 28"

Capt. Marion Perry aboard *Rose Dorothea* won the 1907 Fishermens Cup race, sponsored by Sir Thomas Lipton, to become first fishing vessel to win the coveted Lipton Cup. *Rose Dorothea* (named for Captain Perry's wife) defeated *Jessie Costa* by 1:43 minutes at the finish of the 40-mile race on Massachusetts Bay.

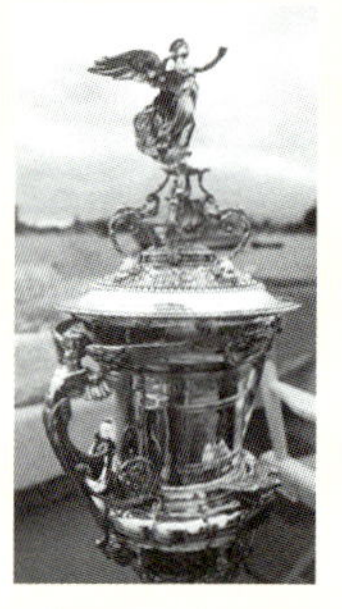

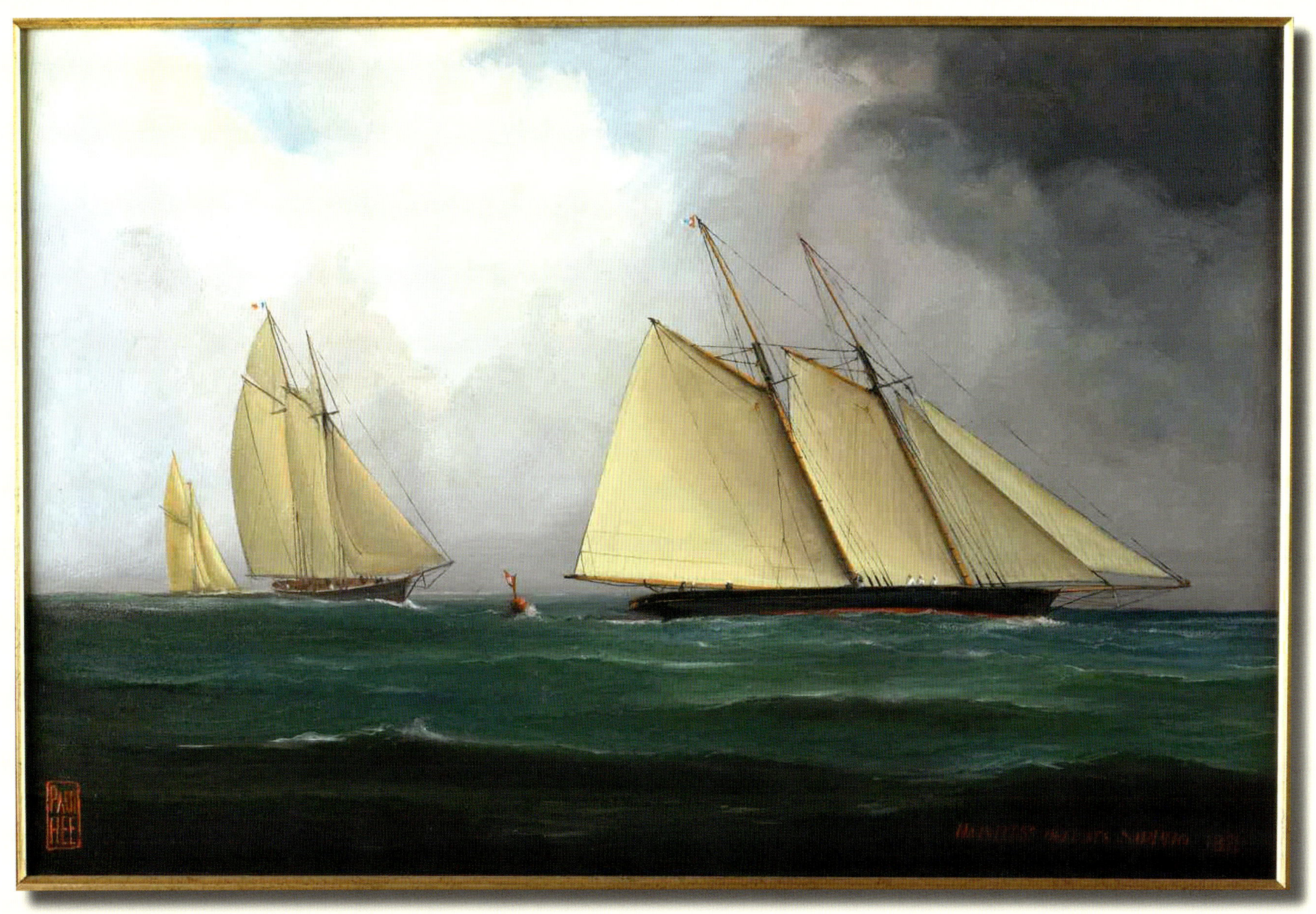

DAUNTLESS VS. SAPPHO
18" x 28"

Dauntless
16" x 20"

Originally *L'Hirondelle*, this sloop was built in 1866 by Forsyth & Morgan for S. D. Bradford, and sold the next year to James Gordon Bennett, publisher of the *New York Herald*. He re-rigged the 121-foot sloop as a schooner, renamed her *Dauntless*, and posted victories over *Jadho* and *Cambria*. An America's Cup contender in 1867, *Dauntless*' best Atlantic passage east was 16 days, 1 hour, 43 minutes. Her best run was 326 miles. In 1882 Caldwell Hart Colt, son of Hartford gun maker Samuel Colt, bought *Dauntless* and raced her until his death aboard in 1894 at age 36. She sank in Hartford in a 1915 gale.

FLYING ACROSS THE SEA

THE DAUNTLESS AND CORONET STARTED.

THE BEAUTIFUL SIGHT FURNISHED BY THE TWO YACHTS AS THEY BEGAN THEIR LONG CONTEST.

The whistle has sounded and the two white-winged competitors in the great ocean race of 1887 are now flying across the Atlantic. The start was a beautiful picture and took place amid every evidence of impartial enthusiam and general good-will.

The Dauntless began her day yesterday with an avalanche of beautiful flowers. Boat after boat came from shore laden with beautiful, towering flower emblems, Capt. Samuels, in his capacity as School Trustee, getting the lion's share. There was a floral schooner, 6 feet high, from the scholars and teachers of Grammar School No. 60; a 5-foot floral anchor from School No. 61; a beautiful floral wheel, 5 feet in diameter, from School No. 62, and on the the bottom of it was the pretty sentiment, "Both Dauntless, vessel and commander." At 9:30 o'clock Mr. Bird came on board with a

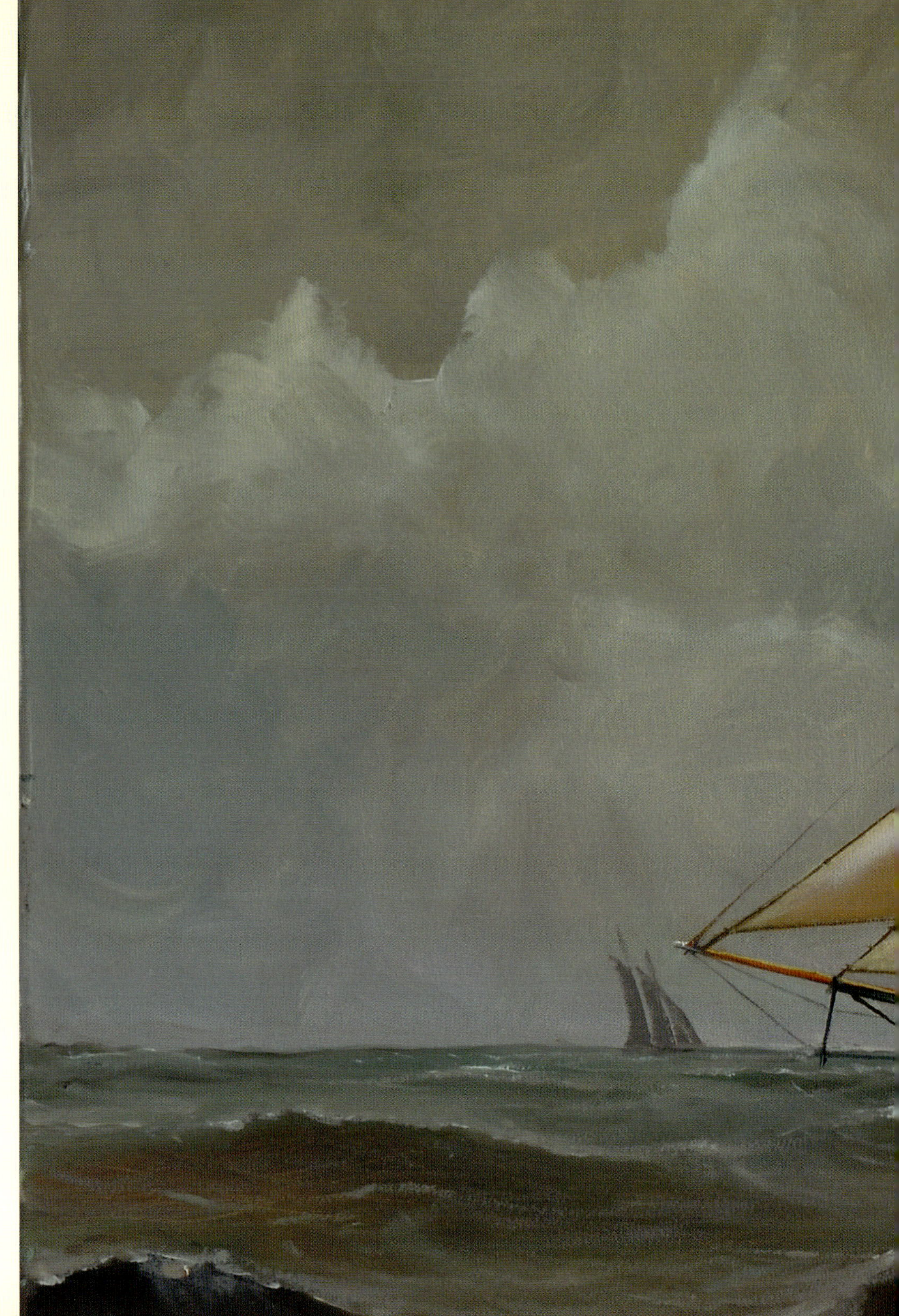

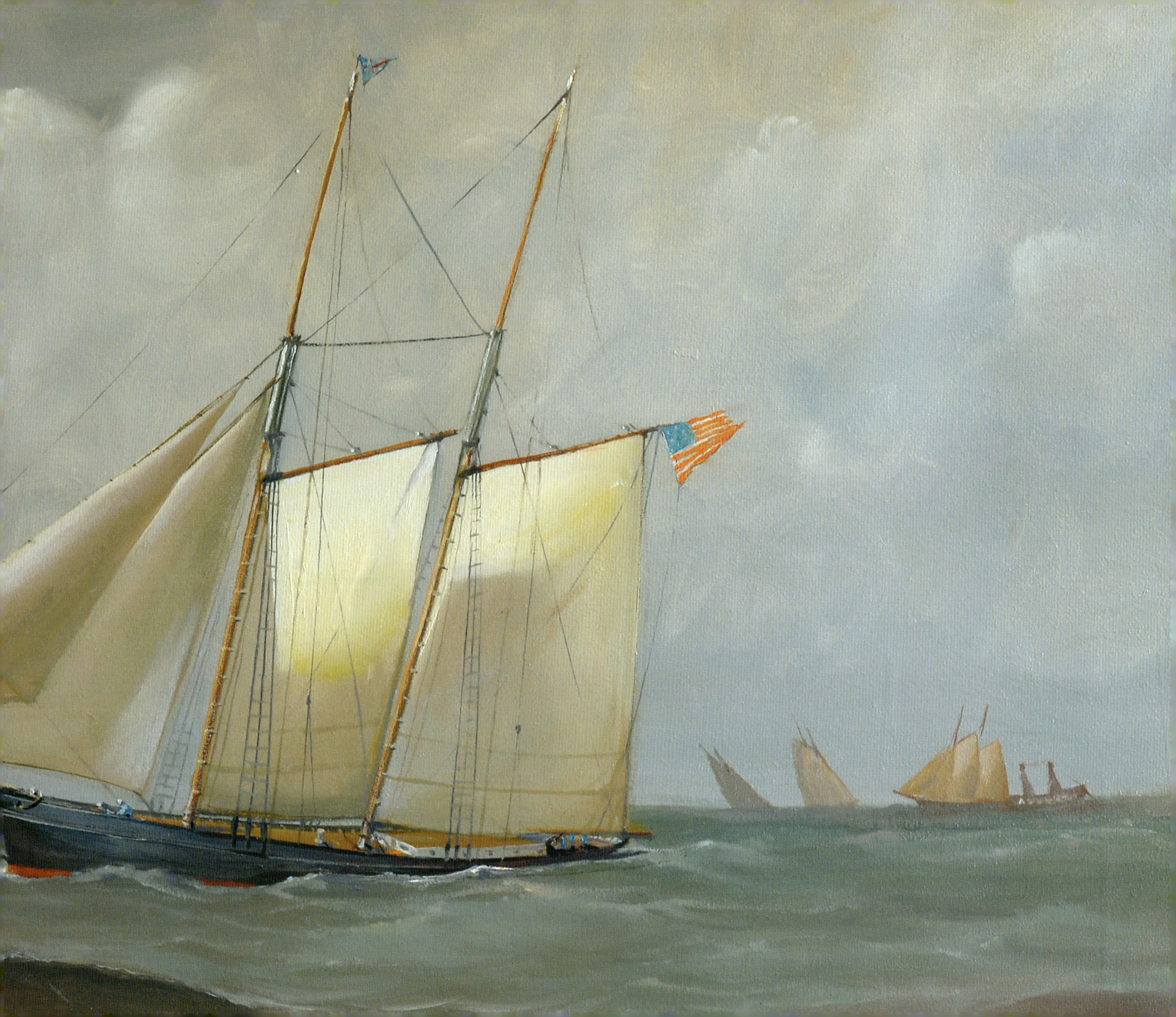

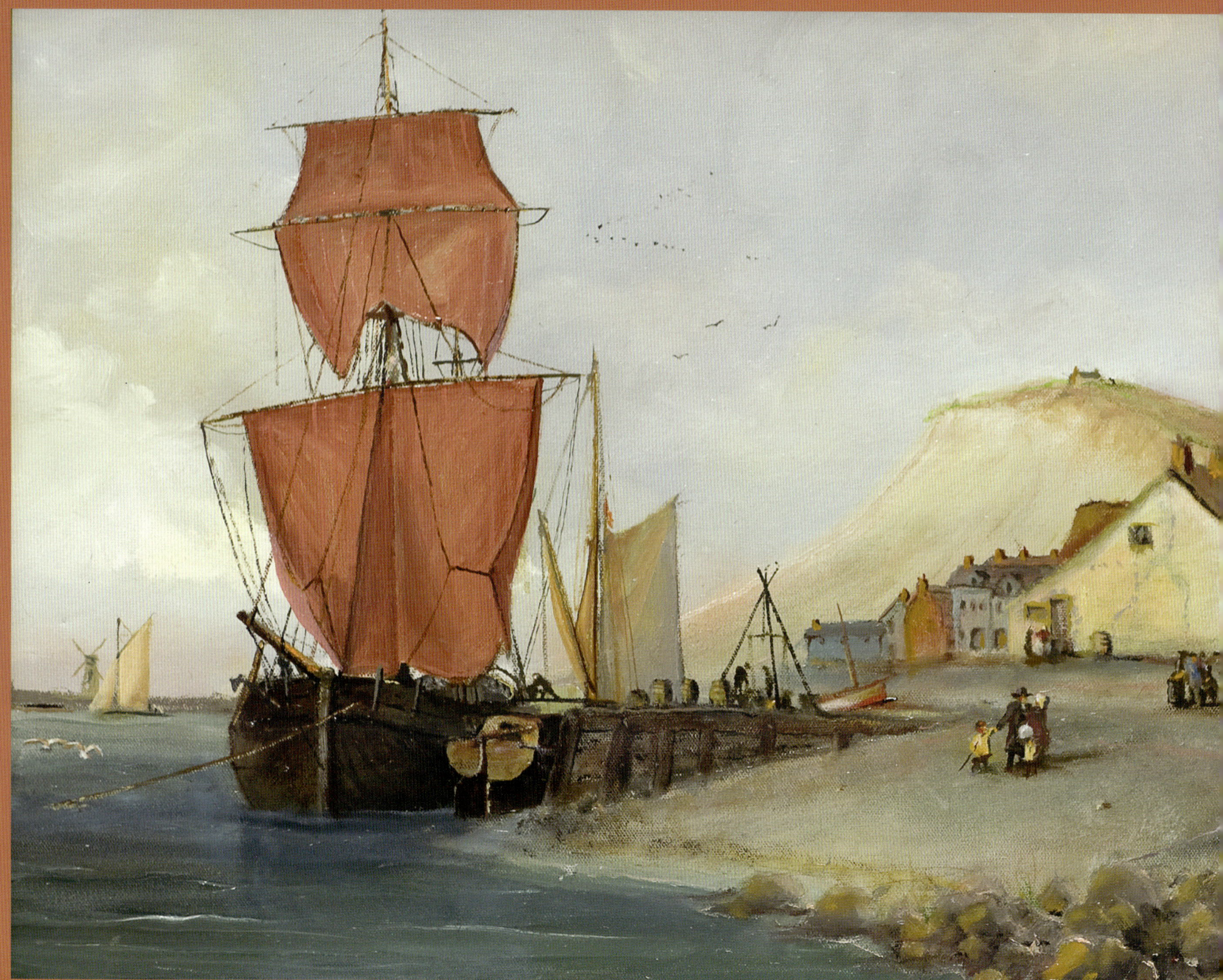

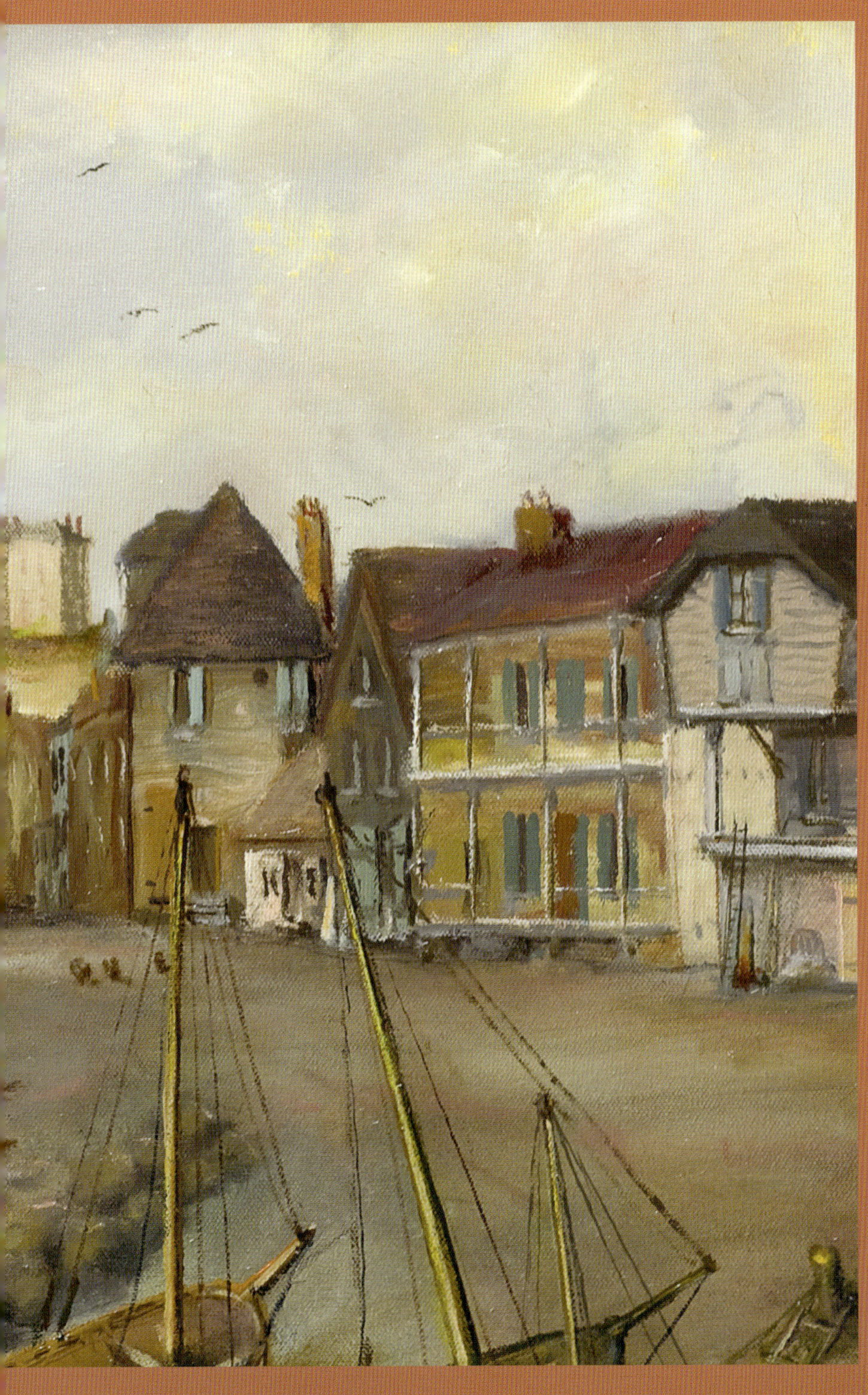

CHAPTER VI

SEASCAPES

Low Water at Folkestone

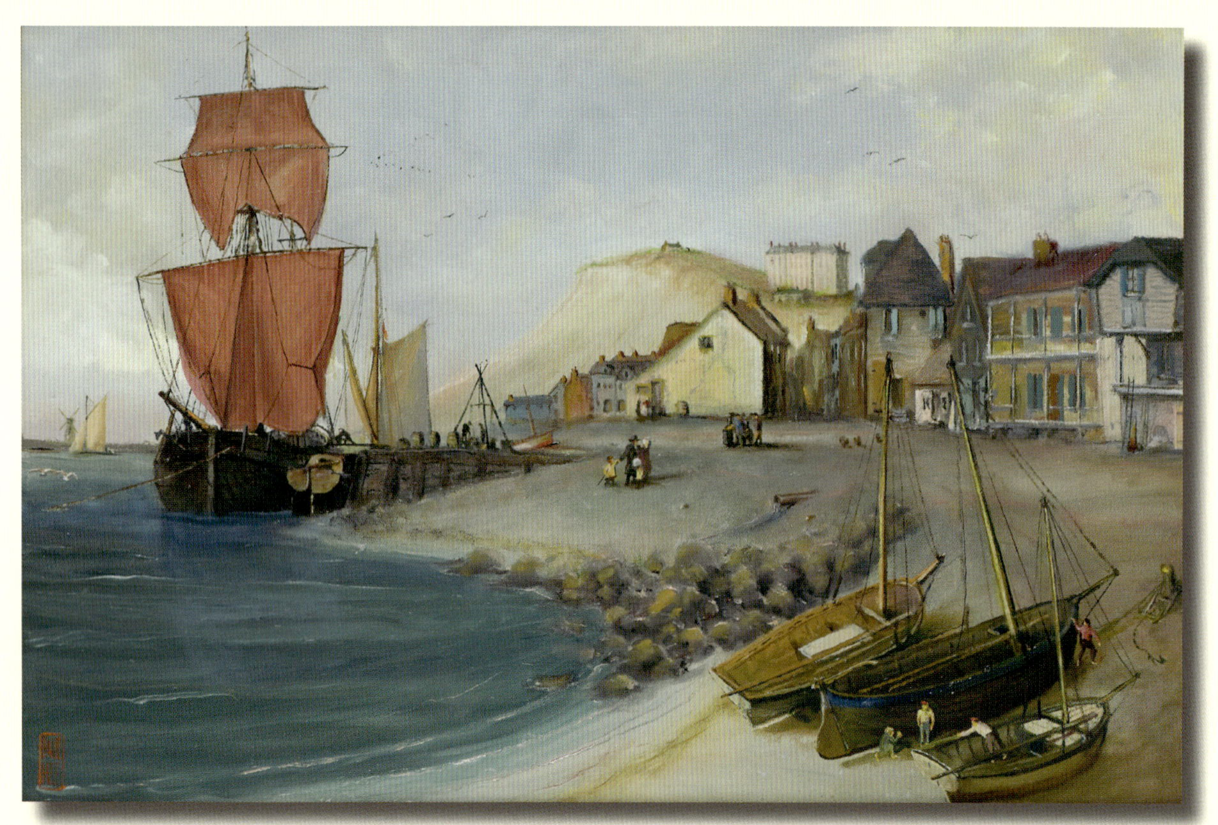

Low Water at Folkestone

18" x 24"

A hand-colored 1831 etching by Edward William Cooke (1811-1880), from his *Sixty Five Views of Shipping & Craft*, inspired this scene of the village of Folkestone, Kent, at low tide. Boys play between dories beached on a broad strand, and a grounded ship awaits the incoming tide.

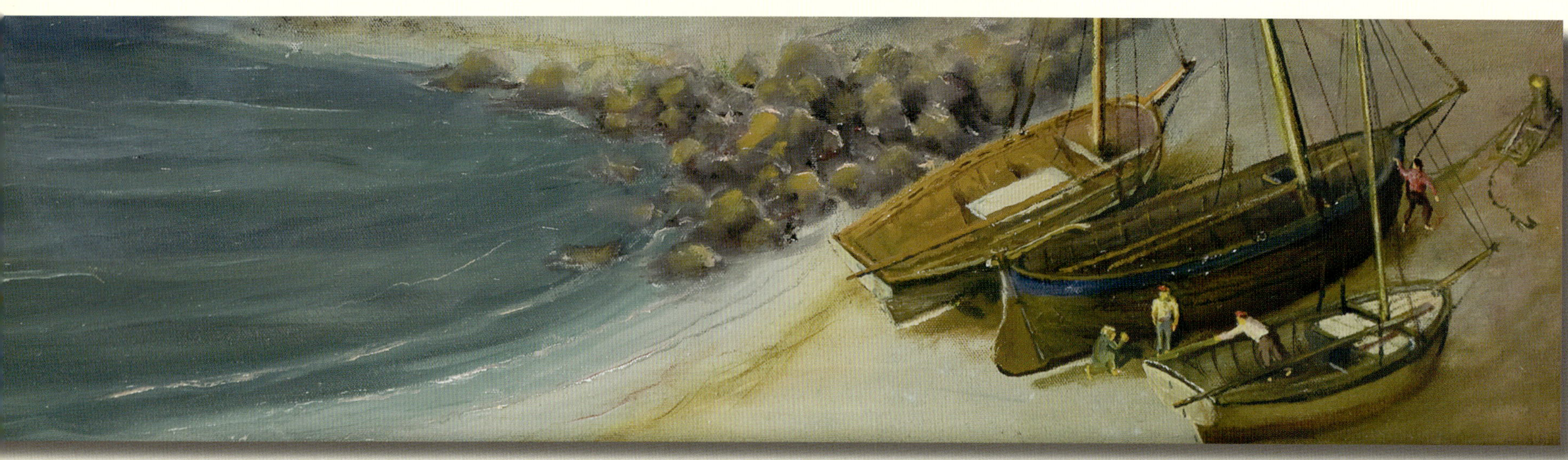

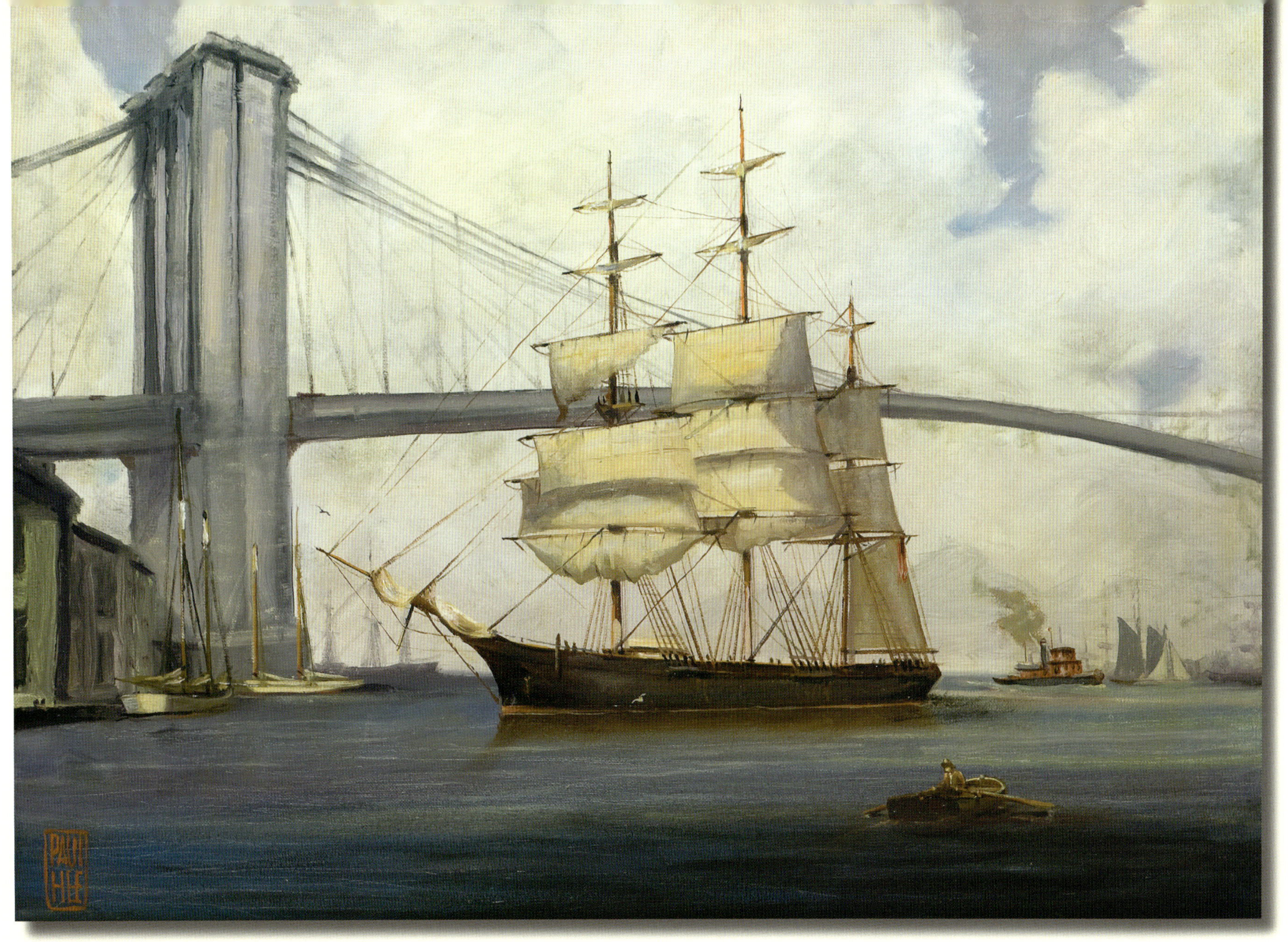

New York Harbor

18' x 20"

A typical day in New York Harbor, 1905.

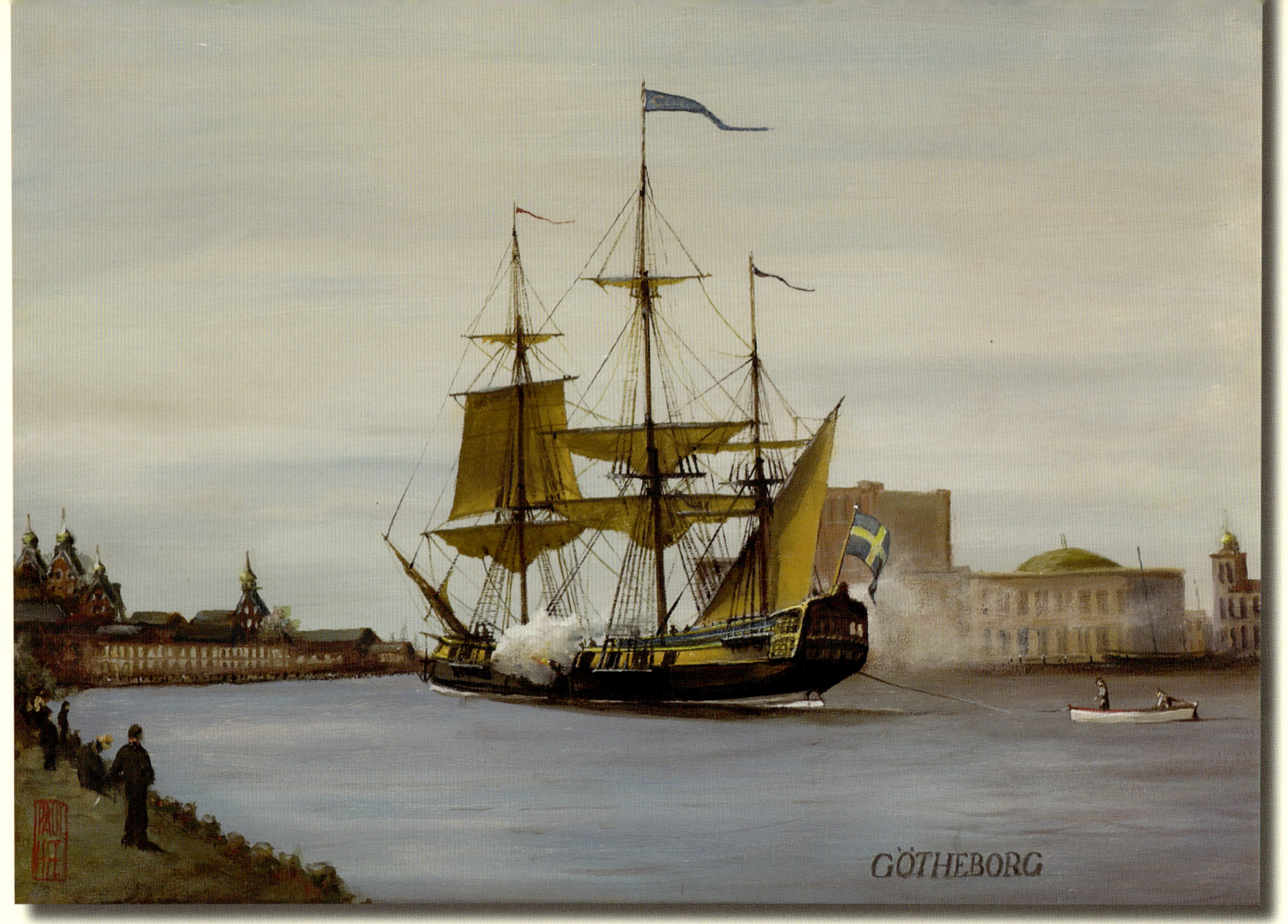

Gotheborg 1745
18" x 28"

After three voyages to China, the Swedish East Indiaman *Gotheborg*, laden with tea, porcelain, silk and spice, ran aground at the entrance to her home port of Gothenborg, Sweden, on September 12, 1745. All hands survived, but the ship was lost. In 1984, wreckage of the 140-foot vessel was found and excavated by nautical archaeologists. A replica was built, for $30 million, and launched in 2003. *Gotheborg* once again sailed for China on the old trade route.

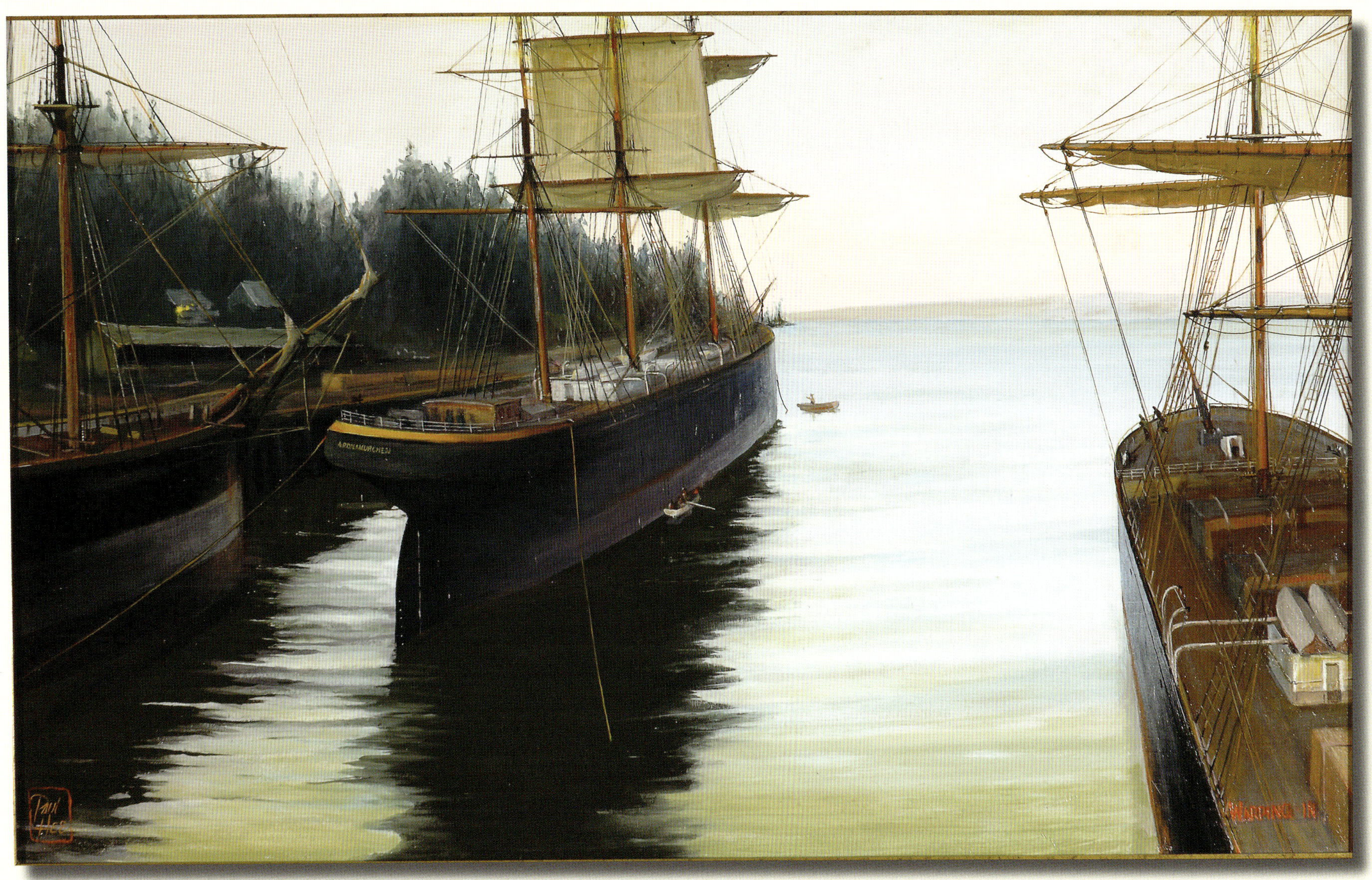

Warping In, Port Blakely

24" x 35"

Port Blakely, on Bainbridge Island in Washington state, became the largest lumber port on Puget Sound, possibly the nation, in the 1880s. In this scene, three large square-riggers wait to load redwood timber from one of the local sawmills.

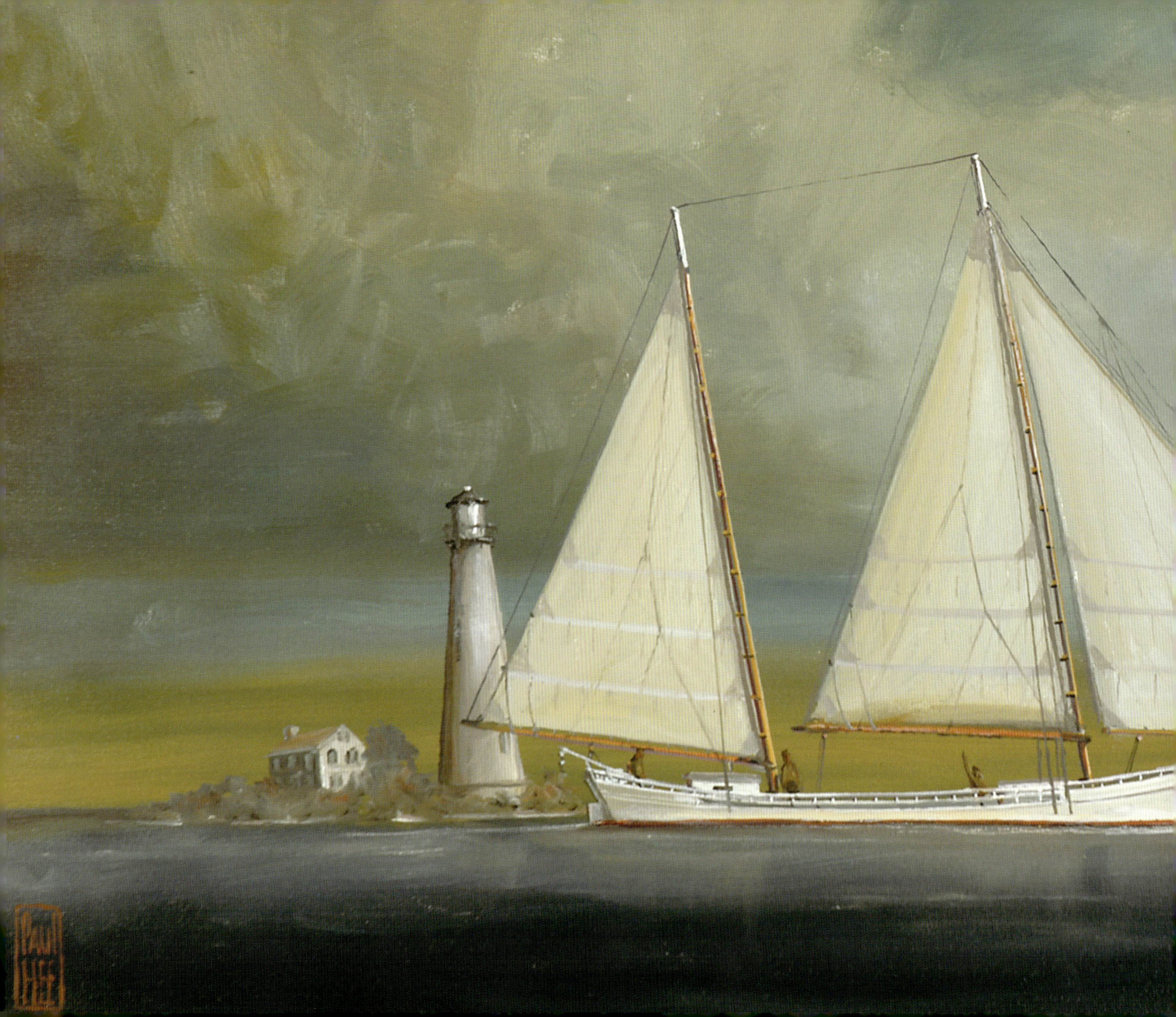

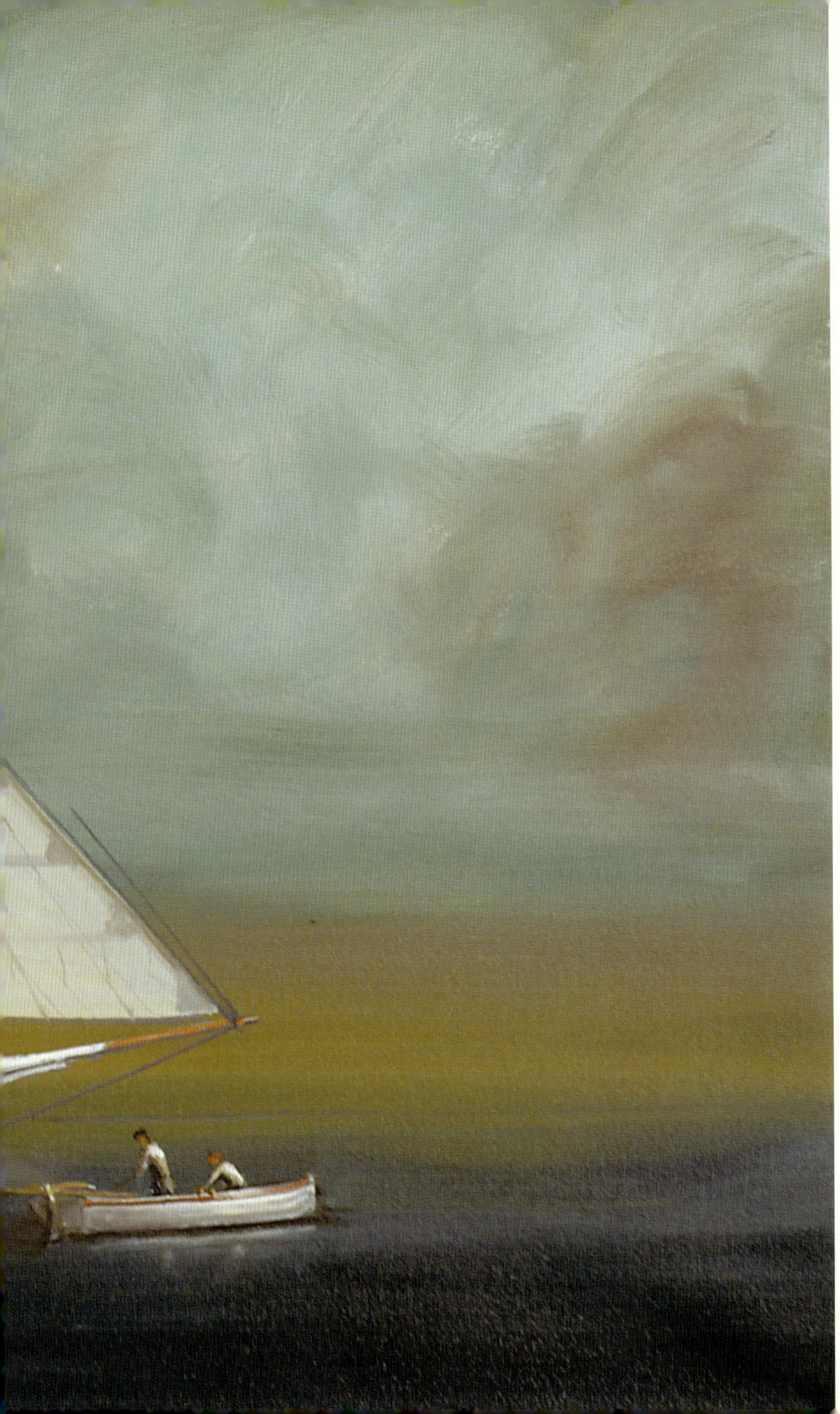

Edna E. Lockwood at Back River Light

18" x 28"

The *Edna E. Lockwood*, a three-sail Chesapeake Bay skipjack (often called a bugeye), sails by Back River Light on Fox Hill, Hampton, Virginia. *Lockwood* was the last of the type to keep her sailing rig and working appearance. Built in 1889 by John B. Harrison in the log, or "chunk" style of shipbuilding unique to the region, *Lockwood* dredged oysters until 1967. Established in 1829 at Back River Point, the 34-foot-high brick lighthouse topped by an octagonal iron lantern remained in service until 1936 when Hurricane Flossie destroyed it on September 27.

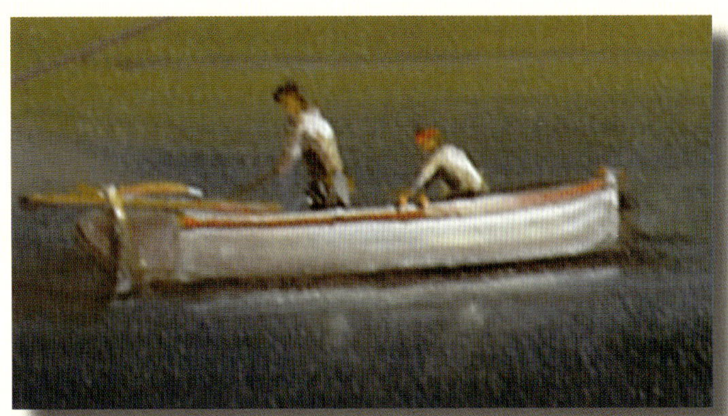

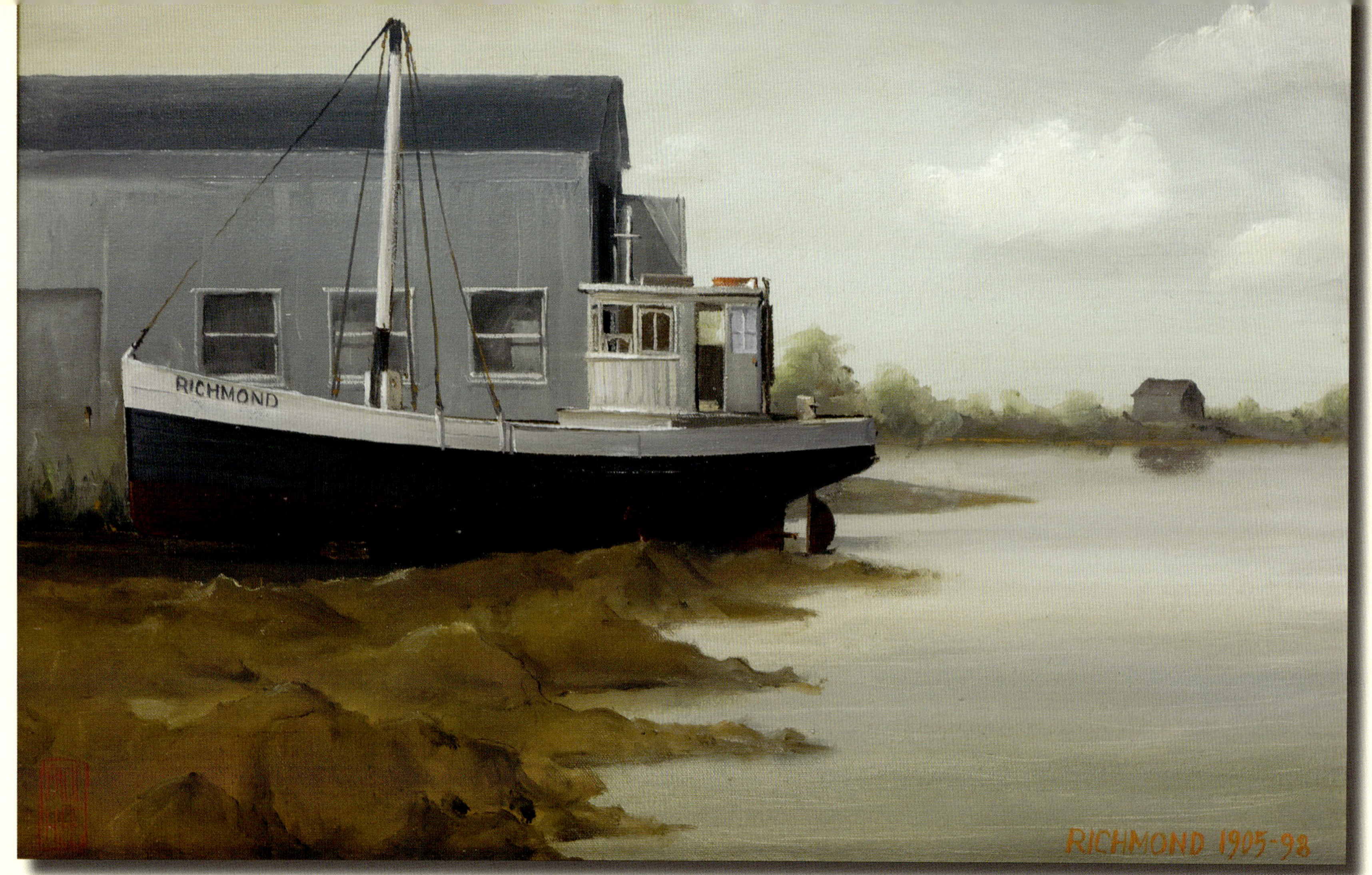

Richmond

18" x 20"

The *Richmond,* a Chesapeake Bay oyster dragger, was built for Captain Royal Toner, the "Oyster King" of Long Island's South Bay. In 1949, Toner raised oysters in 6,000 acres of beds off the shores of Long Island, Connecticut, Delaware, and California. One of the most successful US oystermen, he sold more than 50 million oysters a year, netting $1 million annually. He used six boats, 60 to 90 feet long, to harvest five-year-old, market-sized oysters in depths of up to 80 feet. The 40-foot *Richmond* weighed 20 tons. It sank dockside at South Bay in 2004.

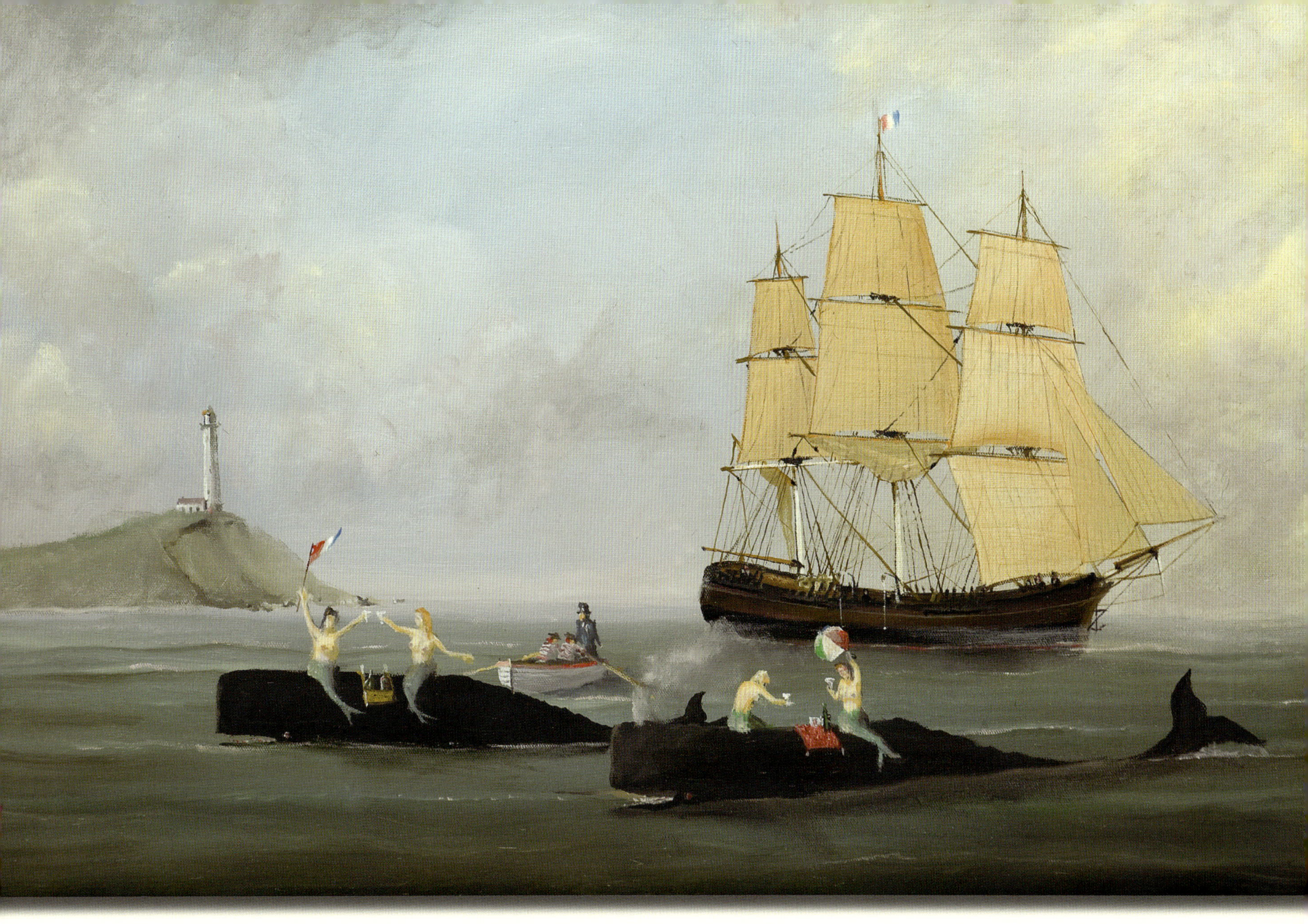

Mermaids & Whales
18" x 20"

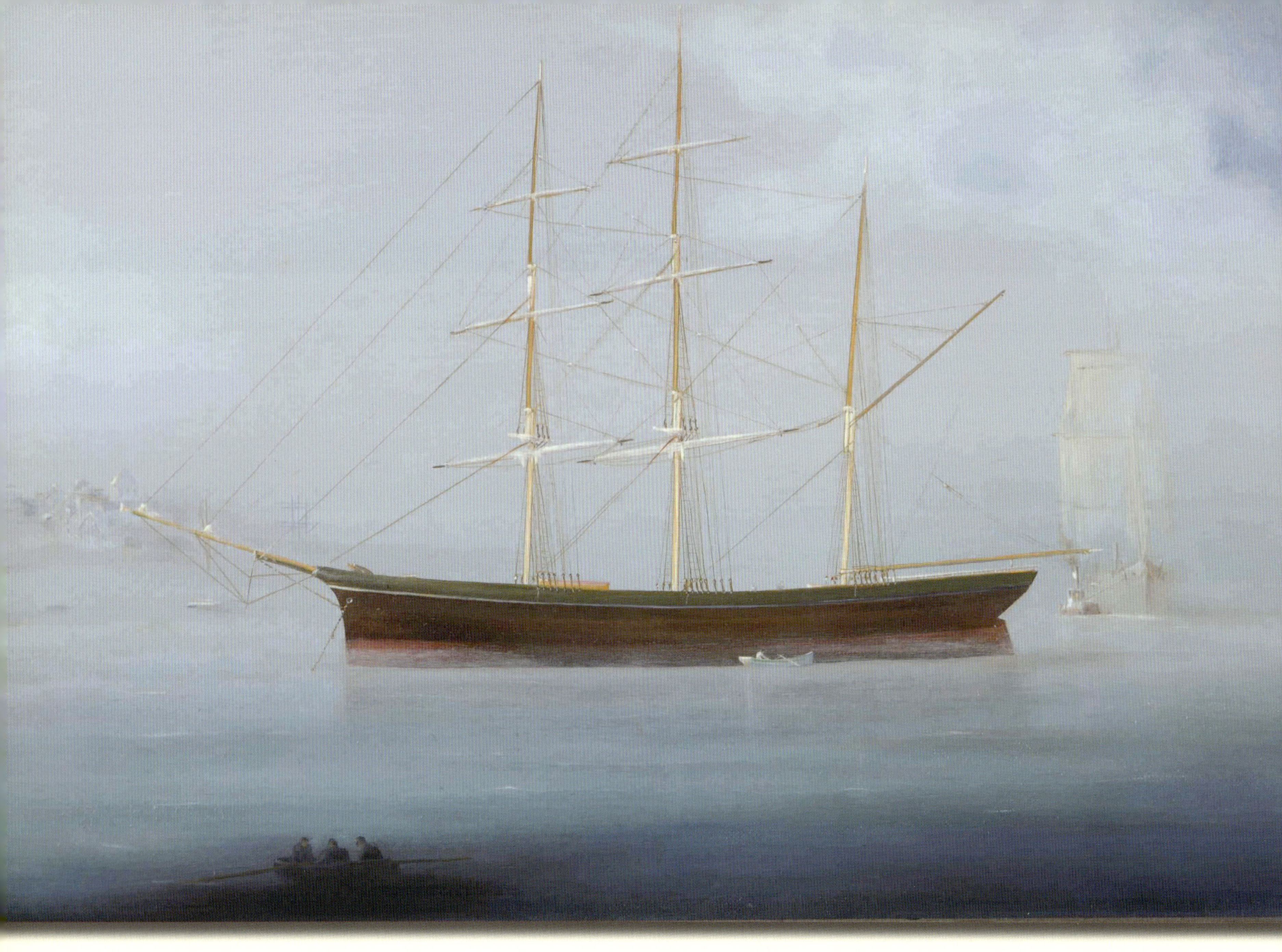

Moored in Fog on Connecticut River
18" x 20"

Horatio Nelson's Ships

18" x 28"

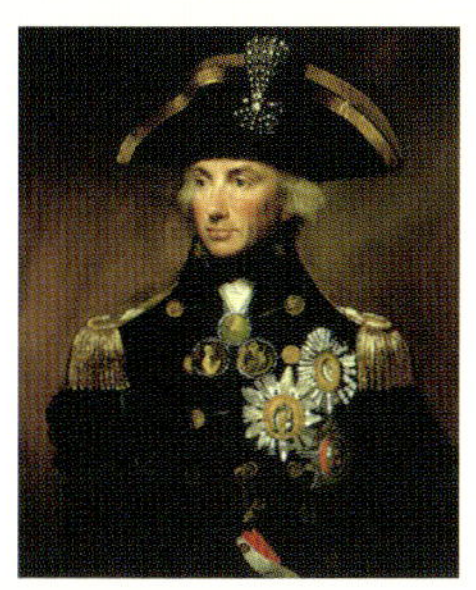

This composite depicts five warships commanded by the British Naval hero Horatio Nelson (1758-1805) who died in the Battle of Trafalgar aboard the 100-gun *Victory*, seen here with the 64-gun ship *Agamemnon*, and the 74-gun ships, *Captain*, *Vanguard*, and *Elephant*.

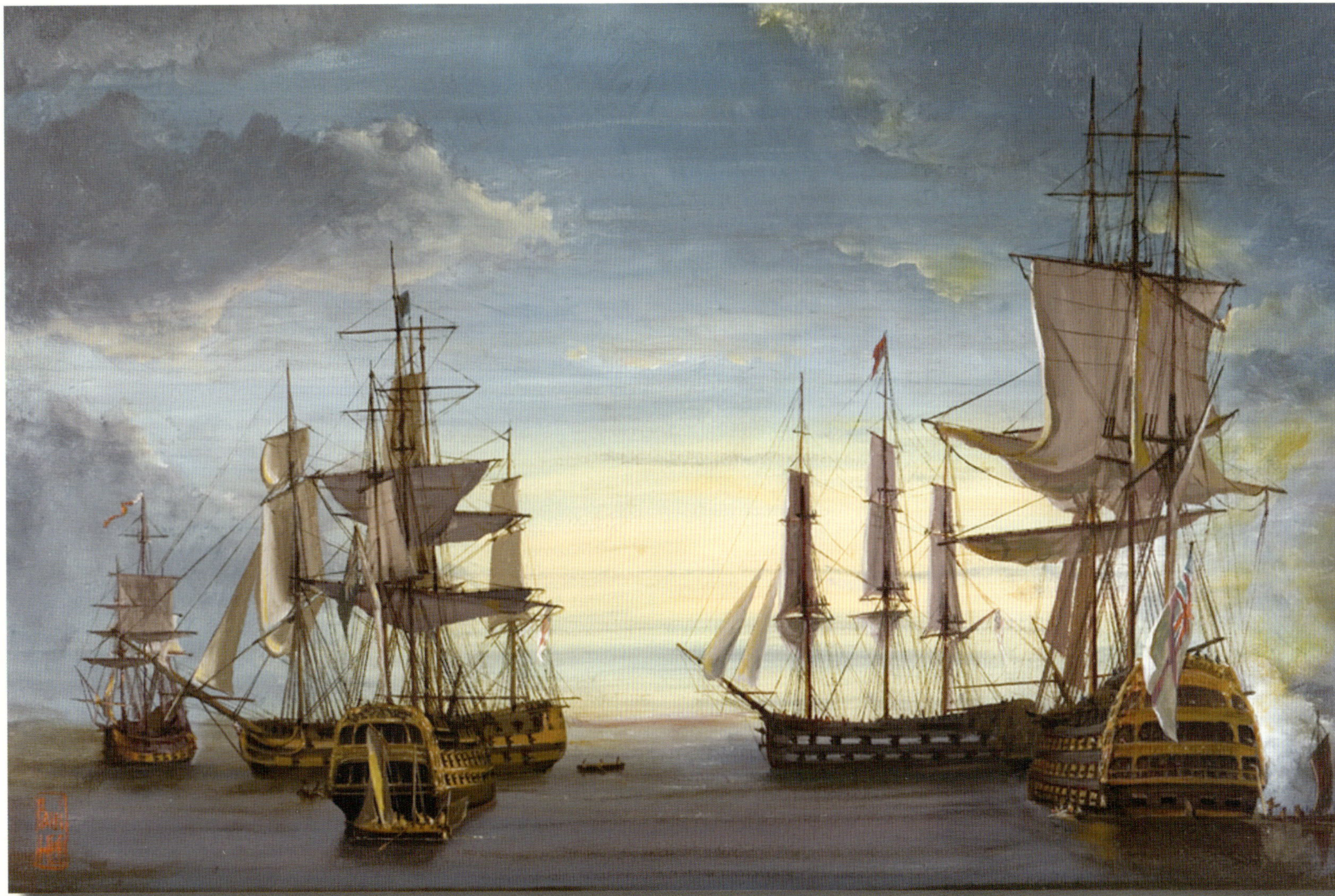

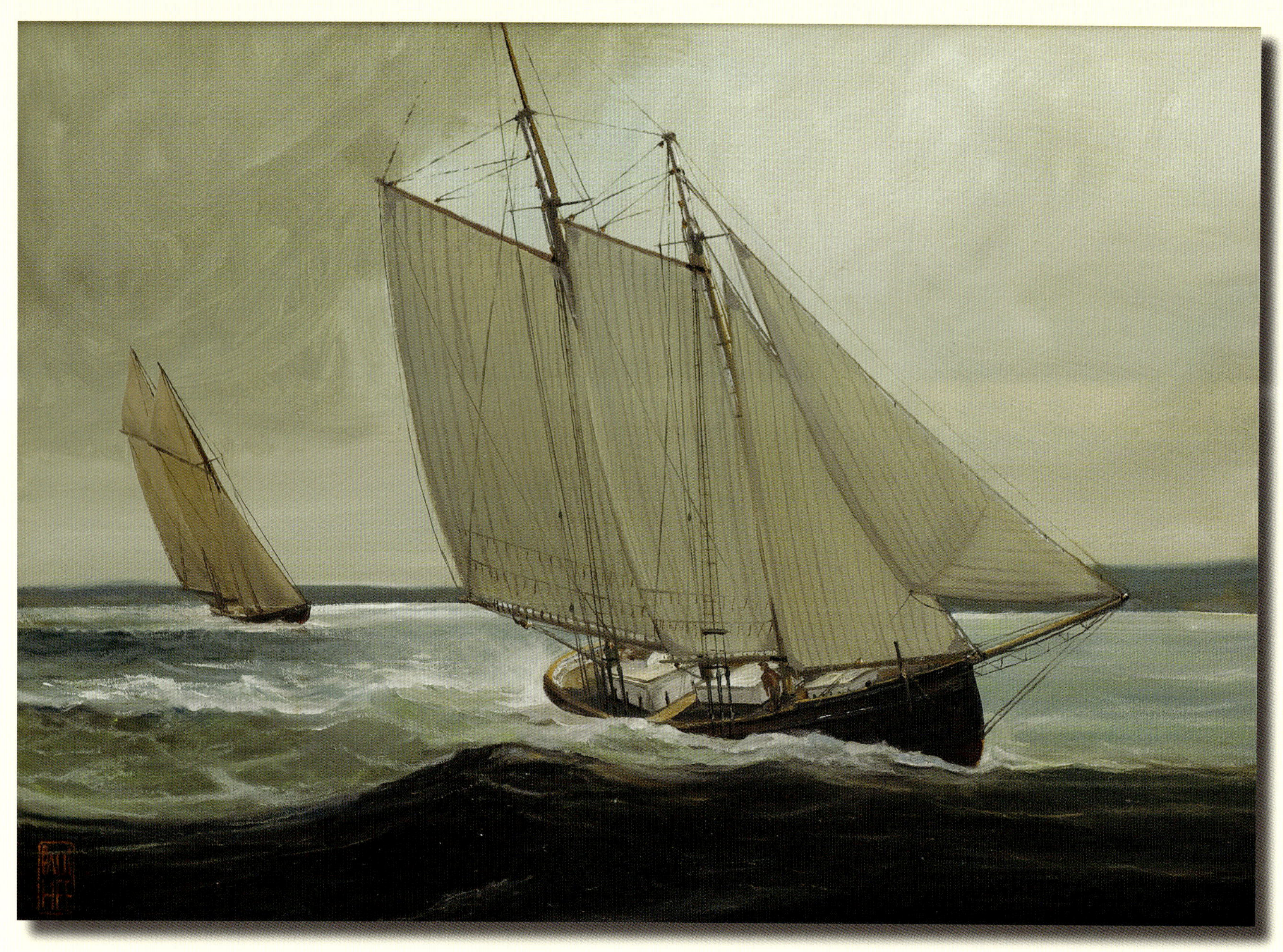

Fishermens Race 1907
18" x 28"

Lenders to Book & Exhibit

Betty Bulla, Beaufort, North Carolina
Michael & Lisa Brodnick
Coronet
Greg & Sheila Brodnick
Pilot Boat in Heavy Sea, *Pride of Baltimore*, Lost Off Hatteras
Carolina Yacht Club, Charleston, South Carolina
Maris
Chris & Rebecca Carden
Dauntless Defeats *Sappho*
Virginia Costlow, Beaufort, North Carolina
Royal George Victorious at Quiberon Bay
Douglas DeBanks, Durham, North Carolina
Dr. Brad & Susan Drury, Beaufort, North Carolina
USS Constitution
William Fuqua, Beaufort, North Carolina
David Gittleman, Louisville, Kentucky
Bruce Hebb, Newport, North Carolina
Susan Haupt, Marshallberg, North Carolina
Whales & Mermaids
Jim & Donna Howard, Beaufort, North Carolina
HMS Revenge
Carol Hurley, Morehead City, North Carolina
Charles & Mary Ingram
Garrick
Dr. Ted Kunstling, Raleigh, North Carolina
Massanuten Off Cape Lookout, *Argus & Pelican* 1812
Charles & Deborah Llewellyn, Beaufort, North Carolina
Edna J. Lockwood at Back River Light
Ross Meurer, Long Island, New York
New Jersey Tug I, Moored in Fog, *Pride of Baltimore*
Andrew Munch, Pine Knoll Shores, North Carolina
John Nelson, Beaufort, North Carolina
Richard & Elizabeth Olsen, Beaufort, North Carolina
USS Constitution, CSS Nashville

Jimmy & Jo Piver, Beaufort, North Carolina
Amistad, Bill of Rights
Karma Rodholm, Beaufort, North Carolina
Olaudah Equiano, *New Jersey* Tug II, *USS Spark*
Dr. & Mrs. David Rowland, East Aurora, New York
Battle of Trafalgar
Joseph Schwarzer, Hatteras, North Carolina
Scott & Lenore Taylor, Beaufort, North Carolina
Massanuten Off Cape Lookout
The Winter Group
BonHomme Richard
Tidewater Gallery, Swansboro, North Carolina
(on consignment)
Arctic Whaling Ships, 1860
Bombardment of Algiers
Christine Leads *Triton, 1884*
Fidelia on The Mersey River
George Taulane, 1905
Richmond
Sinking of The *Central America*
Stag Hound, 1850
Deborah Van Dyken, Beaufort, North Carolina
John Vang, Beaufort, North Carolina
Gotheborg, Low Water At Folkestone
Jason & Michelle Voelpel
Essex
Raymond & Janet Voelpel, Swansboro, North Carolina
New York Harbor, *Niagara* 1902
Mr. & Mrs. Bradish J. Waring, Charleston, South Carolina
Wanderer
Harvey Sharp Wooten
Castillian 1868

Sources

Books

Captain Otway Burns and His Ship Snap Dragon, by Jack Robinson, The Columbia Encyclopedia, Sixth Edition (2008)

CSS Alabama, Anatomy of a Confederate Raider, by Andrew Bowcock, Chatham Publishing, London, 2002

From Sail to Steam the Story of Antonio Jacobsen, Marine Artist: An Artist's Chronicle of the Ships that Sailed the Seas from 1870 to 1920, Staten Island, N.Y., Manor Publishing, 1972

Illustrated Directory of The Old West, by Ray Bonds, William C. Davis, 2002, MBI Publishing Co.

Old Steamboat Days on The Hudson River, by David Lear Buckham, The Grafton Press, New York, 1907

Graveyard of the Atlantic, by David Stick, University of North Carolina Press, 1989

Pen And Pencil Sketches Of Shipping And Craft All Round The World, by Robert Taylor Pritchett, Marine Painter to the Royal Thames Yacht Club, London, Edward Arnold Publisher to the India Office, 1899

Ship, Sea & Sky The Marine Art of James Edward Buttersworth, by Richard B. Grassby, South Street Seaport Museum in association with Rizzoli New York, 1994

The Arctic Whaleman: Winter In The Arctic Ocean, by Lewis Holmes, 1895

The Alabama & The Kearsarge: The Sailor's War, by William Marvel, University of North Carolina Press, 1996

The Book of Boston, by Edwin Monroe Back, 1916

The Confederate Navy: A Pictorial History, by Philip Van Doren Stern, 1992

The Cruise of The Alabama & The Sumter, by Raphael Semmes, 1864, Digitized by Digital Scanning Inc., 2001

The Era of The Clipper Ships, by Donald Gunn Ross II, 2009

The History of the Carolina Yacht Club, Charleston, South Carolina, by Robert P. Stockton. (Charleston: Carolina Yacht Club), 2004

The Life of Admiral Viscount Exmouth, by Edward Osler, London, 1841

The Story of Mt. Deserts Island, by Admiral Samuel Eliot Morison, Sea History 67, Autumn 1993

The Western Ocean Packets, by Basil Lubbock, Dover Publications, 1988

Traditional Work Boats of North Carolina, by Michael B. Alford, North Carolina Maritime Museum, Beaufort, North Carolina, 2004

Tidecraft: The Boats of South Carolina, Georgia and Northeastern Florida, 1550-1950, by W.C. Fleetwood, Jr., WBG Marine Press, Tybee Island, Georgia, 1995

Museums

Chesapeake Bay Maritime Museum, Navy Point, 213 N. Talbot Street, P.O. Box 636 St. Michaels, MD 21663

Los Angeles Maritime Institute, Berth 84, Foot of 6th Street, San Pedro, CA 90731

Maritime Museum of the Atlantic, 1675 Lower Water Street, Halifax, B3J 1S3, Nova Scotia, Canada

Pitcairn Islands Study Center, Nelson Memorial Library, Pacific Union College, 1 Angwin Avenue, Angwin, CA 94508

Pride of Baltimore, Inc. 1801 S. Clinton Street, Suite 250 Baltimore, Maryland 21224

National Maritime Museum, Greenwich, England

Navy History and Heritage Command, Washington Navy Yard, DC

Pilgrim Monument and Provincetown Museum, High Pole Hill Road, Provincetown, MA

US Navy Fact File, Navy Historical Center, Washington DC

Web Sites

Age of Nelson, Database.
http://www.ageofnelson.org

America's Cup
http://www.americascup.com

Brig Niagara
http://www.brigniagara.org

Port Blakely
http://www.portblakely.com

The Ship's List
www.theshipslist.com

HMS Bounty
http://library.puc.edu

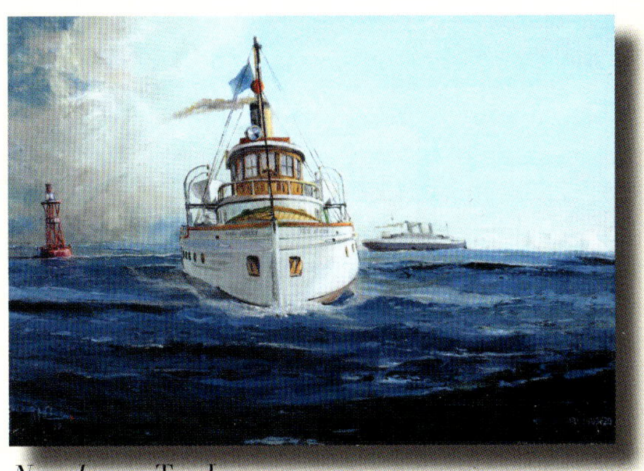

New Jersey Tug I

Photo Credits:

All images of Paul Hee art digitally photographed by Scott Taylor except:

Battle of Trafalgar
Dr. David Rowland

Coronet
Michael J. Brodnick

Maris
Bradish J. Waring

New Jersey Pilot
Ross Meurer

Other images:

Beaufort, North Carolina
Frank Leslie's Illustrated Weekly

Beaufort Map by Mosely
Archives North Carolina Maritime Museum

Bombardment of Fort Macon
University North Carolina Library, Chapel Hill, Carolina Collection

Carribean Sea Chart
CIA

Coronet
Corona & Coronet

CSS Nashville
Frank Leslie's Illustrated Weekly

Don McKay
Columbia Encylopedia.com

Fort Macon, Cannon, Cannon Balls
Rick Carroll, *Beaufort-by-The-Sea: Journey Back in Time*

Louisiana Purchase Map
Goverment Printing Office 1912, Map 4

Louisa Bliss Silhouette
Maritime Museum of The Atlantic, Halifax, Nova Scotia

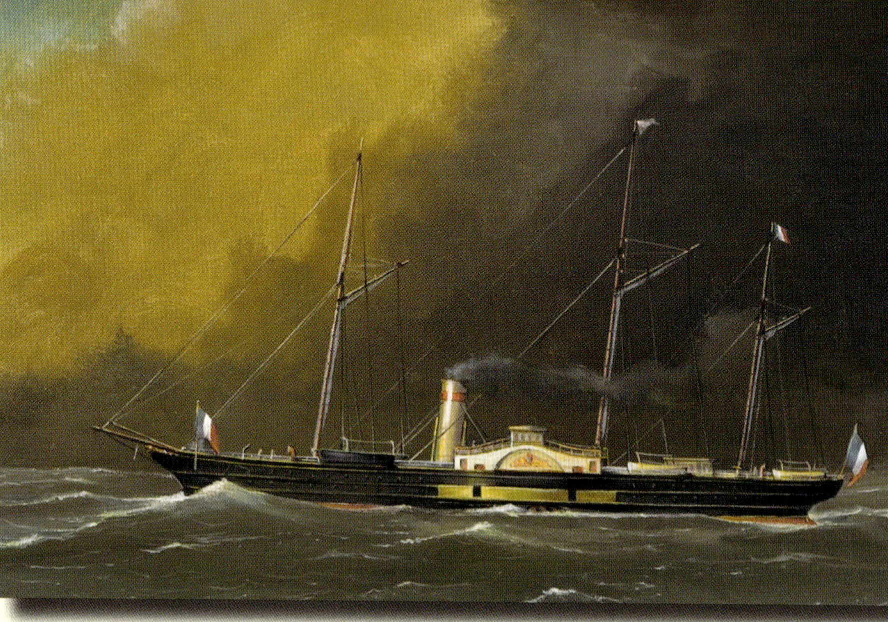

Valmy

Lipton Cup
Robin La Dow, San Diego Yacht Club

Marryat Code
Peabody Essex Museum, Salem, Massachusetts

Otway Burns Tomb
Larry Hedlund, *Beaufort-by-The-Sea: Journey Back in Time*

Otway Burns
Archives, *Beaufort-By-The-Sea: Journey Back in Time*

Stained Glass Door, Coronet
International Yacht Restoration School, Newport, Rhode Island

Tapscott Line Ad 1849
The Ship's List

Viscount Exmouth
Royal Naval Museum, Portsmouth Historic Dockyard

Horatio Nelson
National Maritime Museum, London

John Paul Jones
Surface Navy Association Hall of Fame

Oliver Perry
Surface Navy Association Hall of Fame

Index

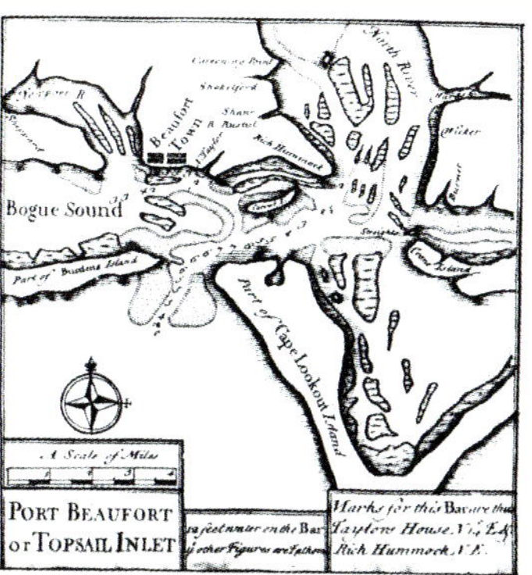

Bogue Sound
Beaufort Town
Port Beaufort or Topsail Inlet

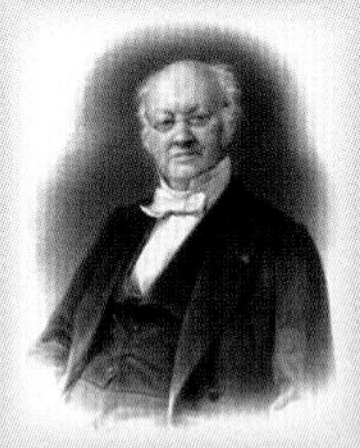

About Didot

Since the name of this three-century seaport is in the French vernacular and pronounced *bow fore* it's apropos that this fine art book is set in the font Didot.

Designed in 1818 by Firmin Didot (1764-1836) the font's strong clear forms, typical of the Age of Enlightenment, give text a classic, elegant feel.

Active in the 18th and 19th Centuries, the Didot family started as booksellers and became printers, publishers, intellectuals, and proprietors of France's most important print shop.

Both Didot and the Italian Giambattista Bodoni exaggerated the height and vertical ascent and descent to give characters architectural grandeur. The font dominated print until the late 19th Century when Arts and Crafts gained popularity.

In 1800 Pierre Didot printed the French Constitution using the typeface Didot and it became the standard book type font in France for more than a century, and is still in use today.

The font became popular in America in the 1950s when art directors of Harper's Bazaar and Vogue magazines selected Didot as the signature font. In 1963, CBS adapted Didot as its official typeface on all stations, and the Evening News "eye" logo.

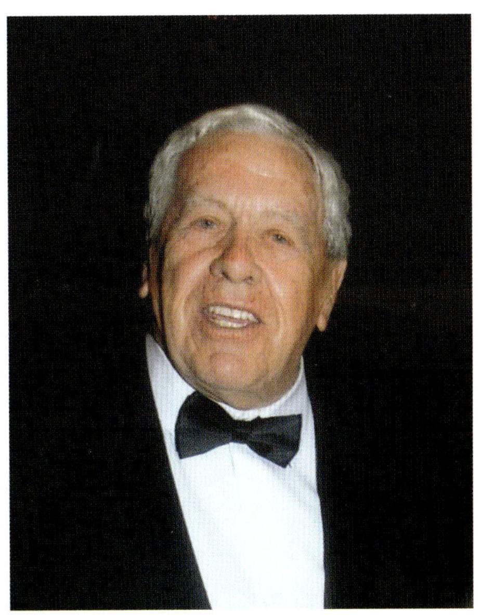

Maritime artist Paul Hee studied art under Leo Stitsky of Fort Lauderdale School of Art after going to sea on U.S. Navy ships and as a Miami-based cruise line executive. Influenced by Antonio Jacobsen (1850-1921) the prolific Danish artist, Hee researches vintage American and British ships to gain exact specifications, then paints the vessels in historically correct, visually stunning oils on canvas. A native of Long Island, Hee lives and paints in Beaufort, North Carolina.

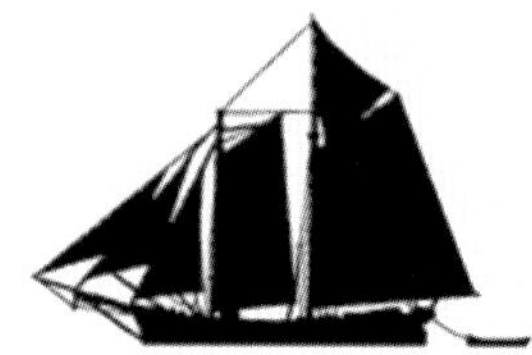